The language-experience approach to the teaching of reading

The language-experience approach to the teaching of reading

RUSSELL G. STAUFFER University of Delaware

Harper & Row, Publishers, New York · Evanston · London

The illustration on page *145* is from Russell G. Stauffer, Away We Go (*New York*, Holt, Rinehart and Winston, *1960*), *p. 101*.
The illustration on page *148* is adapted from C. K. Ogden and I. A. Richards, The Meaning of Meaning (*New York, Harcourt, Brace & World, 1946, and London, Routledge and Kegan Paul, 10th ed., 1949*).

This book was made possible by the many children who participated in our USOE study of the Language-Experience Approach and its embracing of group and individualized instruction and by the many other children before and since who benefited by its eclecticism. Therefore, this book is dedicated to the children; to the teachers and school administrators who contributed; to my students and Reading-Study Center colleagues; and to my wife.

Contents

Preface

The purpose of this book is to provide teachers with a practical and detailed account of how the Language-Experience Approach to reading instruction functions. In many ways, the detailed accounts presented cause the book to take on characteristics of a manual. They provide opportunity to point out sound psychological and philosophical premises that support the approach. In other ways, woven into the fabric of each chapter there are many explanations that reflect cognitive-professionalism and pragmatic-idealism.

The book reflects years (since 1952) of first-hand experience working closely with teachers and children—experimenting, refining, and elaborating on practices and principles. Two United States Office of Education grants (1964 and 1965) to compare the approach with a controlled population and do so on a longitudinal basis provided a superb opportunity to work ever more closely and carefully in classrooms and schools.

As the senior author of a series of basic readers, I learned how difficult it was to construct material at a preprimer and primer level. A year of great effort plus the help of a well-known author of books for children produced only substandard language usage that was no more palatable than any of the similar materials already available. Such materials do not take advantage of children's facility, intellectual abilities, and motivations.

The Language-Experience Approach as detailed in this text does take advantage of the wealth that children bring with them to school—linguistically, intellectually, socially, and culturally. By focusing on language as a means of communication, the transfer from oral language usage to written language is made functionally. Reading does become talk written down.

The phonological wealth of children is converted into a means whereby phonics is used first to decode the children's own spoken language as it appears in print and then the writings of others. Phonics is taught and applied intensively from the very beginning of reading instruction.

The syntax and semantic skill of the children is used in a communication context. This focus on word order and word meaning is practical and serviceable. It facilitates word recognition and retention.

When foundation reading skills have been acquired, attention is given to the development of critical reading-thinking skills. This is done by means of Directed Reading-Thinking Activities in *group* situations in which intellectual and affective interaction is accomplished. Self-selection, identification of interests and tastes, reading, and sharing are done in *individualized* instructional situations with the library as the principal source of materials. Thus group instruction with the interaction of minds and individualized instruction with emphasis on pupil actions are both accomplished. As a result, the library becomes the hub of the reading program, and communication of what is read completes the combining of the language arts.

Extensive reading is initiated in first grade and develops as a major activity. Children read and read and read. Intensive reading is also done as children convert interests into tastes and as they prepare sharing reports. They learn that there are many ways to share but that each requires preparation. All of these activities and abilities foster an attitude toward reading that is favorable and a regard for reading as a means of acquiring knowledge.

Creative writing makes writing, spelling, and creating functional. Good handwriting is required because other children read what is written. Spelling conscience is developed for the same reason. Many opportunities to write invite creative responding and encourage originality. Formal spelling, when introduced, augments the spelling ability developed in creative writing and makes it more functional.

So many people should be named as contributing to the refinement of ideas that pages of names would result. And to all I am indeed most grateful. Some few must be named even at the risk of offending others: Dr. J. A. Vansant, Superintendent at Rehoboth, Delaware, Mrs. Lynn Vogel, Elementary School Principal, and Mrs. Warren Hayes, formerly a first grade teacher there; Dr. Kenneth Madden, State Superintendent of Schools for Delaware and formerly Superintendent of Schools at Seaford, Delaware; Mrs. Mary Phillips, Reading Supervisor at Seaford, Mrs. Marion Pepper, Mr. Peter Mollahan, Mr. Robert W. Thomas, Sr., Mrs. Mary Wiley, Principals; Mr. George Keen and Mr. William Bant, Superintendents at Georgetown, Delaware; Mr. Albert W. Adams, Superintendent at

Harrington, Delaware, and Mr. Solomon Markowitz, Principal at Harrington; Mrs. Evelyn Kay, Elementary Supervisor of Cecil County, Maryland; Mrs. Naomi England, Principal at Rising Sun, Maryland; Miss Elizabeth Maloney, Principal at Holly Hall Elementary School in Cecil County, Maryland; and W. Dorsey Hammond, currently Reading Supervisor for the State of Maryland and formerly the graduate assistant who worked with me on the Seaford project. Above all, I am especially grateful to all the teachers who contributed so generously to the refinement of the method.

The highest form of commendation a teacher can receive is to be called an "eclectic teacher." She is one who takes advantage of good practices whenever she can and regardless of their source. The best label that can be applied to the Language-Experience Approach is "The Eclectic Approach to Reading Instruction." It embraces the best practices regardless of their source and does so in a functional communication-oriented way.

R. G. S.

The language-experience approach to the teaching of reading

I

Language-experience foundations

READER INQUIRY AND REGULATION

This chapter has two major sections and, in addition, a prologue and an epilogue. The prologue discusses how the relationship between the two concepts language and experience is altered when they are hyphenated and categorized at the embracing language-experience level. The first major section of the chapter discusses the oral-language wealth of six-year-olds, not only their stock of words but also their wealth phonologically, syntactically, and semantically. The second section describes how the experience wealth and overall cognitive wealth of six-year-olds are as opulent as their language and vary according to their social-cultural-economic backgrounds. The conclusion restates the enormous importance of the bond between thought, word, and deed and reading, writing, and school learning.

In reading the following objectives and speculating about the answers, you may find that, because of your knowledge, you are to a large degree confirming ideas you already know and refining them. Or it may be that your knowledge and your speculations are limited, in which case you may gain more as a reader because you took the first two essential steps of a scholar-reader: You were intellectually honest with yourself and you committed yourself to answers. This honesty and commitment will help regulate your reading, keep you on course, and sharply increase your retention and understanding.

1. Explain the importance of understanding how the two basic tenets in the evolution of language provide the foundation for reading instruction.
2. Explain why it is that the continual growth of language facility and its exchange is almost more a process than a means of storage.

3. List major studies concerned with the analysis of children's functional speaking vocabularies and compare these vocabularies with word counts of basic readers.
4. Discuss children's linguistic wealth and how it reflects the potency of functional communication.

Upon reading the second section of the chapter, the reader should meet these objectives; but first he must inquire of himself concerning answers and regulate his course by this speculation.

1. Explain how the sensible universe of children can actuate numerous pathways to the central nervous system.
2. Explain how it is that, when children begin to use language as a means of conveying the content of experience and action, there is a developing correspondence between what they see, do, and say.
3. Discuss the theory of the continuity of experience.
4. Describe how children acquire concepts by discrimination, perception, transposition, and generalization.
5. Discuss the four stages of intellectual development as described by Jean Piaget.
6. Explain how symbolic functioning and language play an increasingly significant role in the intellectual development of children.
7. Discuss why Piaget stresses over and over again the importance of "action" and "social interaction."

Language-experience hyphenated

The two words language and experience are the best labels available for the approach to reading instruction that they name. The method is founded on the oral-language facility of children. By the time children are of school age, the overwhelming majority of them have oral-language facility sufficient to provide the foundation for reading instruction. In addition, by the time children are of school age, they have had enough experience to provide the meaning, or concept, base for reading-instruction purposes.

When Albert Einstein enunciated his theory of relativity, he made a major contribution to thinking regarding the concept "relativity," by using a simple hyphen. Prior to his time, men had done much thinking and writing and computation concerned with "time" and "space." Even for the ancient Greeks, the problem of geographical latitude had been an easy one. The problem of longitude was much more difficult, because it required some standard, such as Greenwich time. The impact of Newtonian physics has led to many advances of great significance—an accurate ship's chronometer, mathematical tables of the motions of the moon, the pendulum, the balance wheel, the sextant, the telescope, universal joints, the electric motor, the vacuum tube (26). Even so, the thinking of the world's advance guard of craftsmen and scholars was greatly enhanced when Einstein spoke of a time-space relationship and made it the embracing concept of relativity. Similarly, when the hyphen is placed between language and experience, it creates an all-embracing concept of human communication: not language *and* experience, but "language-experience." The human use of language (concepts), from infancy through old age, is based on experience (percepts and cognition) and on man's need to communicate. The functional dynamism of "language-experience" makes it a sweeping concept.

The intimate relationship of language-experience and social-personal communication is clearly apparent from the early days of human life. The infant who learns to make the sound *da-da* and learns to associate it with the adults about him has learned from repeated experience to use sound to produce a response. As he matures, the number and frequency of experiences needed to learn to use a sound, or set of sounds, to symbolize a concept, decreases as well as varies. It does so according to many influencing variables of personal and social nature. Nevertheless, the learning pattern has been established, and the principles of phonology, syntax, and semantics that he learns remain the same throughout his life. This is so whether or not concepts are learned by the child on his own or are taught to him by someone else.

The Language-Experience Approach to learning to read is developed in this textbook. It is as all-embracing a concept in the life of the educator as time-space is to the physical scientist as a universal symbolism and calculus of reasoning that has led to the symbolic logic of the twentieth century. The practices and procedures of the Language-Experience Approach can be as influential in education in general, and in the teaching of reading and writing in particular, as mathematics and symbolic logic are in the world of the scientist. It should replace, in the design of educational processes, the effects of the misplaced whole word method, or the alphabet method, purism based on a faulty empiricism and a haphazard analysis of the communication process. Both methods represent a cancer of pedagogical narrowness and feebleness whose effects are well seen, both inside and outside the schools.

Language

A study of the evolution of language involves two tenets. First, language as a means of communication is ordinarily thought of as being directed from person to person. Language belongs to man as a member of a social community. Second, it is the means by which man encodes and decodes meanings with signals or symbols. As such, language has the fineness of clear and repeated accuracy needed to make a code. In brief, language is a code that represents the learned behavior of a social community.

To think of communication and language in the person-to-person sense or in the social sense is to think of them functionally. The *function* of language is to communicate. Communication is the primary purpose of language. If language usage—either oral or written—is to be taught effectively, the teaching must be based on the functional use of language—communication.

Human interest in language appears to be innate. Babies, if left alone, will make attempts at speech. A community of people out of contact with other groups emerges with an unmistakable language. The impulse to use some kind of language is apparently intense, both psychoneurologically and socially (5).

Speech is a human activity and a learned activity. Whatever the mode of speech acquired by a social community, it is a particular language that has to be learned in each special instance. Each example of language, dialect, vernacular, jargon, and slang represents man's freedom and ability to use any pronounceable sound code for some meaning or other and to pass on this code from generation to generation.

Speech is sometimes regarded as man's greatest achievement. It permits him to attach significance to sounds, to retain and use a huge repertoire of codified sounds, and to form complex relationships between experience, sounds, and words.

There seems to be a critical period during which speech is learned most readily. Between the ages of one and five, children are particularly adept at learning not only the language of their community but other languages as well. In fact, if speech is not learned at the proper time, the entire social aspect of an individual may be affected.

Most children are responsive to the continuous stream of language influences in the world about them. This means that they are alive to what is happening phonologically and linguistically in their world and that they are participating in a continual development of language and its exchange. As a matter of fact, because of the arbitrary nature of language, it is almost more a process than a means of storage. This is because language is constantly meeting the demands of the time. New words are added, old words are dropped or adapted to new meanings, and new idea structures are formulated.

It has been estimated that, by the time children are of school age, the size of their functional speaking vocabulary ranges from about 2,500 words (22) to 12,000 words (19, 23). A recent study (24) of the number of different words used by first-grade children in dictated stories yielded a count of 3,331. With both extremes in mind, it seems reasonably safe to estimate the number of words known by six-year-olds at about 7,500 (7, p. 32).

It is, thus, readily apparent that six-year-olds bring with them to school a functional speaking vocabulary of almost unlimited wealth. The number of different morphemes (words) they can use is large and far exceeds the number of words usually presented in a first-year basic-reader program, about 400. This makes the magnitude of the ratio of the difference strikingly apparent: 4/75. Even if the least adequately prepared child has a vocabulary of only 2,500 words, the contrast to a first-year basic-reader vocabulary is still striking: 4/25. The teaching and vocabulary circumstance is not materially altered when a co-basal is used (24) or when parallel readers or transitional readers are foisted on pupils (25). The vocabulary poverty of basic readers, singly and in groups, puts school children at a serious disadvantage when basic readers represent "the reading program," as they have been doing for so long now in more than 90 percent of the nation's schools (2).

Linguists tell us that, by the time children have acquired functional speaking vocabularies of the sizes just referred to, they will also have acquired expert phonological skill. When the sound vibrations of speech hit the air and then the inner ear and its connection with the cerebral center, the circuit has been completed and the raw material of language—sound—is serving its purpose. Phonemes are the distinctive basic sound elements of language and have no referential function, but they make up the component parts of the signs of language (morphemes), which do have referential meaning and grammatical functions. The infant learning to use the language of his community needs to differentiate the varieties of sounds that occur in the language. In addition, he must learn that the sounds function as signs only as they represent form differences of communicative value. Because these phoneme-morpheme sign systems represent a high degree of sound complexity, the talking six-year-old has accomplished a most impressive feat. At the same time, his knowledge includes appropriate reaction to the gestures, facial expressions, stresses, intonations, and junctures that ordinarily accompany speech behavior.

All these responses to sound, which children are capable of, do not qualify them as phoneticians, however. Even a linguist, to become a phonetician, must become an expert in the science of speech sounds (phonetics) and be able to *describe* the varieties of sound that occur. To learn to read, children do not need to be phoneticians. What they do need is an opportunity to use the vast knowledge of sound that they already possess when they learn that print is no more than speech written down.

Impressive as this record of the knowledge of sound is, however, it is an accounting of only a part of children's wealth. Words used to communicate are arranged into acceptable sequences, as in a sentence, and these arrangements are known as syntax, or the grammar of a language. It is claimed that, by the time a child of normal intelligence is six years old, he knows practically all the essential grammatical structures of his language. All this language know-how is acquired without formal teaching or structuring or programming. The secret teaching ingredient is <u>functional communication</u>. Children learn to listen and talk and use oral language to serve themselves as they operate in the environs of their social-cultural world.

Most six-year-olds possess a language wealth that is as astounding as the facts provided here indicate. Of course, there are children who have neurological disabilities or speech or hearing disabilities and the like, but they are the exception and, furthermore, can usually be readily identified and given appropriate instruction. It remains, then, for teachers of beginning reading to appropriately capitalize on children's language opulence.

Experience and knowledge

The age of wisdom has been described as being between six and sixteen. At six, children can ask every conceivable question and, at sixteen, they can answer all questions. This ask-all-questions age encompasses the concept we are concerned with here. The asking child is the inquiring mind ferreting out the attributes and relationships in his perceptual and conceptual world.

The experiences of six-year-olds are as numerous as the stars. Many represent frequently recurring happenings that become so commonplace as to breed a dangerous familiarity. Others are unique and rare and so obtain attention. Whatever the circumstance, the sensible universe—sight, sound, smell, touch, taste—activates numerous pathways to the central nervous system, where experience is stored and classified.

Current research in child development, as collated and interpreted in the Russell Sage Foundation's *Review of Child Development Research* (11), can help sensitize teachers to the range and variety of child behavior at different ages and in different settings. The diverse stimuli of the physical and social world are gradually identified by children and grouped into some orderly schema. By so doing, they adapt to and function appropriately toward many objects, events, and people in their environment. From this they develop a system of concepts that, as Irving Sigel says (20, p. 209), "function as an adaptive mechanism through which we cope with reality."

In his classic *Experience and Education,* John Dewey said that it is not enough to insist upon the necessity of experience to education but that everything depends on the *quality* of the experience. He stated (8, p. 17): "The more definitely and sincerely it is held that education is a development within, by, and for experience, the more important it is that there shall be clear conceptions of what experience is." Experiences must be more than immediately enjoyable; they must promote fruitful and creative subsequent experience. Educationally, this must be done in such a way that each pupil's power of judgment and capacity to act intelligently in new situations is in harmony with the principles of growth. This is the theory of the continuity of experience, which means that (8, p. 27) "every experience both takes up something from those which have gone before and modifies in some way the quality of those which come after." This is principally what differentiates civilization from savagery, and, to a considerable degree, the curiosity and creativity of the normally developing child from the overindulged child.

In the years before school, the developing child acquires a complex set of learnings based on perception, discrimination, transposition, and generalization. He acquires concepts—the "crucial links between the environment and the individual" (20, p. 209)—and a set of appropriate behaviors that may become a more or less fixed way of doing things. Concepts and habits enable a child to cope with his environment, to meet and respond to the physical and social conditions of living, and to form emotional and intellectual attitudes. This developmental process gradually frees him from domination by the perceptual and sensory aspects of his environment and enables him, through language, to approach it conceptually.

The stages of intellectual development as described by Jean Piaget (10) provide a schematic description of developmental changes that occur through time. His stages are sufficiently open ended to allow for the fact that children show different levels of ability, knowledge, and skills as a function of the rate and quality of the learning experiences they encounter.

The first 2 years of life are described as the sensory-motor period. The infant, using the inherent reflexes of his biological endowment, interacts with his environment. The interplay of internal and external conditions through stimulation and response characterizes the normal development of infants. From the maze of undifferentiated, unreflective, and unspecified experiences, the child gradually attains rudimentary knowledge. As Sigel says (20, p. 215), to accomplish this, he "establishes a differentiation of himself from objects; he localizes himself in space; he establishes a beginning awareness of cause and effect, of time and space." Most children, by the time they are 8 to 12 months old, have shown intention or goal-directed activity. Purpose or the intentionality of purpose now begins to influence a child's interactions. This is a big stride intellectually, as awareness of "means-end relationships" helps the child to cope with the physical and social complexities of his world. By the end of this stage, the child is well on the way to dealing with his environment symbolically and conceptually. He can already invent solutions in his mind and is no longer required to act them out by trial and error.

It is apparent, then, that in the first 2 years of life children live in a concrete world and in a series of situations. The interaction that is going on between a child and his physical and social world permits him to separate himself from his environment as well as to realize that the environment has certain properties of space, location, permanence, and causality. He is increasingly able to operate symbolically by classes or groups. He can tell that a dog, *Rover*, is a member of the dog family but he cannot deal with the category *animal*.

The next 5 years of life Piaget describes as the preoperational phase (10, pp. 150–163). In this phase, language plays an increasingly important role as the child acquires concepts through a complex set of processes. To attain concepts, he has to become increasingly sensitive to objects in his concrete world. He has to learn not only that they exist but also that they have many characteristics and attributes. In addition, he sees that diverse items can be organized into classes or categories (Rover, collie, dog, animal, vertebrate) and that language can facilitate as well as direct the process of conceptualization.

The third stage, or operational stage, is described as taking place roughly between ages seven and eleven. Because symbols and language play an increasingly more significant role in the intellectual functioning of a child, the second and third stages have on occasion been treated together (5, p. 218). Roger Brown does this because, as he says, in general the same problems have been used to study both periods. At the preoperational stage, children perform less adequately than at the operational stage. It is the development and use of language, though, that suggests the grouping of the two stages together.

Even so, Piaget not only declares the two stages but further breaks the preoperational stage into two periods. The first occurs between ages 2 and 4, the time when the child learns, in Brown's language (5, p. 218), to "name things, to ask questions, issue commands, and assert propositions." At the sensorimotor period, the child makes a giant intellectual stride by the influence of intention or purpose, the sensing of means-end relationships. At this stage, an equally significant stride is made as the sensorimotor infant becomes, through symbolic functioning, a manipulator of representations. The act of symbolic functioning is the result of the generalized capacity to differentiate between signifiers—symbols that stand for something—and significates—the objects. This representational intelligence, through its possession of symbolic functioning, sets the stage for the upper limits of cognition and the manipulation of reality.

At this stage, though, conceptualization is dominated by the world of percepts. To a large degree, the potency of physical attributes determines the concepts formed. Piaget calls this the preconcept period, because children primarily grasp first-level concepts. They can grasp the fact that peaches and pears are food but cannot distinguish between different pears. Or, they can recognize that certain very different things belong together: Daddy's watch, Daddy's chair, Daddy's hat.

Between four and seven years of age, the intuitive period, increased symbolic functioning is possible. Piaget discriminates between symbols and signs as signifiers. Symbols are of the dream-symbol variety or of deferred imitation or of representational play. They are private non-codified signifiers. Signs—linguistic signs—are acquired from the social surroundings and are shared socially. Words are the commonest signs of a codified and socially shared linguistic system.

The use of private signifiers or symbols as well as the early use of linguistic signs provide the focus for Piaget's statement that children are egocentric. They generally lack the ability to take the role of another person and to treat their own thought processes as the object of thought. Over and over again, Piaget indicates that it is in the context of *social interaction* as a member of a learning group that a child, forced to take cognizance of the ideas of others and forced to become increasingly cognizant of his own thoughts and their reliability and validity, emerges as a sociocentric objective scholar.

In addition to grasping images and signs as signifiers, the child learns to use them as anticipative mediators of future actions. Starting with imitative images that serve as anticipative schema, the child begins to direct future action. He begins to evoke acts and deeds in thought rather than actually carrying them out in reality. This ability to anticipate, to conjecture, to speculate, leads to the ability to hypothesize, to deal with variants and covariants, to test logically. In the life of a learner, this is an advance of the utmost importance. It is the pattern of inquiry that George Kneller (15, p. 42) defines as the ability "to analyze the problem and to consider ways of dealing with it—that is, to set up hypotheses." The learner is now becoming more reflective and less impulsive. He is beginning to want proof, to suspend judgment, to think of information as tentative and relative. Rather than seizing on the first idea that occurs to him, he now pauses, suspends judgment, to notice whether or not there are better ways or other alternatives.

Another cognitive advance that occurs at this stage is the ability to use numbers, not only to order things in terms of quantity but also to see that relationships can exist on a numerical basis. In the dimensions of concept attainment as defined by Herbert Klausmeier (14), this is referred to as the ability to deal with formal properties. When *formal* is compared with *intrinsic* and *functional*, its meaning can be grasped more quickly.

Intrinsic properties are observable properties, experienced directly through the sense organs. The common elements—an object or event—are observable. *Functional properties* are classifications of objects based on use. For example, a hammer, a pulley, and a slide rule are all tools, classified by their functional properties. *Formal properties* are products wholly of man's mental processes, such as number systems and alphabets. Number systems, for example, have properties too, in this case formal properties that are agreed upon by mathematicians. The child who can combine two quantities to produce a sum deals with an abstraction based upon formal properties of mathematics.

The latter part of the preoperational stage or the *intuitive stage* finds children making judgments largely on the basis of partial and immediate perceptions or on the basis of objective similarity. They judge by the way things look and usually in terms of just one of a number of relevant dimensions. Even so, three fundamental operations occur. They can think in terms of classes: When presented with circles and squares, they can classify them on the basis of roundness. They can think in terms of relationships: Mr. Jones is the father of Ralph, Mr. Jones is bigger than Ralph, and Ralph is the oldest of three children. They can think in terms of quantity or by handling number concepts.

In the concrete <u>operations</u> <u>period</u>, the thought of children aged seven through eleven is more like that of the adult, in that they think more in logical terms. *Operations* is used by Piaget to refer to mental acts or imminent acts of an internalized nature taking place in the mind. These mental acts represent a process of interaction and development whereby new syntheses are formed by discovery. Attributes are noted, objects are classified, and categories are determined. The syntheses are real in the sense that they not only have a location in time and space but also take place in the mind. In the process of cognitive growth through making discoveries and syntheses, the individual is merely the neural medium in the resynthesis of cultural elements.

Three significant operations described by Piaget are *reversibility*, as in arithmetic ($2 + 3 = 5$, or $5 - 3 = 2$), *classification*, or the organization of objects into classes (desk, chair, table = furniture), and *seriation*, or arranging ideas along a spectrum of increasing values (2, 4, 8, 16, 32). In brief, at this stage the child is able to treat objects as alike (desk-chair, furniture) even though different, to note that they can be in more than one class and that some classes can be subordinate to others, and to count one item as first and another as second.

In addition, the child understands the concept of *conservation*. In other words, he can see that certain properties of objects, such as quantity, can remain invariant even in the face of certain changes. For instance, two circles each with a diameter of 6 inches remain the same even though one is cut into quarters and the other is cut into thirds. Cutting a circle does not alter the amount or quantity of the circle.

To arrange items in a series along a continuum, a child must grasp the principle of *transitivity*. He must understand the sort of ordering whereby he recognizes that, if A is larger than B, and B is larger than C, then A is larger than C.

Interestingly enough, it is reported that the grasping of conservation and transitivity occur sometime between the ages of five and seven

(4, 13, 16, 20, 21). Almy conducted an "excellent psychopedalogical" study (1) of cross-sectional and longitudinal nature to determine the validity of Piaget's account of the principle of conservation and to determine the relevance of such understanding to children's progress in kindergarten and first and second grade. The results underscored the importance of maturational factors and "more generally . . . the transition from thought that is intuitive and perceptually dominated to thought that is systematic, or, in Piaget's terms 'operational.' " The results also supported Piaget's findings on conservation and highlighted the role of experience.

In addition, Almy and her colleagues investigated the processes of children of various social-economic backgrounds and the relationships with measures of intellectual functioning, readiness, and achievement. They found that the sequential development of children in lower-class schools, although similar to that of children in middle-class schools, was at a much slower pace. Also, in general, children who did better on tests of mental ability, readiness, and achievement grasped conservation at an earlier age. To this must be added the findings and interpretations reported by Jerome Bruner and his workers (6). They state that invariance, or conservation of various forms of quantity across transformations in appearance, is possible by very young children as reflected by actions premised on conservation. The "do" rather than "tell" features apparently provide less impediment in learning conservation as a tool of thought.

In the concrete operations stage, the child's thoughts, even though they may be logical and systematic, are limited to the direct experiences he has had. When he has no direct experience, he tends to reason by analogy to something he has experienced. In this regard, verbal ability, as well as physical activity and social interactions with verbal ability, may be crucial in acting as a support to help a child overcome the influence of his visual perceptions. While training designed to increase vocabulary may facilitate the development of logical thinking and help resolve the perceptual-cognitive conflict, it is "equilibration" or self-regulation that takes on greatest significance. To permit a child "to learn an appropriate answer without making certain that he can retrace his steps, or arrive at the same result in another way, is to encourage the erection of a verbal superstructure that may crumble under even minimal cognitive stress" (1, p. 132).

The fourth stage, the formal operations stage, is the time when abstract thinking develops, at about the beginning of adolescence. Now the child begins to deal with the possible without reference to the actual. He begins to grasp the complexity of human knowledge by learning how to construct theories and make logical deductions about their consequences without the need for empirical evidence. As Hunt puts it (12, p. 355), "instead of observation directing thought . . . the adolescent's thought directs his observing." In all this, language, or representational thought, plays an important role, but Piaget is of the opinion that ability to use language to express logic is an outcome of activity and that attempts to improve a child's logic by teaching him in the use of language is not apt to be very successful.

SUMMARY

In essence, the idea of activity—a child's need to reach by his own efforts an understanding of the world in which he lives and the experiences in which he participates—represents Piaget's first critical variable in the teaching-learning experience. A child may accommodate his thoughts to those of others, but, only when *he tries out* the ideas of others to see how they function and retraces the ideas, can he then assimilate ideas and make them his own. For the teacher, this means that each child's readiness to make a discovery or to acquire a new idea must be determined and then instruction must be so paced that the child has both the required knowledge and the cognitive abilities needed to make or acquire it. Almy says that, for curriculum makers and teachers (1, p. 138), "in the early childhood period activity and language need close association. For example, in the case of the socially disadvantaged child, no adequate comparison of quantities can be made by a child who does not understand the terms 'more' and 'less,' or 'most' and 'least.' But comprehension of those terms may not be developed through words alone, but rather through a combination of manipulation and verbalization."

Piaget, in summing up a talk on development and learning, said that all his remarks represented the child and the learning subject as active: "Learning is possible only when there is active assimilation" (17, p. 18). He had said earlier that, if the development of knowledge is to be understood, we must grasp the idea that to him is central—the idea of an operation (17, p. 18):

Knowledge is not a copy of reality. To know an object, to know an event, is not simply to look at it and make a mental copy, or image, of it. To know an object is to act on it. To know is to modify, to transform the object, and to understand the process of this transformation, and as a consequence to understand the way the object is constructed. An operation is thus the essence of knowledge; it is an interiorized action which modifies the object of knowledge.

An operation is an interiorized action that is reversible and never isolated or is always a part of structure: "Knowledge is not drawn from objects, but it is drawn by the actions effected upon the objects" (17, p. 12). Piaget is saying, in other words, that learning is subordinate to development.

When challenged, Piaget says he always has three questions: (1) Is the learning lasting, or what remains 2 weeks or a month or a year later? (2) Can the learning be used for generalization or the transfer of a generalization? (3) What was the *operational* level of the learner before the learning experience and what more complex structures has he achieved through this learning? He asks this because all development consists of momentary conflicts and incompatibilities that must be overcome if a higher level of equilibrium is to be reached. (17, pp. 17–19).

With respect to the point made by question three, Almy and her colleagues say (1, p. 136): "We can think of no better safeguard against meaningless verbalization and rote memorization than a teacher who is able both to appraise the difficulty of the concepts and to assess the children's comprehension of them." Nancy Bayley, writing on the growth of intelligence, has said (3, p. 807): "Intelligence appears to me . . . to be a dynamic succession of developing functions, with the more advanced and complex functions in the hierarchy depending on the prior maturing of earlier simpler ones."

It seems, then, that language development as a part of maturation or all-round mental capacity influences much of a child's progress from thought that is predominantly perceptual and intuitive to thought that is conceptual and logical. A child's verbal accommodation to a learning experience is helpful, but it will produce lasting effects only if, through further self-regulation, generalization to other tasks has resulted. It is not enough just to have had an experience, even verbally, unless it affects a child's way of organizing his experiences.

Social interaction, or sharing by pupils, represents the second critical variable in a teaching-learning experience, according to Piaget. Children must be given the freedom and opportunity to reveal and share their thoughts. Social exchange with their peers may help children learn from each other, overcome their egocentric view of things, and lead to a critical frame of mind: "Cooperation is indeed co-operation" (9, p. 4).

Finally, as Piaget has declared, transition from one level of thought to the next involves principally maturation, social interaction, physical activity, and, most important, the process of equilibration or self-regulation. And, as Hunt says (12, p. 346), in view of the technological developments in Western culture that demand high ability to manipulate such organizational structures as schemata, operations, and concepts in the solution of problems, the "hope of increasing the average level of intelligence by proper manipulation of children's developmental encounters with their environment, a hope which becomes reasonable with the evidences surveyed here and with relinquishing the assumptions of fixed intelligence and predetermined development, provides a challenge of the first order."

Conclusion

The purpose of this chapter is to show how the language-experience-cognitive wealth that children bring with them to school at ages five and six provides a sound, all-embracing foundation on which to construct and develop reading ability. The size of their functional speaking vocabularies is much larger than is usually believed by unsophisticated teachers and parents, and it is more encompassing than is allowed for by basic-reader programs with their numerous primers. A child's experience wealth is proportionately equal in opulence (even though varied) to his social-cultural-economic background. The all-round maturation characteristic of the preoperational and operational stages is cognitively a source of neuro-psychological affluence with tremendous implications for learning and reading instruction.

It is not the purpose of this chapter to deal with the vexing linguistic relation between language and thought. This has been done by others—notably by Carroll (7) and Brown (5). Language and thought are discussed in this chapter in some detail to show that both represent processes that can serve the individual as he manipulates ideas either directly or intellectually to communicate with others or undirectly or autistically to satisfy his individual and incommunicable desires. Intelligence, as it undergoes maturation and a gradual process of socialization, increasingly uses concepts through the bond established between thoughts, words, and deeds. Directed thought is controlled more and more by the laws of language, experience, and logic, and it is influenced enormously by the need and desire to communicate thoughts to others. Carroll says, in speaking of different languages (7, p. 111), that "There are more similarities than differences in the way language codes symbolize concepts, because these concepts are the result of the transactions of human societies with a physical and social environment that has many uniformities over the world." He also says (7, p. 110) that:

Thinking is the conscious or unconscious manipulation of internal processes for oneself, usually in some particular direction such as the solution of a problem. Communication, whether through language or through other means . . . is behavior in which the initiator of the communication seeks . . . to arouse certain internal processes in the recipient of the communication and possibly to secure certain overt responses on his part.

In reporting on studies in cognitive growth, Bruner discusses how certain features of human development and growth are culture bound. He compares Wolof children with Western children and says (6, p. 323) "The difference lies, at the very least, in the extent to which and the manner in which children learn to use language as an implement of thought." When language is used to convey the content of experience and action, there is (6, p. 322) "more often than not a requirement of developing correspondence between what we do, what we see, and what we say. It is this correspondence that is most strikingly involved in reading and writing, in school learning, and in other abstract pursuits."

The bond between word and action and thought, between language and experience, between reading and writing and communication, is of enormous importance. What educationally significant conclusions can we draw from these facts? It would seem that the most functional way to show children that reading is no more than speech written down is to do a great deal more than we do about using their language-experience-cognitive wealth to share each other's intellectual life. Piaget says (18, p. 64), "The mere fact, then, of telling one's thought, of telling it to others, or of keeping silence and telling it only to oneself must be of enormous importance to the fundamental structure and functioning of thought in general, and of child logic in particular."

It now remains, in the chapters that follow, for us to see how the Language-Experience Approach to initial reading instruction, in particular, and to all reading instruction, in general, is an effective means of accomplishing the high cognitive and communicative skills alluded to in this chapter. Numerous examples and details are provided for those who wish to use the approach.

Bibliography

1. Almy, Millie, Edward Chittenden, and Paula Miller. *Young Children's Thinking*. New York: Teachers College, Columbia University, 1966.

2. Austin, Mary, and Coleman Morrison. *The Torch Lighters, Tomorrow's Teachers of Reading*. Cambridge, Mass.: Harvard University Press, 1961.
3. Bayley, Nancy. "On the Growth of Intelligence," *The American Psychologist*, vol. 10, no. 12 (December, 1955), pp. 805–818.
4. Braine, M. S. "Piaget on Reasoning: A Methodological Critique and Alternative Proposals." In W. Kessen and Clementina Kuhlman, eds., "Thought in the Young Child," *Monographs of the Society for Research in Child Development*, vol. 27, no. 2 (whole no. 83), 1962, pp. 41–64.
5. Brown, Roger. *Social Psychology*. New York: Free Press, 1965.
6. Bruner, Jerome S., Rose R. Olver, and Patricia M. Greenfield. *Studies in Cognitive Growth*. New York: Wiley, 1966.
7. Carroll, John B. *Language and Thought*. Englewood Cliffs, N.J.: Prentice-Hall, 1964.
8. Dewey, John. *Experience and Education*. New York: Macmillan, 1938.
9. Duckworth, Eleanor, "Piaget Rediscovered." In *Piaget Rediscovered*, edited by Richard E. Ripple and Verne N. Rockcastle. A Report of the Conference on Cognitive Studies and Curriculum Development (March, 1964). Ithaca, N.Y.: School of Education, Cornell University, 1964.
10. Flavell, John H. *The Developmental Psychology of Jean Piaget*. Princeton, N.J.: Van Nostrand, 1963.
11. Hoffman, Martin L., and Lois Wladis, eds. *Review of Child Development Research*. Vol. 1. New York: Russell Sage Foundation, 1964.
12. Hunt, J. McV. *Intelligence and Experience*. New York: Ronald Press, 1961.
13. Kessen, W., and Clementina Kuhlman, eds. "Thought in the Young Child," *Monographs of the Society for Research in Child Development*, vol. 27, no. 2 (whole no. 83), 1962.
14. Klausmeier, Herbert J. *Concept Learning and Problem Solving: A Bibliography, 1950–1964*. Technical Report No. 1. Madison, Wis.: Research and Development Center for Learning and Re-Education, University of Wisconsin, 1965.
15. Kneller, George F. *Logic and Language of Education*. New York: Wiley, 1966.
16. Kooistra, W. H. "Developmental Trends in the Attainment of Conservation, Transitivity, and Relativism in the Thinking of Children: A Replication and Extension on Piaget's Ontogenetic Formulations."

Unpublished doctoral dissertation, Wayne State University, Detroit, Mich., 1963.

17. Piaget, Jean. "Development and Learning." In *Piaget Rediscovered*, edited by Richard E. Ripple and Verne N. Rockcastle. A Report of the Conference on Cognitive Studies and Curriculum Development (March, 1964). Ithaca, N.Y.: School of Education, Cornell University, 1964.

18. Piaget, Jean. *The Language and Thought of the Child*. New York: World Publishing, 1965.

19. Seashore, Robert H. "The Importance of Vocabulary in Learning Language Skills," *Elementary English*, vol. 25, no. 3 (March, 1948), pp. 137–152.

20. Sigel, Irving E. "The Attainment of Concepts. In *Review of Child Development Research*, edited by Martin L. Hoffman and Lois Wladis Hoffman. New York: Russell Sage Foundation, 1964.

21. Smedslund, J. "Transitivity of Preference Patterns as Seen by Pre-School Children," *Scandinavian Journal of Psychology*, vol. 1, no. 2 (1960), pp. 49–54.

22. Smith, Madorah E. "An Investigation of the Development of the Sentence and the Extent of Vocabulary in Young Children," *Studies in Child Welfare*, vol. 3, no. 5. Iowa City, Iowa: State University of Iowa, 1926.

23. Smith, Mary Katherine. "Measurement of the Size of General English Vocabulary Through the Elementary Grades and High School," *Genetic Psychology Monographs*, vol. 24, 2nd half (1941), pp. 311–345.

24. Stauffer, Russell G. "A Vocabulary Study Comparing Reading, Arithmetic, Health, and Science Texts," *The Reading Teacher*, vol. 20, no. 2 (November, 1966), pp. 141–147.

25. Strickland, Ruth B. "The Contribution of Structural Linguistics to the Teaching of Reading, Writing, and Grammar in the Elementary School, *Bulletin of the School of Education* (Indiana University), vol. 40, no. 1 (January, 1964).

26. Wiener, Norbert. *The Human Use of Human Beings*. Rev. ed. Garden City, N.Y.: Doubleday, 1954.

2
Dictated experience stories

This is one of the longest chapters in the book because it provides detailed accounts of how to get started as well as numerous illustrations.

The chapter is in four major parts. The first tells how to initiate a language-experience program in the first grade on the first days of school. The second part explains how to move from whole-class dictation to group dictation and on to individual dictation, undoubtedly the most fruitful. The third part describes stimulus interest areas or the acres-of-diamonds approach to learning to read. This part has seven subparts with numerous illustrations of children's dictation. The fourth part is concerned with how to preserve for the children the force and dignity of their own language.

Proceed as you did in Chapter 1. Read the following objectives and speculate about the answers. Again, it may be that because of your considerable knowledge in this area what you read may largely confirm what you already know. On the other hand, your knowledge may be limited and your speculations sparse. Remember, though, that your comprehension may be vastly improved if you proceed as a scholar by being intellectually honest with yourself and by committing yourself to answers. This honesty and commitment will help regulate your reading and increase your retention and understanding.

1. Explain how the Language-Experience Approach is the all-embracing approach to reading instruction.
2. Describe how getting started or getting ready to dictate takes full advantage of the sensible universe—sight, sound, smell, touch, taste—and the functional use of language by thought, word, and deed to show that reading is no more than talk written down.

19

3. Name sixteen things that occurred as a result of the recording of the first pupil dictation. Name seven things that a teacher discovered about her class on the first experience-dictate-read circumstance.
4. Describe how in many respects a teacher is able to make an informal inventory of pupil readiness for reading during the first week or two of school.

Upon reading the second section, the reader should meet these objectives if he first inquired of himself concerning answers and regulated his reading course by this speculation:

1. Explain how organizing a class into groups facilitates the obtaining of individually dictated stories and accounts in sufficient quantity to make learning to read a stimulant to learning to talk.
2. Describe how pupil action and group interaction provide the foundation for learning.
3. Explain the purpose of word underlining and story illustrations.
4. Tell how each dictated piece gives teachers an opportunity to "see" pupils' essential characteristics because dispositions are in continuous flow.

Upon reading section three, the reader should meet the following objectives if he first inquired of himself concerning the answers and regulated his reading course by this speculation.

1. Explain how every classroom, school building, and school playground represents literally an acre of diamonds.
2. Describe why the worlds of "I," "my," "me," and "home," and "neighborhood" can provide an innumerable supply of stimuli as well as a catharsis.
3. Explain why reading, when thought of as a process rather than a subject, utilizes to advantage the total curriculum.
4. Tell how a record book containing a chronological listing of dictated materials serves many purposes.

Upon reading section four, the reader should meet the following objectives if he first inquired of himself concerning answers and determined how to regulate his reading by this speculation:

1. Discuss four points presented on the language children use.
2. Distinguish between public language and formal language.

Introduction

Most teachers of reading agree in the belief that there is no single method of teaching reading to all pupils. Teachers who follow the Language Arts–Experience Approach heartily endorse this educational axiom. They do so, not in spite of their belief in the Language Arts–Experience Approach, but because of it. The approach represents an integration of conditions, all of which are rightly a part. <u>Language arts</u> encompasses the four facets of language and is founded on the social-personal condition of purposeful communication. <u>Experience</u> encompasses an individual's perceptual and conceptual world, his interests, curiosities, and creativity, his culture, and his capacity to adjust, learn, and use.

Other conditions, even though quite commonplace, warrant repeating and reestablishing. *First* is the fact that among typical six-year-olds the range of individual differences is at least 5 years. This means that, if reading instruction is to be paced even in part on ability grouping, the range and frequency of pupil distribution has to be determined and considered. *Second*, reading is not only to be thought of as a communication process but is also to be taught that way. Meaning is the important thing—not saying words. Reading is a thinking and not a parroting process. *Third*, individualized reading procedures as well as group reading procedures are to be used. *Fourth*, written materials must convey meaning in much the same way as does the oral communication of six-year-olds. Stilted artificiality must be avoided and no excuse can be trumped up for its use. *Fifth*, the vocabulary, concepts, and cognitive processes that children have developed for oral communication purposes must be utilized to the fullest degree possible by linking written words as the stimulus to trigger the same concepts. *Sixth*, word-attack skills must be taught as a first-aid to meaning. Words must be introduced in a communication context so that, as the reader moves along, meaning clues to recognition may also be a first order, functional source of help. Phonic elements must be taught in a pronunciation unit or in context, not in isolation. *Seventh*, pupil interests, experiences, and knowledge must be used as a basic source of funds and must be extended and refined. *Eight*, reading skills must be taught and paced in such a way that individuals are able to assimilate and use them. *Ninth*, the rules of the psychology of learning must be observed. *Tenth*, the freedom and responsibilities of self-selection must be initiated from the beginning. *Eleventh*, a love of and appreciation for what reading can do for people must be fostered.

Getting started

Most children come to first grade eager to read. The few who can read want to show that they can. Others are eager to show that they want to try. An immediate or at least an early start should be made. The object of the start is to show pupils that reading is no more than talk written down.

A good way to accomplish this is by means of a pupil-dictated experience story. Arrange to have available in the room some item that will catch and hold interest. One teacher began in a unique way by using a white mouse; its uniqueness contributed to its value as an attention-getting device and a means of stimulating oral language. There are many other similar ideas that could be used: a puppy, chick, baby rabbit, turtle, or parrot, a novel toy, a well-illustrated book such as *Hop on Pop*,[1] or a story well told.

With the mouse, the teacher placed its cage in the center of a pupil-viewing-level table. The pupils gathered around and watched the mouse move about in its cage. They saw it stand up on its back legs with its front feet up on the side of the cage. They saw it eat from a food tin. Then the teacher took the mouse out of the cage and allowed it to walk along the top of the desk. She showed no concern about handling the mouse and her confidence and poise very much influenced the class.

As the pupils watched, they talked and exclaimed: "Look, he's standing up!" "He has pink eyes." "See how long his tail is!" When this comment was made, the teacher asked the class to say how long they thought the tail was. Estimates were given that ranged from 6 inches to 4 feet. Regardless of the accuracy, the question had caused all to look again and examine with a different and specific purpose.

"What should we name him?" asked the teacher. This evoked a number of responses such as "Whitey," "Snow White," "Pink Eyes." Of the different names given, the class preferred "Snow White." The choice was made by a show of hands, which allowed all to participate, express an opinion, and operate in a democratic atmosphere. Group cohesion as *esprit de corps* was being developed.

The teacher put the mouse back into the cage, covered the cage, and

[1] Dr. Seuss, *Hop on Pop* (New York: Random House, 1963).

set it aside, and then she gathered the class around an easel on which she had tacked a large piece of newsprint. (Newsprint is lined paper approximately 2 feet by 3 feet in size.) After printing the mouse's new name, "Snow White," on the top line, she invited the class to tell about the mouse, indicating that she would print what they said, just as she had recorded the name.

Dick said: "Snow White scratched around in his cage." Jane added: "Snow White has pink eyes." Alice said: "He stood up on his hind legs and looked at us." And so on.

As each child offered an idea, the teacher recorded it, using appropriate printing and a heavy black crayon. Pupils noticed immediately that she could not write as fast as they talked. Even so, she wrote at a good pace and the waiting time was not long. After each idea had been recorded, she read it back to the group in general and to the pupil dictating in particular. Thus she proceeded, recording the ideas of six different pupils and completely filling the newsprint sheet. All this took but a few minutes; the pupils were fascinated by the performance and were eagerly attentive. The account when she finished read as follows:

Snow White
Dick said, "Snow White
scratched around in his cage."
Jane said, "Snow White has pink
eyes." Alice said, "He stood up
on his hind legs and looked at us."
Jerry said, "His tail is two feet
long." Bill said, "Snow White ran
around on the table." Nancy said,
"Snow White is soft and furry."

Now the teacher read the entire story to the class. As she read, she pointed quickly and briefly to each word. Then all the class read the story together. The teacher pointed to each word as they proceeded, saying each word and the pupils saying it with her. Even though the pointing and the repeating after by the pupils made for some arhythm, a surprisingly even paced performance resulted. The tone and intent of the teacher's voice helped bridge the slightly arhythmical gaps.

Next, she gave each pupil an 8½-x-11-inch sheet of white paper and asked them to make a drawing of Snow White. While the children were drawing, she went about the room, printing the words *Snow White* at the top of each paper. She gave some a chance to show that they had already learned to copy her printing as they proceeded to label their paper by themselves.

Some of the things that resulted from the experience are:

1. Pupils saw that reading is no more than talk written down.
2. They saw that the teacher could read back all the story or just parts of it.
3. They followed the reading process from left to right.
4. They made return sweeps from the end of one line on the right to the beginning of the next line on the left.
5. They saw that different letters are made differently. Some were capitals. *Snow White* always started with capital letters.
6. They saw the use of punctuation in a meaningful language context.
7. They experienced the thrill of "reading" as they read with the teacher.
8. Some of the pupils saw their names in writing and their ideas in writing.
9. They had displayed *curiosity* as they watched and examined the mouse and *creativity* as they told about their reactions.
10. They were stimulated to oral-language use as they reacted to seeing the mouse.
11. Ideas were shared in the dynamics of a class situation and in response to an immediate experience.
12. The teacher's questions had caused them to observe more carefully.
13. Each had opportunities to listen to others speak, to hear their ideas, and to discover how others reacted to the same circumstances.
14. Each had an opportunity to vote and express preference for a name for the mouse and to learn how to accept the decision of the majority.
15. Each had an opportunity to make his own drawing and thus show the attributes of the mouse that he was reacting to.
16. The name "Snow White" written on each drawing gave pupils an opportunity to link two symbols for one referent: a printed name and a picture.

In addition, the teacher had had an excellent opportunity to discover some things about her class:

1. their curiosity about the mouse
2. their concern or lack of concern about seeing the mouse out of the cage and on the table and their reluctance or readiness to touch the mouse
3. their willingness to move about the table and among each other
4. their oral-language usage and, particularly, their choice of words

5. their attention span, persistence, and cooperativeness;
6. whether some could read (as the story was being read back by the class, some continued to read ahead correctly)
7. their ability to use crayons and to illustrate ideas (the illustrations were some index to maturity and were revealing in ways similar to the Goodenough-Harris Drawing) (4)

For all concerned, this was a profitable experience. To be sure, the parents heard about the event. They also heard that reading had been done. "I read a story about Snow White," said one girl to her mother. "Oh," was the pleased reply, "You read about Snow White and the seven dwarfs?" "No, Mother, we read about a white mouse. We named him Snow White. See, here's his name on my picture. He's standing up looking at us."

The next day, the teacher divided the class into three arbitrary groups. In each group were two of the children who had dictated lines for the Snow White story. Then she had each group take a turn sitting with her in the back of the room around the story of the previous day.

She started each group session by rereading the story to them. Then they all reread it together as she pointed to the words. Next she invited Jerry to stand by her and read the chart with her. She started by merely pointing to the name of the chart and Jerry immediately supplied "Snow White." Each time the name *Snow White* appeared in the story, Jerry hurried ahead and read the words. He also recognized his name. "Reading" for Jerry had been a booming success.

Jane stood by the teacher next. Jane read the title, too, as Jerry had. But, each time the words *Snow White* appeared thereafter, Jane hesitated. All the teacher needed to do, though, was point in each instance to the same words in the title and Jane responded immediately. She also read her own name.

Others in the group were given opportunity to "read," too. The teacher stayed alert to the interest of the group and the activities of the rest of the class. Some were looking at books that had been placed on the library table. Others were in the house corner, playing. Still others were drawing. Some sat together; some preferred to work alone. The teacher was careful not to overplay the attention span and interest of the group sitting with her or of others in the class.

In the next group, Nancy did a fine reading job. She read "*Snow White*" each time it appeared. She read the name of each pupil and the word *said:* "Dick said," "Jane said," and so on. When they got to the sentence she had dictated, she read all of it: "Nancy said, 'Snow White is soft and furry.'"

Dick took his turn and needed a little help with the story name. All the teacher did, though, was make an *s-s-s* sound, and Dick caught on. This help was needed each time. A pause on his name was sufficient to prompt him to remember that this was his contribution and therefore his name.

In the third group, Alice performed as Jerry had. Bill, however, astonished the group. He read almost the entire story, needing help only with *scratched* and *furry*. Now the teacher went a step further. She asked Bill to locate certain words. First, she said, "Point to your name." This he did quickly. Then she had him point to *Dick, Jane, Nancy, Jerry,* and *Alice* in that order. He found each name almost as quickly as he had located his own. Next, she asked Bill to count the number of times *Snow White* appeared in the story. He proceeded to count as he pointed, starting with the title, and gave the number five.

By this time the teacher had gathered the entire class around. Next, she had Bill locate the words *table* and *around*. Both appeared in his contribution, so she had felt reasonably confident about these two requests. Then she said, "One of those two words appears at some other place in the story. Which one?" This was a challenging question. Bill had to compare words and make a decision. In a few seconds, though, he had located *around* in the second line.

Now the teacher tried one more thing. She saw that all this was holding the attention of the class and she realized that she was being given an ideal opportunity to make points about how interesting reading can be. She printed the word *table* on the chalkboard and asked Bill to read it. This he did instantly, even though it was in isolation. Then she wrote the number *two* on the board and he named it. Next, she wrote the word *pink*. He could not say the word but he apparently recognized its configuration or knew it iconically. On his own he walked to the chart and located the word. Then he announced that the word was "pink." How did he do this? The power of communication had taught him to recognize words not only by their configuration but also by their total language context.

Many things occurred during this second day with the "Snow White" story that were very desirable, both for the pupils and for the teacher. For the pupils, the following observations are particularly relevant.

1. They had an opportunity to work in a group as well as work on their own or with some other classmate.

2. When they were not in the reading group, they had an opportunity to decide what they would do from a list of opportunities prescribed by the teacher.
3. They could do some "book selecting" at the library table.
4. They could read. As is revealed by the performance of the six children who dictated, reading performance varied according to ability.
5. They could listen to others read.
6. Each pupil who had a chance to read also had a chance to succeed. Some read only the title but some, like Nancy, read six or more words.
7. The range of words read varied from Dick, who knew two words with a bit of hissing help from the teacher, to Bill, who knew thirty-five of the thirty-seven different words and who read fifty-four of the fifty-six running words.
8. Visual discrimination of words was accomplished early in the school year, *without* drawing shadow boxes, an extremely artificial crutch. The teacher did not have to frame any of the words with her hands, this, too, a weak sort of aid.

9. Visual-auditory discrimination occurred each time the pupils located a word the teacher had spoken and each time they read with her.
10. The sounds that letters represent were linked in a phonetic word attack. When the teacher helped Dick recall "Snow White" by making the *s-s-s* sound, the attack linkage became more specific.

In many respects, the teacher was able to make an informal inventory of pupil readiness for reading. Each pupil's performance allowed her to make notes about their skills. For example, she learned that Bill could read many words; he had already indicated that he knew thirty-five words. This total is higher than what is found in the first two preprimers of most reader series. He knew words in isolation as well as in context. But above all, he knew how to use context clues and word meaning as an aid in word recognition. When Bill returned to the story and located and identified the word *pink*, he showed command of one of the most important skills in any word attack—the use of meaning clues or the power of comprehension.

Jerry, on the other hand, indicated that he recognized only three words: *Snow*, *White*, and *Jerry*. He knew *Snow White* each time it occurred, showing clearly that he had a visual image for the word. It also provided evidence that he linked the right auditory image with the right visual image.

It is to be noted again that the total performance of the class stands in sharp contrast not only to the result of the use of the content of pre-primers but also to the memoriter skills-in-isolation approach to word learning. This teacher did not give the class a list of words to take home, so distaste for reading was not reinforced at home as well as in school. Instead, she got their attention through an old psychology-of-learning trick: She used a *novel* experience, *different* and *vivid* and within their grasp. Then she allowed the pupils to react by letting them talk rather than by imposing her ideas. She arranged to have recontact or reinforcement of learning within 24 hours, when forgetting occurs at a rapid rate, both in logical and in rote learning. Each time a pupil read the story, others in the group had recontact with the words.

By the third day, this teacher had reproduced the "Snow White" story on hectograph and had a copy available for each pupil, giving them an opportunity to pour over the story as much as they wished. This day, she moved about from individual to individual, and in private person-to-person sessions she read through the story with each pupil. This time each word that a pupil could read on his own was underlined by the teacher. Some had only the title underlined, whereas Bill had every word underlined. In addition, the teacher wrote the name of each pupil at the end of the story. In a few instances, pupils were able to write their own names.

On the classroom library table was the story of "Snow White and the Seven Dwarfs." Pupils gained a great deal of scholarly pleasure from the fact that they could read the words *Snow White* in a book. In addition, the teacher had a booklet about a snowman, and some pupils discovered they could read the word *snow* there, too. Some could read the entire word *snowman.* One little girl had brought with her from home a copy of *Jack and Jill* magazine, in which, in a story with a winter setting, the word "snow" appeared a number of times.

So these children were encouraged to make immediate transfer of their reading knowledge to different contexts—manuscript writing and print in books. Interestingly enough, they made the transfer without raising any questions about the differences in the printed form and shape of letters with different type-face styles and in manuscript writing.

In addition, the teacher had found time to accomplish all the other pupil-getting-acquainted activities that are a part of the first days in school: recognizing names and name cards, locating seats and desks, closets and lavatories, meeting the teacher next door, the school nurse, the principal, and so on. She read orally to the children, told stories, had them listen to music, and soon had them settled into the business of school life.

Grouping as an aid to individualized instruction

Not all the time during the first weeks was devoted to getting acquainted, nor was all the time devoted to reading. The teacher did, however, continue with other experience stories in which the pupils dictated in response to a shared and immediate firsthand experience. The school librarian stopped in one day and told a story to the class, and this story was used as a prop for other pupil-dictated stories. A group of eight-year-old children came in one day and performed a puppet show. This was an excellent source of stimulation for dictated stories.

By the end of the first 3 weeks, this teacher had acquired much understanding concerning the language facility, the interest and tastes, the intellectual maturity, and the social-personal poise of each pupil. Now, to differentiate reading instruction and pace the learning of each one as individually as possible, she organized the class into groups, thus permitting opportunity for enough individually dictated stories to make them useful. Moving around the room from pupil to pupil was not as efficient for systematic help as working with small subgroups, so the teacher placed Bill and five others in Level IV group, Nancy and seven others in Level III group, Jerry and eleven others in Level II group, and Dick and five others in Level I group. In most instances the groups were otherwise formed spontaneously along interest lines.

In the Level IV group, Bill was advanced well beyond the others. He already had a sizable reading vocabulary and was having a grand time reading his way through the books in the library corner. The teacher, with her modified individualized reading approach, had made provision for Bill and the other budding Bills. He was keeping a record of the books he read and was sharing his enthusiasm and book knowledge with others in the room. He shared informally with his friends, and he discovered as well that he could share interests with other classmates. Two others in his "dictating" group were catching on fast, learning words and reading.

Dick and the pupils in his group, on the other hand, seemed almost miles apart from Bill. Even so, they were doing just what Bill was doing. They were dictating stories, oftentimes about the same stimulus or experience areas as he did. This was especially true when the interest was one in which the whole class participated. They "read" their stories on the two-voice (teacher-pupil) level. They read, and that was the important thing! They took books from the library shelf and "read" them. Then, too, at times Bill would sit next to Dick in the library corner and, in a low whisper, read a story to him. Furthermore, at times Bill would help Dick with words when he was "rereading" his old experience stories or reading a library book.

Everyone in the class knew that Bill was just about the best reader and that Dick was not. But they also knew that Dick was coming along. Dick knew this too. So did Dick's parents and so did Bill's parents. The climate that prevailed in the classroom was best measured by the rising enthusiasm, good will, and self-reliance.

Once the class had been organized into dictating groups, the teacher was able to sit with each group for pupil dictation on an average of twice a week. (The cycle will be enlarged upon later.) It seems timely to study how the teacher worked with groups IV and I.

Group IV, Bill's group, had six members. At the appointed time, they came to the dictating corner. The pupils sat in a semicircle facing the teacher in the center. This is how the group assembled and prepared for the *individual* story-dictating session.

In this instance, the source of interest was a turtle that one of the boys had brought to school. Earlier in the day, all the children in the class had gathered around to watch the turtle and to hear Bob tell how he had found it. The turtle was in a box that looked like a suit box. Grass and twigs and a small rock were in the box, as well as a pie tin containing water and stones to help anchor it. The group was gathered about this natural science exhibit, watching it and talking about it.

The teacher moved to the dictating table, a small table at pupil height, on which she had placed sheets of lined paper, approximately 11 × 15 inches in size, and a black crayon. A small screen provided some privacy by partially separating the table from the rest of the classroom. Then, one at a time, the pupils took turns sitting with the teacher and dictating. Bill dictated the following story:

The Walking Fort
I called the turtle
"The Walking Fort" because
that is what he is. He
carries his fort on his back.

When he walks along, if he
sees some trouble, he pulls
in his neck and his feet.
Then he is safe in his fort.
I told my dad about the
walking fort and he said
the turtle was like an
army tank. But I like
"The Walking Fort" better.

After Bill had dictated the story, the teacher read it back to him to see if everything was in order. Bill said the story was correct as he had dictated it. Then the teacher gave the story to Bill, and he returned to his regular classroom seat to do what he chose with it. He could do a number of things. First, he reread the story. Bill was already so facile at learning new words that he was asked to underline only words he did *not* recognize or was not sure about. In this instance, he could read the entire story. He paused at the word *carries* but was able to recognize it when he read on and the sentence-meaning provided recognition closure. Even so, he lightly drew a line under *carries*.

This done, he turned to his vocabulary book, or new-word book, as he called it. Bill's mother had bought this alphabetized notebook for him, but he could have alphabetized it himself because he already knew the alphabet and could write the letters. Some that he was not too sure about he copied from the alphabet chart on his desk. In his book he entered only words "new and interesting" to him. From this story he chose *turtle, fort, carries, trouble, neck, army, tank, better*.

While Bill was doing this, the five other members of the group were taking turns dictating. Edna dictated the following:

Race
I could run a
race with the turtle.
He has four feet but
he can't go fast. I
have only two feet
but I could win the
race.

The story was read back to Edna and then she went to her seat. Even though no one in the group was as advanced as Bill, they had progressed to the point where they too could underline only words they did not know or were not sure about. In this story, Edna underlined *could, can't,* and *only.* Then she started to draw a picture to accompany her story.

She had just started with her picture when the four others in the group had finished dictating their stories. Then the six reassembled with the teacher and took turns reading their stories to each other. One at a time they stood by the teacher and read the story aloud to the group. This allowed the teacher to follow the oral reading and to note which words were underlined so she could be ready to supply the unknown words if necessary. This helped the oral-reading performance and helped the listener hear and understand the story. Edna needed help with *could* and *only.* Rereading the story aloud led her to recognize the word *can't.* Somehow, the demands of oral reading, language rhythm, and the flow of ideas often serve recall this way.

When the group meeting ended, all returned to their seats. Bill continued with his vocabulary book. Edna and the others continued with their illustrations to accompany their stories.

At another time that day, the teacher sat with Dick's group of six. They, too, assembled around the turtle box and talked again about the turtle. Bob was in this group and he told again how the turtle came out of the water when his dad was fishing. With this group the teacher did more perceptual prodding as the pupils watched the turtle move about in the box. She made such comments as "See how he pulls his head in" and "See how he goes around the rock." Then she set up the easel with newsprint thumbtacked to it and proceeded to record what the members of the group had to say. She used a group-story approach with these pupils because none seemed verbal enough or responsive enough to dictate a more detailed account on his own. The stimulation of one upon another helped elicit a story. The account recorded in this instance was as follows.

Bob's Turtle

My dad saw the
turtle when he fished.
The turtle is little.
The turtle can pull
his head in. He has
spots on his back.

> Bob
> Mae
> Gale
> Jimmy

The names on the end were those of the four pupils who gave sentences. The fact that not all the children in the group contributed was of little concern. Some days all added an idea; some days only a few did. Some days the group selected one member to tell the story for the group.

After the story was dictated, the teacher read it back to the group, pointing very briefly to each word as she proceeded. Then different pupils took turns standing by the easel and participating in a two-member (teacher and pupil) oral reading of the story. Bob was up first. He knew his own name and said "turtle" when he read the title. When he came to the word *turtle* in the first sentence, he did not recognize it again. Instead of telling him the word immediately, the teacher pointed to the word in the title. He recognized it and made a discovery association—the two words were the same. The teacher's resourcefulness prevented the need to tell him the word. Bob knew the word *fished* when they got to it and he recognized *turtle* the next two times it occurred in the story.

Two more pupils read through the story with the teacher. Then they all returned to their seats to draw pictures to accompany their story. Bob drew a picture of his father fishing, Jimmy drew one to show the spots on the turtle's back, Dick drew a turtle on a rock, and so on. They knew that by the next day the teacher would have reproduced a copy of the story for each.

By the time the teacher was through reading the story with the group, Bill had read it silently at his seat and so had Edna. They had both been prompted by interest in reading and curiosity about what the others said. And, of course, Bill was interested in how Dick was doing.

The next day, Jerry's group of twelve met around the turtle box. At this early stage, this group occasionally dictated a group story, as Dick's group had. Whenever a story or account had been dictated as a result of a firsthand experience, however, individual stories were obtained.

Teachers sometimes voice concern about time, when so many individual stories are to be obtained. Such concern is not unfounded, but the best thing to do is to meet the situation and thereby discover that it can be carried through. Time need not be a factor. It was not in this case. Teachers working with comparable groups have been timed. In one instance, a demonstration in the Seaford, Delaware, Central Elementary School was observed by five first-grade teachers. Their presence added some pressure that might have interfered.

A group was assembled and the interest area was briefly discussed with the pupils. Thinking was stimulated and ideas were shared. Then, one at a time, the pupils sat down with the teacher and dictated. The stories averaged about three sentences in length. In this demonstration, done late in September of the school year, the pupils had already had some experience dictating stories and expressing their own ideas. Even so, they were not unusual, verbose, or creative. Each pupil had his own ideas, however, and voiced them in his own way.

After each child had dictated, he returned to his seat with his story and reread it silently. As he read, he underlined with a single black line each word he felt he *knew*. Guesses were not to be underlined—only words the pupils felt sure about.

When each child had dictated a story and the last one had had a few minutes to reread and mark his story, they all reassembled, and, one by one, they read aloud with the teacher as Dick's group had. The teacher clipped each child's story on the easel and pointed to each word as she proceeded, allowing for enough hesitation to encourage the child to say the word if he knew it or thought he did. Again, as with the Level I pupils, the language pattern and context of the story often helped the pupil recall words that he did not recognize on his own.

The time for the whole group was 33 minutes. Dictating and writing took 23 minutes; oral rereading and sharing took 10 minutes. Even so, the whole procedure was unhurried.

Some typical stories are:

Mr. Turtle
Mr. Turtle walks on
four feet. He is very slow.

The Funny House
The turtle walks around
in his house. His house
has a hard roof. It's a
funny house.

Slow and Easy
I like a turtle. I
like to watch him crawl
around. He is slow and
easy.

Spotty
The turtle has spots
like my cat. I called
him Spotty. That's my
cat's name.

The Turtle
When the turtle eats,
he sticks his heat out.
His eyes are open.

The words underlined are the ones that the pupils felt they knew when they reread their stories silently at their seats. Underlining this way is a positive approach to word learning, because the emphasis is on what is known. Also, it calls for a facing up to the facts: One either knows or does not know, or one guesses. Underlining therefore requires a certain amount of intellectual honesty. The need to "prove knowledge" occurs at the time of the oral reading. The teacher pauses a bit longer on each underlined word. If the word goes unrecognized, the teacher supplies the word and the underlining is marked:　 ⁄ ⁄ ⁄ ⁄ ⁄ ⁄

These pupils now prepared a picture of a turtle or a turtle scene. (Pictures of turtles may be available in magazines. If the magazines are expendable, the pictures may be cut out. Drawings by the pupils are to be preferred, however.)

Next Nancy's group, the Level III group, was assembled. All eight gathered around the turtle to watch and talk and share ideas. Then one by one they sat down with the teacher and dictated their accounts of their turtle observations and their ideas. Some were much like those dictated by members of Bill's group, insofar as length and originality were concerned. Others were more like the Level II accounts. Nancy dictated the following:

The Lonesome Turtle
I believe the turtle
is lonesome. He walks
around so slow and looks
so sad. Sometimes he
looks out at us and
then he pulls his head
in again. I believe he
is lonesome.

Nancy returned to her seat and underlined words she did *not* know or was not sure about. Nancy was a cautious person, more inclined to underestimate her knowledge than to overestimate it, as is reflected by the underlined words.

Nancy's reaction to the turtle also reflects her personal dispositions (1) and motives. Her response to the turtle suggests strong regard for the welfare of others. The one little turtle in the big box being watched by so many people, poking his head out and pulling it in again, apparently aroused her flow of ideas. Nancy's general disposition found many stimuli that were functionally equivalent and that guided her to a form of behavior that was already being labeled as: "That's Nancy for you." This was not only Nancy's way of reacting to her environment but her way of meeting it.

It seems opportune here to repeat Ben Jonson's counsel in his statement: "Speak, that I may see thee" (8). Dictated stories give pupils an opportunity to speak and show themselves. Similarly, they give teachers an opportunity to learn what the pupils' essential characteristics are, because dispositions are in continuous flow. As Gordon Allport has stated: "Interests, ambitions, compulsions, phobias, general attitudes, inclinations, hobbies, values, tastes, predilections—all are personal dispositions (some only secondary) and are at the same time motives" (1, p. 373). Thus Rick, dictating the following story, revealed his personal dispositions.

The Explorer
This turtle is an
explorer. He goes
around exploring. He
came out of the water
to explore. He explores
our box.

In this section of the chapter, three ways of obtaining pupil-dictated experience stories have been described: whole class, group, and individual. The first few days and weeks of school are opportune moments for obtaining whole-class stories, and any number of teaching-learning effects can be accomplished by starting early.

Children interacting as members of a class have the opportunity to get acquainted with each other linguistically, socially, culturally, emotionally, physically, and intellectually. Each stimulus permits the children to move about, to listen and talk to one another, to show or acquire regard for the rights of others. The whole-class story becomes a possession of each pupil, even though only five or six may have contributed literally. Their language unfolds what is cognitively and linguistically latent in all, because it is brought into operation functionally and dynamically as firsthand experience.

Much the same can be said for smaller groups, although there are a number of important differences. Each time a different group is formed, whether spontaneously or by the teacher, different kinds of social-personal arrangements occur: Understandings, habits, and practices relating to social choice and individual values and the reconciling of conflicting individual and group desires or interpretations all become powerful sources for promoting adjustment and emotional reinforcement. In our mobile society, such opportunities should help children adjust to changing functional organization related to learning and communication.

In both the class and the group, each individual may be stimulated to do his own thinking and reacting but, as a member of a group, he is susceptible and responsive to the language habits of others. He is one among many and subject to the polarization that occurs along different lines at different times. But adaptability to change, particularly the free exchange of ideas, is latent in the flexibility of the shifting group membership.

Individual stories yield the best return to an individual and are best for achieving the reading skills aimed at by the teacher. The shift from whole-class and group stories to individual dictation should be made as soon as possible. Many of the benefits associated with group circumstances will continue if procedures such as those just described are followed. The sharing of experiences and the oral interchange of ideas is particularly valuable.

Furthermore, the opportunity for each child to express his own ideas in his own way is most productive. He has the teacher's attention; his words are recorded; he is the author. At a later time, he can share his account of an experience with his classmates and he can share their accounts. The likelihood that he will recognize and remember words in his recorded accounts is greatly increased, because the words are of his choosing and represent his oral language-experience commitment.

Stimulus interest areas

Many people are familiar with the "Acres of Diamonds" story told so often by Russell Conwell, founder of Temple University in Philadelphia. He told about the man who searched around the world for an acre of diamonds and was unsuccessful. He returned home and started cultivating his garden and there he found his acre of diamonds. This is a most fitting introduction to the question of interest stimuli or what the children shall dictate about. Every classroom, school building, and playground represents literally an acre of diamonds of ideas. If to this is added the experiences children bring with them to school, it becomes readily apparent that acres of "interest" diamonds are available—personal, home, neighborhood and community, school, historical and cultural specialties, current and seasonal events, books and papers, TV and theater, and so on.

PERSONAL

This is the world of "I," "me," "my," and "mine." What I am and what is mine have been impressed on me by each of my years of experience. As I have grown I have walked, talked, laughed, cried, eaten, slept, played, worked, given, received, loved, hated. Now that I am six, I know who I am and what is mine. What I know may not be what you know or how you see me, but it is my summation. I am developing my style of life. I may not be a well-rounded person, but already many rough edges have been rounded. I have my likes and dislikes, my fears and anxieties, my feelings of adequacy, my attitudes and biases, and a will to live and be loved. The effects of my experiences have shaped my affections, my expectations, my needs. If you want, I will tell you about them. (What child does not want? Some may require special reassuring that "you want," but that is all that is needed.) Already I have secret thoughts. I may reveal some and conceal others. But if you see me as a person—my hair and the way I wear it, my eyes, my nose, my smile, my walk, my talk, my friends—then I am more apt to be free and alert and willing to share my most precious possession— my self. The following stories dictated by children from either Seaford or Rehoboth, Delaware, are illustrative.

All About Me

I like to ride my bicycle.
There is a hole at home and I
like to play in it. I make
mud cakes. I play with my
dollbaby, and sometimes she
cries, and these are real
tears. She blows bubbles in
her bubble pipe. I play in
my house, too, with my books.

Debbie

Myself

I have brown hair. I can
read some books. I am in the
first grade. I like to unfold
my picture. It is called a
snapshot. I like to build with
my Tinker Toys. I like to watch
television. I like to watch
Superman. I am six.

Jimmy

Me

Me and my brother ride into
Seaford to play at the Seaford
school and my Dad drives my
little brother in and he plays on
the swings. Me and my
brother, we go over there on
the trapeze to play. And on
the monkey bars. One night we
went over to the football field.
And tomorrow we are going up
home.

Michael

Me

You don't know who my girl-
friend is. Guess, Penny B. or
Beverly. It is Beverly. She
is pretty. She goes on my bus.
My brother's name is Tony and
so is Jeff's. My best boy
friend is Jay Clark and I got
some more. My hobby is sports
cars. Tony collects sports car
models.

Keith

I Come and I See

I come to school on a
school bus. I see plenty of
birds. I see all color leaves
on the trees. I see green grass.
I see people at the big school.

David

Me

I cried all the time when I
was a baby. I didn't want to go
to bed.

Conrad

No matter what the stimulus, a pupil has only his own experiences, first hand or indirect, to call upon when he is invited to respond. It is easier for him to respond when he is asked to react to a direct experience. When he is asked to project, though, what he says is the product of a process that takes place in the pupil's mind. To a degree, each dictation has some of the revealing qualities that Henry Murray sought when he used a series of pictures to elicit from a subject data about himself (9). He suggested that a person's perceptual reactions yield information about the ways he looks at his world. He labeled the method the Thematic Apperception Test (TAT): Thematic refers to the themes dictated and apperception describes the perceptual-interpretive use made of a stimulus.

In a way, each dictated story is a TAT. Each is revealing, and the alert teacher can become increasingly more sensitive to the psychodynamics displayed. It is generally said that a TAT can yield information about seven aspects of adjustment: (1) thought organization, (2) emotional organization, (3) needs, (4) the subject's view of the world, (5) interpersonal relationships, (6) the subject's conception of and attitude toward himself, and (7) the dynamics of development and illness (6, p. 211).

This reference to the TAT and its use as a clinical test is not to suggest to teachers that they become amateur clinical interpreters. The stories and accounts children dictate are not TAT protocols. On the other hand, to a sensitive teacher the stories reflect the moods and traces of recent experiences, the psychodynamic features of a pupil's intellectual and emotional functioning. They can be revealing and helpful. Each dictation opportunity may provide a catharsis that may be quite helpful to a pupil and revealing to a perceptive teacher.

HOME

Be it ever so humble, there is no place like home. Stories about home and the family are easy to obtain. It is a place dear to each one, and each in his way is ready to talk about some aspect of home. Home consists of mother, father, sister, brother, grandparents, uncles, aunts, cousins, pets, toys, bedrooms, bathrooms, living rooms, family rooms, kitchens, play-rooms, yards, sidewalks, elevators, garages. All these for some children, only a few for others. In almost every instance, be it ever so humble, pupils feel warmly about their homes. As stated earlier, the following stories were dictated by children from either Seaford or Rehoboth, Delaware, and are examples of the variety of topics children choose when dictating about home.

My Mother

My mother is nice.
She does nice things. She
is pretty. She loves me.

                    Steven

My Father

My father works in
Oklahoma. My father loves me
and I love him too. He buys
me a lot of toys. He is nice.

                    Steven

My Father

My father is in the army.
When he is not in the army, he
teaches school. He sure is
brave.

                    Jack

My House

My house is made out of
bricks. My house is on Old
Meadow Road. I like the living
room because I have set up
trains. My house has a basement
and an attic. My house has three
holes in the chimney.

                    Jimmy

My Pet Turtle

I have a turtle. It crawls
around in the aquarium. I feed
my turtle. Mopsy is my turtle.

                    Conrad

My Baby Brother

My little baby brother has a
broken collar bone. When Tommy
was little he used to cry a lot.

                    Scott

My Mother

My mother cooks breakfast
for me. Then she takes me to
school. She brings me in a
car.

                    John

My Daddy

My Daddy sits at the fire
place with me and drinks coffee
with me. He cooks outside
sometimes.

                    Scott

My Pets

I have a stray cat. I have
a dog. Her name is Corky. My
dog has a house and a pen is
around it. I am going to build
a house for my cat. I like to
let my dog out, but he jumps up
and I can't let him out.

                    Jimmy

My House

We like our house. I play
with my dog, and we go in the
house when it is time for supper.

                    Michele

Baby

I have a baby sister. She
plays with me. My baby sister
gets me up for school in the
morning.

Steven

My Family

I got a little sister,
Donna Mae Davis. That's all
except me, Debbie Davis. My
mother's name is Evelyn and my
father's name is Arthur.

Debbie

Nothing

I have a cat named Nothing. He
comes at the window and we let him
in. We named him Nothing because
he is Nothing. He has fleas and
he gives me them. We had him
since he was a kitten. Nothing is
three years old. He is a big Tom cat.

Laurie

My House

My house is big. My house is
gray. Sometimes we sit on the steps
at my house. Me and my mother sit
on the steps. From far, far away it
looks little. I don't have any stair
steps. I do not live alone in my
house. I live with my aunt. Her
baby's name is Wade. I have a kitchen,
a living room, a bathroom, and two
bedrooms. One bedroom is yellow
and one is pink. The kitchen is
gray. My bathroom is pink. I
sleep in my bedroom.

DeeDee

John the Slug

I have a slug snail. And I
like to look at it. He was in
the yard.

Ricky

My Brother Pushed Me

When I go down the hill my
brother walks. I ride in my
wagon. My wagon is red. My
brother pushes me full speed and
I fall off. I didn't cry because
I had my football suit on.

Conrad

The stories above were dictated by white and black children. Generally
speaking, it is difficult to determine who dictated which story. Of the

home stories, though, the last one presented was dictated by a six-year-old black girl. Note the warmth and good feeling apparent, the sensitivity to color in the various rooms, the quality of the language and the orderliness of the ideas. All that most children need is an opportunity to talk and the receptivity of a teacher who understands and encourages.

James Hymes, writing about discipline, made a statement that seems appropriate here (7, p. 49):

> Some youngsters have never really known a friend. They have been hit and hurt. Their parents even urge you to hit them if they are bad. Adults have never shown a warm side to these boys and girls. You will see the effect of this treatment at the very first. But don't forget: Their human nature is on your side. The fact that they have never truly known a kind person, a decent person, someone who could laugh and joke and talk with them, makes them all the more hungry for what you have to offer.

All the stories recorded in these pages were dictated during the first 2 months of school by six-year-old first-graders, most of whom were attending school for the first time. A few had had kindergarten experience. Children talk if appropriately encouraged to do so. Equally important is that they enjoy doing so and look forward eagerly to each opportunity.

NEIGHBORHOOD AND COMMUNITY

Everyone lives somewhere. Everyone has neighbors and a neighborhood. The city child knows his block and can tell you when he is near his neighborhood. Suburbanite and village children can do the same. The child in the country knows his home area and can tell you about it.

Each interest and stimulus provokes its own feelings and responses, its own vocabulary. Each has its own horizon. Note how this is reflected in the following stories:

The Acme

When my mother carried me to the Acme Market, I saw some toys and a tommy gun.

Frankie

Crickets

I like to find crickets.
One is five and one is six.

Ronald

We Go Hunting

I like a BB gun that shoots BB's. That is my favorite thing. I like to shoot birds. I kill 'em with my BB gun. I go hunting with my daddy. My daddy has got a real rifle.

Conrad

My Street

I live on the street that
there was a river on, and when
summer comes I am going to go
out and pick up some sea shells
that were in the river. My
mother does not know there was
a river. She thinks I found
the Atlantic Ocean. I live on
the same street that Laurie lives on.

Wayne

Where I Live

I live in Nanticoke Acres. I
like Nanticoke Acres because I
have friends there. My house is
brown. In the summer my father
paints the house. I help my
father paint the house. Pat Hill
lives by me. Pat's house is red.
The Bice's live by us. Their
house is gray. They have a little
swimming pool in their yard. Our
road is made of stones.

Scott

The Centennial

Seaford is one hundred years
old this week. We had lots of
practices and yesterday our
mothers came to see us out in
the court. We had a program to
celebrate the centennial. Keith
and Raymond wore centennial hats.
Some of the girls wore long
dresses. We danced in the
program. We had to have partners.

Mary

I Help Daddy

I rake up the yard and Daddy
helps me and so does my brother.
We burn them up, and Daddy likes
it. When we come home from school
we have to rake the other side.

Jack

Things I Did Over the Weekend

I went to church on Sunday.
I went out to lunch on Sunday. I
went to the English Grill. We
had a big meal.

Jimmy

Stop and Go

One day Dad was driving our
car. He was driving in Maryland.
He saw the red light and he stopped.
Then it turned green. He started
slow and then he went faster. The
cops were after him. They
caught him and gave him a ticket.
He was going too fast.

John

Trip to the Firehouse

I went to the firehouse. And
I went on the firetruck. I saw
the boots and the coats and the
hats.

Jane

Firemen
I like firemen. They put out
fires. They wear strong hats, and
they wear these hats so that nothing
can hurt their heads.

Sam

Neighborhood and community resources are so numerous that ideas could supply an entire year's dictating program, ranging from the home to the zoo, the park, the theater, the courthouse, the mayor's office, churches, and the YMCA. It should be realized that some do not require field trips, and, for those that do, valuable time should not be lost or wasted by unwise planning or making trips too frequently.

CURRENT AND SEASONAL EVENTS

As all teachers know, the school year has a number of fixed events: Halloween, Thanksgiving, Christmas, Lincoln's Birthday, Valentine's Day, Washington's Birthday, Easter. Some schools have even more. For the teacher using the Language-Experience Approach, these events are a boon rather than a liability. The interest stimulated by them can be used to advantage for communication.

In addition, current happenings are a constant and ready, as well as novel and variable, source of stories: Ships to the moon, inauguration of a President, a bridge collapse, a hurricane, a snowstorm, a centennial, a fire, an accident, and so on. They command attention and turn up in discussions in school corridors and cloakrooms. The alert teacher brings the discussions into the classroom and takes full advantage of the intense motivation they provide.

The Easter Bunny
The Easter bunny's ears are long.
He is gray. The Easter bunny has a
little round tail. He gives all of
us Easter eggs for Easter.

Pearl

Spring
In the spring we see flowers.
There are pussy willows. We see
daffodils. They are yellow. We have
spring showers. Last night we had a
thunderstorm. I saw some lightning

in my window. We have seen a robin.
This is a sign of spring.

Arlene

Valentine's Day

On Valentine's Day we went riding.
We went to see where my boyfriend lives.
We had fun.

Mary

The Pumpkin

Mrs. Johnson brought a pumpkin to
school. The pumpkin is little. We
put it on a shelf. We will make eyes
in it and a mouth. Nathaniel said to
put a tongue in his mouth then we will
have a jack-o-lantern.

Frankie

Santa Claus

Me and my brother went to see Santa
Claus last night. Santa Claus gave me
a candy cane. I told him what I wanted
for Christmas.

Ronald

The Inauguration

We watched TV. We saw Mr. Johnson.
He was made President. He put up his
right hand and put one hand on the Bible.
A man prayed. A woman sang. The people
stood up and we did too when the band
played.

Beverly

Dental Health Week

I brush my teeth at school. I brush
them every day. So does Jimmy. He
waits for me. We saw a filmstrip about
Tommy Tooth. Billy lost a tooth. He
put it under his pillow. The next
morning he found a quarter under his
pillow.

Martin

The Pilgrims

The pilgrims came over on the Mayflower.
The pilgrims found out that there were
Indians on this land. I heard about
the pilgrims and the Indians had a
Thanksgiving dinner.

                                    Bob

Going to the Circus

We went to see the Hawks on Friday.
We ate supper early. On Saturday at
10:30 we went to see Ringling
Brothers and Barnum and Bailey Circus. We
saw a man jump rope on a highwire. We
saw some clowns and a mother clown with
a baby clown.

                                    Scott

Abraham Lincoln

Abraham Lincoln has a memorial in
Washington, D.C. His statue is in the
memorial. He was our sixteenth President.
His birthday was February twelfth. He was
born in a log cabin. When he was President,
he got shot. Lincoln was in the theater
watching a play and somebody came and
shot him.

                                    William

The Coal-Mining Country

Mother and father and me went up to
the coal-mining country. We went to
see my uncle and aunt. I got some coal
and I got some slate. I seen the big
diggers. Some of the things they put on
the diggers are big enough to drive your
car in. They have big trucks to haul
the coal in. They go in the coal mines.

                                    David

Holiday Inn

We had a turkey at the Holiday Inn.
We ate him. My mother had a drink. I

had a drink of a little soda. My mother
had another drink. We had little
swords with our drinks.

Lucy

Rocket
We watched the rocket go off. Part
of the rocket came off. We watched it
go off. When it comes down it goes
under the water.

Jane

SCHOOL AND CURRICULUM

In 1963, when the directors of the twenty-seven studies concerned with different approaches to first-grade reading instruction met in Minneapolis, one of the variables they wished to stabilize and control was reading-instruction time. No decision could be reached at that summer meeting. When they met again, in December, it was thought urgent that reading-instruction time be defined. Still no agreement could be reached (10, p. 564). A principal reason for this was that the language-experience people insisted that reading is a process and that a teacher can use any content as a source of reading material. In other words, all phases of the curriculum can provide material for reading instruction and require the use of reading skills.

Advocates of basic-reader programs, phonic programs, linguistic programs, and the like limit reading instruction to a fixed time in the school day. In addition, their instructional materials consist primarily of the contrived plots and exercises provided in their basal reader collections, no two of which use the same stories or even the same themes. The vocabularies differ and words are taught in different sequences with different controls for word introduction. Word-attack skills are taught in varying order. Yet, the instructors all agreed on a specified time limit to the otherwise "nonagreement" reading instruction—approximately 90 minutes.

The language-experience people, and to some degree the ITA advocates, agreed that all parts of the curriculum provide materials and motivate interests that can be used for reading instruction. A look back at the wide variety of stories dictated by children provides much evidence to support this contention. In addition to the topics being widely varied, the vocabulary, syntax, grammar, and semantics clearly far exceed what is found in any basic-reader first-grade reading program. If this has not already been noticed, it can be seen in the following pupil dictations.

Hatching Chickens

Today Jody had an incubator at school.
It had eggs in it. The incubator had a
light bulb in it to keep the eggs warm.
One egg has hatched. The chicken was wet.
The heat will dry its feathers and keep
it warm.

Pam

The Guinea Pigs

Today Mrs. Ennis brought in two guinea
pigs. She let us pet them. We had fun.
One was black and white. The other one
was all white. They eat carrots, celery,
and apples. They live in a cage.

Jean

A Magnifying Glass

A magnifying glass makes things look
big when you hold it over them. My daddy
has a magnifying glass to look at pennies
when he wants to put them in his book.
There is a magnifying glass at school
that has a black handle. I look at pennies
with my magnifying glass, too.

David

What Animals Do in Winter

The snowshoe rabbit turns white in the
winter. This protects him in the winter
from other animals. When he is white, he
can hide in the snow. Some animals get
very fat. Then they hibernate or go to
sleep for the winter. The woodchuck and
the badger sleep in a tunnel that they dig
with their front paws. The bears sleep in
a hollow log or a cave. When it comes
spring, they wake up and come out. The
chipmunks and the squirrels gather up nuts
for winter and store them in their nest.

David

Our Flag
We have a flag in front of the school.
We have one in our room too. The day before
yesterday, Mrs. VanTine took our flag down.
When I brought my flag, she put my flag up.
The flag has fifty stars. It has six red
stripes and seven white stripes. All the
stripes together are thirteen.

          Bill

The Intercom
I saw the intercom. Mrs. Pepper
showed us how it works. She called our
room. Larry and Linda and Nancy talked
through the intercom.

          Mitch

Election Day
Me and my brother rode down on his
bike and my bike. My father voted for
Johnson. He voted through the machine.

          Pete

Science Fair
I saw a skeleton. I saw a egg in the
water. If you put a lot of salt it will
float up. I saw a turtle. I saw a big
shell. Then we saw a alligator. We saw
our chicks. And in the box there were
two popped out and there were more to
hatch. After we went back to the room, we
saw a puppet show.

          Karen

Seeds
When the seeds grow bigger, we are going
to take the flowers home. We put seeds in
the cups. We put some dirt in it and
some stones in it. When the flowers come
up, they will have roots on them.

          Betty

Magnet
We played with the magnet. Everything
that was metal it would pick up. It
picked up a bar. It was metal. It
picked up the bobby pins. It picked up
screws.

Mary

My Project
The project I brought in for the
Science Fair was the disappearing gas. I
used some vinegar. I soaked steel wool in
the vinegar for a few minutes. I stuck it
in a bottle and added a little water to it
and put a balloon in the top of the bottle.
It will blow up inside the bottle.

Conrad

Julie's Frog
Julie brought her frog in today. Mrs.
McWilliams got a box to put the frog in.
Kenny and Julie went out to get grass to
put in the box. When they got the grass,
the frog got out. Kenny caught the frog.
The frog is big. The frog is green and
it has black on it. It is pretty. I
like the frog.

Carla

Animals
I like a cow because cows give you
milk. A baby cow drinks milk from the
big cow. We went on a trip to the farm.
I saw some cows. They were black and
white. The little cow was brown. They
say "Moo."

Sara

Bicycle Safety
Sergeant Wells told us how to ride a
bike. He showed us a movie. He showed
us how to slow down or stop, and to turn

right and left. The girl crashed into a
car. She had to go to the hospital. After
she was fixed, she obeyed the rules.
                        Steve

These children are not confined to a Procrustean preprimer or primer. They are not asked to tell again and again some silly plot about Dick Scott and Jane Foresman. Their reading-talking-thinking-sharing world is bound by all knowledge. From the very beginning of their reading days, they are reading about things they themselves have observed or heard or felt or smelled. Their attitudes toward reading are being shaped by experience and knowledge and not by forced plots with substandard language.

STORIES, DREAMS, AND WISHES

The best school and community with its many firsthand opportunities cannot provide all the resources that children are able to use to stimulate and express their ideas. Children are creative and love to improvise and, when encouraged to do so, they create with an eagerness and a zest that clearly suggests pleasure. Talking about dreams and wishes requires self-revelation—my dreams, my wishes. It suggests that someone else wants to know about them and will be interested enough to read about them or listen to them tell about themselves. Telling about "my wishes" may cause many pupils to stop and think about themselves in a way they have not done before, and it may lead to better self-understanding. Books like *Is This You?* by Ruth Krauss[2] may help a child see himself in a different way and enjoy the ridiculous as good fun.

Creating stories is a wonderful way to stretch life. Stories begin as all invention and make believe does, with an idea, frequently a once-upon-a-time idea. How the ideas interact with things, people, and processes depends upon each child's experience and ability to create and spin a yarn and, of course, upon the degree to which the teacher invites and encourages story writing. It also reflects the amount of reading to the children that the teacher does. The following stories obtained from first-grade-level children are illustrative.

What I Want to Be
I wish I could be a cat so I could
have babies. My cat has babies already.
I would keep my babies warm. I would get

[2] Ruth Krauss, *Is This You?* (New York, William R. Scott, 1955).

a lot of weeds and make a nest. I would
give them milk. I would climb trees and
get birds and bring them to my babies. I
would not let them die.

Caroline

When I Grow Up

I want to be a road builder. I like
trucks. I want to drive a road scraper.
It is hard.

Eddie

A One Time Magic Garden

We read a story and it had a magic
garden. I liked this story and I wish I
had a magic garden. I would plant some
basketballs and some trucks. I would
plant a car that I could ride in with a
motor. Children could come along one
time because no one can come two times.

John

What I Want to Be

I want to be a Soap Box Derby boy.
Right now my father and I are thinking
about making a car. We don't have to make
a motor because the starting place is on
a hill. I want to have a motor because
I want to run the car on a street. If I
keep the car, I can race and I might win
in the Soap Box Derby.

Harold

My Favorite Dream

One day I had a dream about some
monsters. Near my house I saw a ten-foot
monster and I ran into my house. The
monster was following my foot tracks and I
locked the screen door and put a chair in
back of the door.

Bill

The Pirates

The pirates were fighting some other men
because they wanted the treasure. The other
pirates shot back at them. When the last
war was over, one of the captains was
killed. The other pirates broke through
the gates of the treasury and got the treasure.
The treasure was from a treasure ship that
sank down into the water a long time ago.
Now some of the pirates were rich and some
were poor.

Jack

My Pocket

I have a pocket on my dress. I carry
tissues in my pocket. My pocket has a
big red apple on it. I have two pockets
on my dress. Sometimes I carry my mother's
mail in my pocket. Sometimes I carry my
toys in my pocket. The pocket I have on
my skirt has a tree on it.

Carla

The Man Who Didn't Want to Fight

One day a man said, "I don't want to
fight but other people do." Then he said,
"What shall I do? I know what I will do.
I will build a house with a door that locks
from the inside and no one can open it with
a key. I will have no windows at all. I
will have a hole for an air conditioner and
a hole for two fans." So the little old
man built the house. It was very cool. He
built his house in the woods. The little
old man lived happily ever after because
he did not get in any more fights.

Pete

The Little Red Hen

The Little Red Hen found some wheat. She
planted it. After the wheat grew, she took

it to the mill. Then she made some bread.
She asked Mrs. Duck if she wanted to help
her make the bread. She asked Mr. Turkey
if he wanted to help her. They both said,
"Not I." When she got ready to eat it, she
asked if they wanted to eat it. "Yes,"
they said. But Little Red Hen said, "You
did not help me make it. My children and
I will eat it."

Pam

RECORD BOOKS

Each child in first grade can keep a record book in which to place all the dictating he does for the year. A standard $8\frac{1}{2}$-×-10-inch notebook will serve the purpose well. If the stories are typed, the typed copy can be taped or pasted into the book. If the dictation is recorded in manuscript by the teacher, it can be done directly in the notebook. Each story is dated, providing the pupil with a chronological record of his dictation. Throughout the year, a pupil can reread any or all entries. (As one boy said in February when he reread a story he had dictated in September, "That's the way I talked when I was little.") Drawings for each story can be made on the pages facing the pasted-in dictation, a drawing on the left and a story on the right. Notebooks can be exchanged and classmates can read each other's stories. The notebook serves many purposes and is especially valuable as a learning-to-read aid.

The titles of the entries in one boy's book are illustrative of the variety of interests and themes that children derive:

How I Come to School
The Funny Man
Jane Jumps
Helping at Home
My Weekend Story
The Halloween Story
The Trip to the Coal-Mining
  Country
Dandelions
Dick, My Brother
The Fireman's Big Truck
Help

Something Funny
The Lost Money
What I Want to Be
The Pilgrims
Santa Claus
When I Was Sick
What Animals Do in Winter
Teeny's Two Puppies
My Birthday
The Hands-Down Game
Going to the Reading Confer-
  ence

The Late Snow

The Boy and Girl Who Ran
  Away

The Mousetrap Game

Our Family Garden

The Man Who Didn't Want
  to Fight

The Man Who Wanted a Family

Thanksgiving

Guess What This Is

The Book I Like Best

The Holiday I Had Off

The Puppet Show

Three Little Horses

Lincoln and Washington

A Magnifying Glass

What I Am

Two Guinea Pigs

The Easter Egg Hunt

A Funny Thing Happened

Note that some of the titles listed here are the same as those used earlier in this book. On occasion children select a common title for all to use and frequently reflect joint ventures, such as field trips.

This list represents only David's record of dictated stories. In addition, he had a long list of creative writings that he started in November and continued throughout the school year. Furthermore, not all his dictated accounts were placed in this notebook. Some were gathered in a science book, others in a health book.

In summary, it should be strikingly apparent that the abundance of stimuli with which to motivate dictation is limitless. Ideas and props are as extensive and numerous as experience and knowledge, not only of the immediate geographical area—home, community, and school—but also of the curriculum. Any teacher can tap this tremendous reservoir. In so doing, she gets the children to examine more carefully the world about them, to see new horizons, to view the past and the future, and to act upon it all intellectually.

A look at the vocabulary displayed in the stories in the preceding pages shows how wide-ranging it is. Nomenclature in them is used correctly, concepts are refined and attained, and intellectual growth is stimulated and accomplished. Above all, attitudes toward knowledge and communication are fostered, as is the spirit of inquiry. Knowledge comes first. Reading and books are viewed as one means of obtaining ideas. Reading is learned as it is taught, not as an end in itself, but as a means of obtaining information or entertainment.

Individual language and experience levels

Without a doubt, the chief use of language is to communicate meaning. Sounds have no intrinsic meaning of their own:

A stream of speech consists of a succession not only of units of sound, but also of units which convey meaning to the speakers of the language. How do we know they contain meaning, and how can we test for meaning? The only way we can test with absolute assurance is by collecting large quantities of specimens of continuous speech from a speaker of a given language (5, p. 13).

The illustrations of children's dictation provided in this chapter are indicative of the stream of language children use to convey meanings. Morphemes (words), unlike phonemes (sound units), have meaning and catalogue the vast universe of experience. The stories here show the range of experience of children, the influence of instruction, and the use of language to tell others about experiences and ideas.

Furthermore, it should be noted that, by and large, the children communicated their ideas quite effectively. They learned to make themselves understood within the framework of the linguistic patterns pertaining in their society. If they lack adroitness in using the right expressions, this is a matter conditioned largely by opportunity to speak, by considerations of prestige within their social-cultural-linguistic environment, which now includes the classroom and the school, and by the taste, temper, and maturity of each pupil. To say that these children speak in nonstandard fashion is nonsense. Certainly they speak differently from the way they did when they were four years old; they change continuously and at varying rates in different groups. And such change will continue as fostered by the new opportunities provided by the school and if it is not stifled by a premature demand for "correctness." Finally, it is on the point of correctness that much confusion exists. Linguistically, what the children normally say is "correct." If one considers the forms that are admired and accepted by certain groups, though, then the language of the children does not really find favor. The conventions of society are inescapable and represent a form of correctness that is a good thing. But, at this stage of a child's communicating life, attention must be focused on communication so that the "why" and "when" of communication become soundly inculcated. Then language refinement, or how to conform to the best language patterns, becomes significant. Until then, children must manage to say practically everything they ever have a need to by learning to handle with ease the language that is their own.

If the language is a public language in which short simple sentences abound, few subordinate clauses used, sequence limited, adjectives and adverbs rigid and few in number, and reasons and conclusions confounded, then the rate of change will be slow and attempts to make for change will meet with resistance. If the language in the peer group in school approximates this kind of communication only, then change to a more formal language will be slow:

To ask the pupil to use language differently, to qualify verbally his individual experience, to expand his vocabulary, to increase the length of his verbal planning function, to generalize, to be sensitive to the implications of number, to order a verbally presented arithmetic problem, these requests when made to a *public* language user are very different from when they are made to a *formal* language user. For the latter it is a situation of linguistic development whilst for the former it is one of linguistic change (2, p. 99).

The task of reading instruction appears to be to preserve for the children the force and dignity that their language possesses while making available to them the possibilities inherent in a linguistic form oriented toward higher conceptualization. Their cognitive and affective states must be channeled in such a way that disequilibrium does not result. Small classes, individual attention, frequent opportunity to think, speak, listen, opportunities to use language not only to label and enumerate but also to categorize objects, events, and people, along with many opportunities to internalize the role of the speaker as well as the listener are all required in the task.

This is what the use of the Language-Experience Approach provides so abundantly. There are numerous opportunities for children to see, react, think, speak, be listened to, read, share, acquire increasingly more acceptable forms of language. This is what the stories reproduced here reflect so clearly. Notice again the quality of the sentences, the range and size of the vocabulary, the use of sequence, prepositional phrases, and personal pronouns, the use of divergent and convergent thinking, the use of logical qualifiers, and the processing of relevant data to reach acceptable conclusions.

Conclusion

The purpose of this chapter is to describe how teachers can use the dictated experience stories of children to initiate and maintain instruction in how to read. Most teachers are uncertain about how to get started in the beginning of the school year. To help them understand the how, when, and what of getting started, procedures were described in detail. Of special significance is the fact that, if on the first or second day of school instruction is initiated as described, all the children can go home feeling that they have read. Favorable attitudes toward reading will be fostered from the very beginning.

The use of a whole class as a base for obtaining dictation serves a useful purpose and is a means of getting started. But the best procedure is to obtain individually dictated accounts. Transition from whole-class stories to individual dictation can be made quite effectively through groups that reflect some arrangement by ability or that are randomly organized. Children can see how an interest or stimulus is dealt with in the whole class or in one story, when three or four groups result in three or four similar but different stories about the same theme, and in individual dictation resulting in perhaps thirty versions. Teachers will find that they can direct and obtain individual stories with greater ease if they operate out of group situations. As any teacher who tries the approach soon discovers, individual stories are most productive and have the best utility for instruction.

What to talk about or how to get children to talk has been described and illustrated with numerous children's stories. The big question is not what to use as a stimulus but how and what to select from among the innumerable possibilities. All living provides a ready source, with the curriculum and its many concepts as a structural fountainhead.

Certainly the language levels of children will vary from some command of a public language to good control of a formal language. Use of the children's language and acceptance of their level is the important guide line. Great care must be taken not to stifle their language by demanding "correctness." At this point in their language development, the purpose of language as communication is paramount. Of course, this is true throughout life, and at a later time the formalities of language will have to be taught, but not at this early stage.

Above all are the manner and degree to which the use of children's language and experience fosters a favorable attitude toward reading. Because they are learning to read much as they learned to talk, functionally, the children are forming intellectual and emotional dispositions that will result in reading habits. As Dewey said (3, p. 57), "the intellectual elements in a habit fix the relation of the habit to varied and elastic use, and hence to continued growth." This is precisely what occurs—children acquire the reading habit and practice it constantly because they enjoy doing so. This is the aim of sound reading instruction.

Bibliography

1. Allport, Gordon W. *Pattern and Growth in Personality*. New York: Holt, Rinehart and Winston, 1961.
2. Bernstein, Basin. "Social Structure, Language, and Learning." In *The Psychology of Language, Thought, and Instruction*, edited by John P. DeCecco. New York: Holt, Rinehart and Winston, 1967.
3. Dewey, John. *Democracy and Education*. New York: Macmillan, 1916.
4. Goodenough, Florence L., and Dale B. Harris. *Goodenough-Harris Drawing Test*. New York: Harcourt, Brace & World, 1963.
5. Hamp, Eric P. "Language in a Few Words: With Notes on a Rereading, 1966." In *The Psychology of Language, Thought, and Instruction*, edited by John P. DeCecco. New York: Holt, Rinehart and Winston, 1967.
6. Holt, Robert R. "The Thematic Apperception Test." In *An Introduction to Projective Techniques*, edited by Harold H. Anderson and Gladys L. Anderson. Englewood Cliffs, N.J.: Prentice-Hall, 1951.
7. Hymes, James L., Jr. *Behavior and Misbehavior*. Englewood Cliffs, N.J.: Prentice-Hall, 1955.
8. Jonson, Ben, "Oratio Imago Animi," *Timber: Or Discoveries Made upon Men and Matter*. In *Ben Jonson*, edited by C. H. Herford and P. Simpson. Oxford: Oxford University Press, 1925–1952.
9. Murray, Henry. *Thematic Apperception Test*. Cambridge, Mass.: Harvard University Press, 1943.
10. Stauffer, Russell G. "The Verdict: Speculative Controversy," *The Reading Teacher*, vol. 19, no. 8 (May, 1966), pp. 563–564.

Building a word bank

This chapter enlarges on the practices recommended for the development of a basic reading vocabulary or, as it is sometimes labeled, a sight vocabulary. First steps in the process have already been described in Chapter 2, in the discussion concerned with underlining words in the experience stories (pp. 34–35). A point of special interest in this chapter is the use of the word bank for creatively structuring ideas and for developing word-attack skills.

Read the following objectives and conjecture about the answers. If you are well informed about word banks, the chapter may only confirm your ideas. If you are not, then you need to give close attention to *why* and *how* you read. Remember to take the two essential steps in the life of a scholar-reader. Be intellectually honest. If you do not know how word banks serve, face this frankly. Then conjecture about how they might serve. This honesty and conjecturing will regulate your reading and magnify your understanding.

1. Explain how plans for underlining *known* words may be adjusted to the learning rate of pupils.
2. Tell how recognition and retention of words is facilitated for a child if he produces the words and ideas orally.
3. What are the advantages of using a card window to test recognition and facilitate retention?
4. Explain when, how, and why word-bank alphabetization is introduced and how it readies pupils for dictionary use.
5. How does a six-year-old word-banker put to work his bank deposits during any one school day?
6. Describe the creative use of a word bank.

7. Explain how a word bank is invaluable in the development of word-recognition skills.

How to develop a reading vocabulary

Among the many things a child can do when he has his own copy of a story is underline words he recognizes or can read. Each member of the class can be given a copy of a whole-class story. Then each pupil can be asked to underline each word that he knows. Bill, in the report in Chapter 2, could read all the words in the story except two. Dick, on the other hand, could read only *Snow White* and his name. But both could underline words they knew.

The number of words underlined varies with each individual. Similarly, the number of words recognized varies from pupil to pupil, especially during the early learning phases. Plans for underlining known words may be adjusted to the learning rate of a pupil, a group, or an entire class. A class with many bright children with excellent language facility may be asked to underline each known word immediately after they receive a copy of the story. Thus, underlining is done when chances for recognition and retention are best and before much time has elapsed for forgetting. Sometimes, even among bright children, words are underlined at this point but are not recognized 24 hours later. A useful safeguard that does not curb a child's desire is to have him draw a second line under each known word a day later. This helps develop scholarly honesty. Pupils who are less able than others should be required to draw a second line as a means of promoting retention.

Sometimes it is wise to ask pupils not to underline known words until the second day. If recognition persists over a 24-hour period, then retention and recall over an even longer term are apt to be good. When this procedure is followed, a second underlining should be required on the third day. The purpose of double underlining is the same, but the double-checking time or the forgetting or remembering time has been extended.

Pupils may sit by the teacher one at a time and identify the words they have underlined. Or the teacher may move about the room and point to underlined words, asking pupils to identify them. The likelihood of recognition is greater when words remain in the story context than when they are isolated from the story. A window card provides an easy way to isolate the underlined words and check recognition. A window, cut into a 3-×-5-inch card, is placed over the underlined word so that the card occludes the other words and ideas in the immediate area.

Children who recognize words readily in a whole-class story give an early indication of aptitude. This is true particularly if they recognize words that they did not dictate. To do this is equivalent to recognizing words in a book. The words were not produced by the learner. Some children recognize only words they dictated and perhaps a few key words such as *Snow White, turtle*, and the like.

Recognition and retention are facilitated for a child if he produces words and ideas orally. Hence, the opportunity to dictate becomes important. In a whole-class story, opportunity to dictate is limited to a few pupils. When group stories are obtained, the number of pupils who contribute to a story is increased. If the class is divided into three groups, as many as twelve pupils in a class of thirty may have an opportunity to dictate in one dictating session.

The best procedure is to obtain *individually dictated* stories. This can be done with greater ease than a novice teacher might believe possible. The account in Chapter 2 told how readily individual stories can be obtained.

A stimulus for the day might be a big red apple, as in one classroom. First, all the children talked about the apple and speculated about how it tasted. Pupil experiences with apples were related. Next, the teacher selected eight childrn to meet with her and take turns dictating about the red apple. Bill dictated the following story. Note that it is more imaginative than just a description of an apple:

A Red Apple
Look! There's an apple on a tree.
I am going to climb the tree and eat it.
Bill

Bill underlined five of the seventeen different words in this September dictation. Two of the words that he recognized occurred twice and he underlined them each time. He also recognized his name. He knew these words on a second day, as is shown by the double lines.

In another class, the teacher used crickets as a stimulus, and Ronald dictated the following:

Crickets

I like to find crickets. One cricket
is five and one is six.
                              Ronald

He underlined only the word *cricket* but did so each time it occurred. Even though two uses of the word were plural and one was singular, he recognized each correctly. He also knew his name.

Jane dictated the following story and underlined the words as shown:

Coming to School

I come to school on a bus. My bus
driver's name is Mrs. Hastings. My bus
number is twenty-three. There are big
children and little children on the bus.
                              Jane

Jane used twenty-three different words and recognized each one. She did this with such ease that she was asked to underline the words only once. Her recognition was checked with a window card placed over different words in the story in random order.

Recognition of words isolated by a window card may be facilitated if the words are exposed one at a time by following the word order in the story or by occasionally skipping a word. Some children recognize words better this way, because they sense the idea sequence and the word order of the story they dictated. A sign of growth in recognition skill occurs when such a child can recognize words presented in random order, for example, by shifting the window about, showing a word in the last sentence, then one in the first sentence, then one in the middle, and so on. Random-order recognition can be aided if at first only the substantives, or nouns, are exposed, then the action verbs, then the adjectives, and so on.

The use of a window card is a very important part of word-attack-skill learning. Each child can be given a window card to use at various times throughout a school day to test himself. Children love to do this and do it almost constantly for a while. If they do not recognize a word instantly, they sometimes amusingly take cautious peeks under the card in search of the global ideas.

At this stage, children love to test each other. This provides many action-centered opportunities for children to pair up in different ways and play window-card games. Some planned arranging can be done by the teacher, too, by deliberately placing a very good reader with one who needs many opportunities to see and remember.

Psychologically speaking, window recognition, with the described procedural steps, is an exercise in cue reduction. The number of cues for recognition of a word is gradually reduced through (1) use of total story context, (2) teacher pointing finger to different words, (3) window-card isolation of words in story sequence, (4) window-card isolation of words in random order. The number of cues provided by the original stimulus is reduced each time, until only a fleeting glance at a randomly isolated word may be sufficient for instant recognition.

For the stories just given, the children drew an illustration to accompany their dictation. Bill drew a big red apple hanging on a small branch of a tree. Ronald drew two stick-figure crickets, a big one and a small one. Jane's picture was of a large yellow bus with the number 23 on it.

Given an opportunity, children often display the pragmatic approach of associate-test-remember to word learning. Their pictures usually represent key concepts of the story context. The illustrations help them recall the story or words in the story; pictures can be a semantic or meaning clue to word recognition as much as story or language context. Both pictures and language as forms of association are more logical, meaningful aids to recall than rote memory. Both forms have atomic potency when the child is the original creator by story dictation and illustration artistry.

WORD BANKS

The reading market maintains its steady climb upward as it reflects the interaction of word-learning skill and reading attitude and interest. It shows a sudden point-three rise, though, as a result of response to the word-bank idea. Investment in personalized word banks is wise and sound. It provides short- and long-term funds in what can become an upward-year bullish market. Optimism prevails, and the tightening demands for accurate recognition and reinvestment through functional use cannot dislodge the security confidence.

The bank stability removes peak-and-valley forgetting periods that are the frustrating liability of attempts at rote memorization of fixed word lists. Rote memorization has been categorized by repeated experience as an exercise in futility. The word bank, by contrast, with its dynamic, utilitarian pragmatism, results in the accumulation of a sound and functional vocabulary, invested with meaning and logical associations that facilitate retention and recall.

Every individually dictated story represents a personalized record of word usage. In the eyes of the pupil, the words in his story are "My words in writing." Possession is sometimes spoken of as nine-tenths of the law; similarly, in word learning, it represents nine-tenths of retention.

Every time a pupil marks a word in his story as a known word, he is underlining a "my spoken word, my printed word" idea. In a way, he is awarding himself his own gold star. Each underlined word represents an achievement he himself understands. He recognizes the word and he draws the line. Should he forget the word, as he may humanly do, the story context as well as his picture may provide the meaningful clues needed for rerecognition.

The underlined words that are recognized 2 and 3 days after dictation provide the deposits and reserves of the word bank. Deposits are made by a pupil through the teacher. Every underlined and recognized word is printed by the teacher on a small card (⅜ in. by 1½ in.). The words may be typed in primer-size type or handwritten. In either case, lower- and upper-case letters are used as the circumstances of good language require. Proper names, for instance, begin with capital letters. Typed words provide clear, well-shaped, and uniform letters. If script is used, the same conditions should be observed. This makes for ease of recognition and for transfer of recognition to other contexts.

A word bank may be a small metal box of the kind made available commercially for filing 3-×-5 cards. Or it may be any similar box—a shoe box cut down, a box for Christmas-tree ornaments, a candy box, and the like. It should have a lid or the accident proneness of young folks may result in a lot of spillage.

In the beginning, the small word cards are placed in the word bank in random order—that is, not in alphabetical order. This random filing is purposeful, however. All the known words are kept in the bank and can be withdrawn readily. As long as the number of known words is less than thirty or so, the need for alphabetizing is usually not urgent. Once the number exceeds thirty, then pupils become irked with the inefficiency of the filing plan and are receptive to a better one.

When alphabetical filing is introduced, the best plan seems to be to place each letter in a small envelope, except X, Y, and Z, which are placed together. The capitals and lower-case letters are written on the outside of the envelopes: Aa, Bb, Cc, Dd, and so on. Envelope size depends to some degree on the bank size; envelopes for thank-you notes or party invitations will usually do. Children deal with the alphabetizing in a very mature way. They are invariably impressed by the efficiency of the system and its functional orderliness. They quickly learn to file each word card in the correct envelope according to the first letter of the word.

Now, much practical knowledge is acquired in a short time. Alphabetical order is appreciated in a way quite different from rote repetition of the alphabet. Now the order of the letters serves a function; parroting the alphabet serves only to impress proud parents and naïve teachers. Children begin to note the relationship between letter placement: *B* is toward the front, *S* is near the back, *M* is in the middle, and so on. When all the known words are filed, they see that some envelopes contain more words than others and that some are empty. When Pam started her alphabetical word bank, she had forty-four words to file. Sixteen of the letter envelopes received words and eleven did not. In the *T* envelope, she filed seven different words, with five in the *H* envelope. Pam said she liked her *B*-envelope words best—*bus, big, bicycle*. She started her alphabetical file in the latter part of September.

After the children have started alphabetical word banks, they can be introduced to a dictionary; any abridged dictionary designed for use in elementary school will do. Now the children can compare their word-bank words and letter order with that of the dictionary. They notice that the *B* words in the dictionary are in the front of the book and that the *S* words are near the back and so on, just as they are in their bank. Children are very responsive to being asked to locate in the dictionary words from their files. Some do this easily; others need help. Introduced this way, children do not develop fears and anxieties about using dictionaries. Their attitude is favorable from the start, and its utility value is impressively fostered.

WORDS, WORDS, WORDS

Up to now, we have been concerned with only a small aspect of word banks. A word bank provides the security of a sound investment. The account can be drawn on at any time without depleting the principle. The interest on each word investment far exceeds anything available on the world economic scene.

Each dictated experience story becomes a treasure, even if it is dictated by the whole class or a group. Each individually dictated experience is even more treasured. The notebook with its chronological entries becomes a bank, too, a story bank much like the word bank. Both are cherished possessions.

How do these six-year-old bankers spend their day? Their banks are open Monday through Friday, usually from around 8:45 A.M. until around 2:45 P.M. They are occasionally open through the lunch hour. The word bankers are neither miserly nor avaricious but frugal, prudent, and benevolent. All day long, they deal with words in one way or another, their own words and the words of peers. An atmosphere of industriousness prevails. "Busy work" is not needed; the teacher's after-school hours are not spent spinning fool's gold in a Rumplestiltskin effort, only to see her effort spent each day in a lavish time waste yielding little learner return.

What do the six-year-old word-bankers do all day with their treasure? A search that yields tremendous pleasure is to locate word-bank words in other places. One of the most thrilling places is a book in the classroom library, or any library for that matter. One day in September, Pam found forty of her forty-four bank words in one book. Pam's excitement and satisfaction spread to others in the room and similar searches were soon initiated. Sheila had only ten words in her bank but she found five of them in one book.

The children learn that books are exciting and it is thrilling to find known words there. But equally exciting is the thrill of finding words in newspapers. A newspaper has considerable status—Daddy reads it; so do Mother, Sister, Brother, everyone. A big advantage of newspaper words is that they can be cut out and kept in a special file. Sheila, for instance, found all her word-bank words in newspapers and magazines. She was almost as proud of her cut-out words pasted on an 8½-×-11-inch sheet of paper as she was of her word bank.

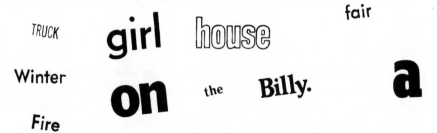

Pam not only found most of her words in newspapers and magazines but she had prepared special lists. She had six different sizes and shapes for the word *bus;* one was all capital letters of about 36-point type, another all lower-case letters of about 8-point type; one had a capital *B;* one was in green, another in boldface, and one in italics:

BUS   bus   **bus**
Bus   bus   *bus*

Sheila and Pam and all the others assembled their own word pictures— the picture-dictionary idea, in a sense. Pam cut a picture of a bus out of an old magazine. Sheila cut out a picture of a fire truck and put the words *fire truck* on the back of the picture. Pam did not bother doing this; labeling was already too elementary for her. Sheila, on the other hand, used her words and pictures as a test. First, she read the words. If she did not know a word, she would turn the picture over and look at it. Some interesting developments occurred; one boy, for example, said he "knew" some of his words so quickly because he knew by the size of the paper what picture was on the other side. Obviously, not all words could be pictured—*the, then,* and the like. The children soon discovered this and set up special lists of "no-picture words," "helper words," and the like.

Children were astounded to find that they could sometimes read every word on a page. Now the stilted and barren preprimers took on some value. Children were pleased when they could read every word in them. Of course, they wanted to read to others to display their prowess, so they worked with partners or met in small groups and listened to each other read aloud.

This kind of action-packed cutting, pasting, reading, and sharing requires freedom to move about. Children are quick to recognize and respect the need for orderliness and quiet. They move about in the room and share with each other as respectful good citizens. Naturally, because they are six-year-olds, this kind of conduct does not always occur. Teacher authority still prevails but only when pupil freedom exceeds the limits of social responsibleness.

CREATIVE WORD USAGE

The thrill of being an author, a composer, or an arranger is deeply felt, inspiring, and ego filling. Already the six-year-olds discussed have experienced much of the pride of the originator and innovator. Now they are receptive to another experience—the creative use of the words in their word banks for communication.

The words in a word bank can be arranged and rearranged on the desk top. A word-card holder[1] is helpful to hold the words in place. First, pupils can be taught how to use words and arrange questions on the holder, as for example:

May I have a pencil?
May I see the new book?
Where is the newspaper?
May I have the scissors?
May I hear you read?

[1] Russell G. Stauffer, Pupil Word-Card Holder, produced by Holt, Rinehart and Winston, 383 Madison Avenue, New York, New York 10017.

Children may discover that they do not have all the words they need to ask certain questions. When this happens, they can ask the teacher for help. The pupil sets up part of the question—"May I have ——?"—and then supplies "pencil" orally. Within view of the pupil, the teacher prints or types the word "pencil" on a word card and gives it to the pupil. This is usually an excellent way to add words to a word bank. The words requested are utilitarian because they serve a clearly recognized purpose, and they are readily remembered. When pupils begin to ask questions and use words creatively, the teacher must be ready for a barrage of requests, but this soon eases up as the novelty wears off and as a vocabulary of key words is built up. Pupils can now set up questions on a word-card holder and, without uttering a sound, hold them up for the teacher to see. She in turn can shake her head *yes* or *no,* completing the communication.

From questions to statements to sentences or even stories is an easy step. Often all occur together rather than in sequence as implied here. Here are some samples from a first-grade room late in October:

Nancy	Nancy and he go to my house.
Gail	Gail go to school on the bus.
Judy	I had a scarecrow.
Cindy	Janet's typewriter is old.
	The air comes down beside my daddy.
Clarke	My mother is a doctor.
Dawn	FALL
	Mother sits on the swing.
	Houses are pretty.
	We like leaves.
	I saw some little acorns.
Charles	I go to school on a bus.
Sandra Dee	I like to look at trees.
	I saw some red and yellow leaves.
Benny	I saw a jeep and a boat.
Steven	My dad likes to take us to the Tasty Freeze.
	We like to eat hot dogs.
Missy	My family goes places.
	We go to the store.
	We go to Hunting Island.
	We shoot our BB gun.
J. D.	We ride the fire engines.
	I see the rescue truck.

The amount of thought and effort required to make sentences like these may be far more demanding than seems apparent on the surface. First, each pupil had to think about what he wanted to say, controlled in part by the words in his word bank. Creativity was bounded and restrained accordingly.

Within the limits of the word bank, once the what-to-say had been decided upon, it had to be remembered until the idea was completed and the necessary words had been assembled. Nancy, for instance, probably had no difficulty locating her name. Locating and identifying the other words may have required her to handle each word in her word bank. This kind of decision making requires top-flight, functional word recognition. It is a far cry from the flash-card rote drilling that occurs in some other approaches.

To find the word *and*, Nancy could either move in random order through her word bank or know that *and* was filed under *A*. Because she did the latter, the establishing and reinforcing of word-recognition skills had been most commendable: She remembered the beginning sound of *and* and the letter that represented that sound. This was true of each of the other words she used. This act represented a practical use of word-attack skills in a semantically and phonologically rich circumstance.

This kind of idea structuring not only developed word-recognition skills of the highest order but also began the "writing [makes] an exact man" technical expertness that Francis Bacon referred to.[2] An attitude of correctness (correct thought, "I must say what I want to say") and persistence ("stick with it until I've said what I want to say") was fostered. But above all, "what I want to say is functional only if someone else can read what I compose and understand what I say" was learned. So this structuring took place under the tremendously potent influence of a communication act—someone who writes does so for someone who reads. The author who knows his audience and writes for it is more apt to communicate effectively than the one who does not.

In addition, syntactic power acquired through oral language usage was applied, reinforced, and developed in the composing act. In the first sentence of the list above Nancy decided to write about "herself" (subject: *Nancy*) and "he" (subject: *he*). Then, through the logic of discursive order, she had to decide what about "Nancy" and "he" (predicate: *go*). Now she had established the subject and the subject's action, so she

[2] Francis Bacon, "Of Studies," *Essays or Counsels, Civil and Moral.* In *Works*, edited by J. Spedding, R. L. Ellis, and D. D. Heath (New York, Garrett Press, 74).

arranged the words in syntactical order. She also declared the "where" aspect of "go"—*to my house.*

Dawn's creative act reflects a more complex use of language and communication. She chose the topic "Fall" and wrote ideas related to it. This imposed an order of ideas about fall as well as a syntax order for each sentence.

It is far more important at this stage that children create and produce rather than have their attempts "purified." Interest in written communication must be maintained as high as possible, so that the children will become absorbed in the thrill of this kind of communication.

How much time each pupil requires is moot. Nancy may have worked on her sentence off and on throughout the day; Dawn may have done her constructing in an hour's time. The word bank was constantly available, and since no deadline was declared each pupil could pace his own work throughout the day. At different times during the day, the teacher declared brief sharing periods. A child who had completed a composition could share his material orally. This encouraged children to create throughout the day, day after day.

The children were free to move about in the room and read the compositions of others. They love to do this. They enjoyed helping each other. At times, two worked together to compose a sentence but using only the words in the word bank of one of the two. Pupils occasionally pooled their word-bank resources, but the separation task later was so tedious that they tended to avoid this.

WORD-RECOGNITION SKILL

The word bank provides one of the most valuable sources available for the development of word-recognition skills. As has already been shown, the word bank supplies sight words that can be used to develop visual-auditory discrimination skills.

The use of word-attack skills to unlock a word not recognized at sight involves the use of context or meaning clues, phonic or sound clues, and structural or sight clues. A major benefit of the Language-Experience Approach to learning to read is that the development of word-attack skills is based on these three from the very beginning of the learning-to-read stage.

Auditory discrimination is taught on the first day (see Chapter 5). As soon as a sight vocabulary has been acquired, auditory-visual discrimination skills can be learned.

The words in the word bank provide an excellent source of sight words.

For instance, by mid-September, Pam recognized twenty-five words at sight. Two—*bus* and *big*—started with the letter *B*. In this beginning position, the sound represented by the single consonant *B* can be heard readily. The teacher could do (and did) a number of things. She could tell Pam to find a word in her bank that began with the same sound as the word "baker," for example. This word was spoken by the teacher, thus providing the auditory clue. Then Pam located the word *big* to provide the visual clue. The teacher could then ask Pam to find a word that began with the same sound as "mother" (auditory). Pam found *my* (visual).

Now with both words on her word-card holder, arranged one above the other $\left(\begin{smallmatrix}\text{big}\\\text{my}\end{smallmatrix}\right)$, another auditory-visual activity could be done. This time, the teacher could give Pam an auditory stimulus and ask her to decide which one of the two words had the same beginning sound as the one the teacher spoke. The teacher could now say in rapid order "money," "boat," "bell," "may," "mix," "boy," and so on, and expect Pam to point each time either to *big* or to *my*. At this point the teacher paused to make certain that Pam knew the names of the two beginning letters. She had already determined that Pam knew the sound that each represented when it appeared as a beginning single consonant in a sound unit or word. Knowing the sound represented has phonically the most useful value.

Pam was not the only child in the room who knew the words *bus* and *my*. All had dictated individual stories "Coming to School," and all had used *bus* and many had used *my*. So group instruction could be done, too.

This kind of auditory (stimulus word spoken by the teacher) visual (response word read by pupil) training can be initiated very early in a language-experience reading program. In this instance, the teacher introduced it in mid-September. The activity has much functional value. It helps children:

1. focus attention on beginning sounds
2. notice how beginning sounds are alike and different
3. identify the letters that represent beginning sounds
4. avoid confusing letter names with the sounds they represent
5. learn to recognize sounds and letter names in context rather than isolation
6. make and act upon decisions about letters and sounds
7. facilitate the filing of words in their word banks

Once this kind of auditory-visual training has been initiated, pupils can be teamed to continue it. Pam soon caught on to the teacher role; she was allowed to look over a classmate's word bank and then provide a stimulus word orally. Two or three or more pupils could meet around a table or on a rug in the magic rug corner and engage in this auditory-visual activity. The children loved doing this and did it frequently throughout a day. Again, it is to be noted that the children were active and that what they were doing has much functional value and requires teacher action on the scene and not after school. All the teacher needed to do was use to full advantage the word wealth that the children had acquired. As a result, her role took on more value. She was now free to direct and supervise small-group and individual word-attack skill training.

Pupil participation became different, too. They operated from the known (the words in their banks) to the unknown (words yet unlearned). Their chances for success had increased because of this, as had their motivation. Most important, though, is the fact that the pupils could serve as teacher and help refine the skills of their classmates. To do this pupils must know the *why* and *how* of the skills they teach. And, as every teacher knows, the best way to learn a skill is to teach it to others.

Word beginnings and word endings can be grasped and recognition can be refined by auditory-visual training. By the fourth week in September, Pam, a typical girl, and David, a typical boy, knew forty-four and fifty words, respectively. By using their banks, they undertook various activities that went well beyond learning single-consonant beginning sounds:

*b*us	*dr*iver	*m*y
*l*ittle	*tr*ick	*p*ony
*t*wenty	*bl*ack	*r*ide
com*ing*	bla*ck*	p*u*t
driv*ing*	fa*st*	*a*t
		big

Children are quite responsive to this kind of word-attack skill training because they work at their own levels. They know the printed words and how to set up similar activities. *Why* they are doing the training is no longer a skill-book busy-work mystery. Following directions is no longer the bug-a-boo it tends to be in skill-book activities prepared for the masses, because the children know not only how to follow directions but also how to give directions. Everyone works together throughout the day—partners, teams, groups, the whole class. Partners and teams are not fixed but vary from day to day and from activity to activity. The *esprit de corps* that results from work together toward a goal (learning to read) is tremendous.

Biweekly checkups might be made to determine how readily the children recognize the words in their word banks. The children enjoy putting their words out on their desks and systematically going through them and showing the teacher how many they know. This can be a whole class activity, or the children often enjoy working in pairs or small groups.

If, on occasion, a pupil forgets a word in his word bank, he is confronted with a unique relearning opportunity. He is not daunted, because he knows what to do about it. He knows that the best thing to do is to locate the word in the story in which he first used it and first underlined it. The use of logical, or context clues to recognition, is most praiseworthy and stimulates tremendous recall efficacy. It is not at all uncommon to find a child double checking his accuracy by referring to the original story. A practice found helpful with the slow learners was to number the stories and then number, on the back of the word cards, the words learned in each story:

front	*back*
little	2
bus	1

In other words the word *little* was underlined in the second story, *bus* in the first story, and so on. As has already been stated, the numbering of words was a crutch to learning or, better yet, a small intermediary step for the slow learners, but a cumbersome and unnecessary mincing of steps for the rapid learners.

Conclusion

The word-bank file is a personalized record of words a pupil has learned to read or recognize at sight. The source of the words is a pupil's functional use of oral language to tell about an experience or relate an imaginary tale. Each pupil identifies the words he recognizes and, if he reidentifies them on at least 2 successive days, provides good evidence that he will retain, and recall, the written word over a long period. Recognition is facilitated by identifying the word in written contexts such as books, newspapers, and magazines. Recognition is facilitated most when a pupil uses words functionally to construct sentences, ask questions, or develop a story. He does this by using small word cards and assembling the words syntactically on a word-card holder or spread out over the top of his desk.

Filing words in alphabetical order in a word bank contributes to orderliness and ease, to dictionary use, and to word-recognition skill training. Composing stories is a practical use of word-bank wealth. In addition, the use of the words for word-attack skill training is almost priceless. Auditory, or sound, discrimination (the basis of phonics) activities (see Chapter 5) starts with the first day of school. Auditory-visual discrimination activities, or sound and sight activities, start with the first words in the word bank. This leads to a functional distinction between letter names and the sounds letters represent. It also prepares pupils for consonant substitution activities, the development of word families, and the use of phonetic respellings in a dictionary.

4
Creative writing

This chapter recasts the Language-Experience Approach into a comprehensive approach to reading instruction to evoke a more intensive focus on how all the facets of language serve learning goals.

The chapter is divided into eight parts. The first part deals with how pupils acquire skill in handwriting and how teaching is individualized. The second part explains the functional learning of sounds that letters and letter names represent and how words have a fixed letter order. The third and fourth parts describe early writing-spelling attempts of individual words and the advancment to the writing of accounts or stories and ideas. Children tend to become preoccupied with writing once they get started, so ways of promoting writing are detailed. The fifth part explains concept development in the motivation of writing. The sixth and seventh parts present many illustrations of children's writing, showing their handwriting, spelling, syntax, sense of story sequence, and illustrations. The eighth part describes how children acquire the modesty and capability of scholars who know the power of change and growth and the function of oral and written language.

Again the reader is urged to read the following objectives and conjecture about the answers. His honesty and commitment will help regulate his reading and increase his comprehension.

1. Define creative writing as it is done in this chapter.
2. Explain how skill in handwriting is taught functionally and how this creates a favorable attitude toward handwriting.

Upon reading the second part, the reader should be able to meet these objectives:

1. Explain the meaning of functional learning.
2. Describe how oral and written letters represent sound.
3. Tell about the function of letter names.
4. Explain how sensitivity to letter order is acquired.

Upon reading the third and fourth parts, the reader should be able to meet the following objectives:

1. Describe first attempts at writing a word.
2. Discuss the importance of the teacher's integrity once creative writing is fully launched.
3. Explain how a teacher can give spelling help without violating creative-writing principles.
4. Explain how the teacher's direction promotes the use of opportunities for creative writing within the curriculum.

Upon reading the fifth part, the reader should be able to meet the following objectives:

1. Explain how children's love for words can be used to advantage in creative writing.
2. Describe how children's concepts can be extended and refined.

Upon reading the sixth and seventh parts, the reader should be able to meet the following objectives:

1. Explain how the spelling, syntax, grammar, and semantics of children's writing reflect their language-experience wealth.
2. Explain how each writing opportunity provides the conditions for spelling reinforcement.
3. Describe how children develop a spelling conscience while becoming increasingly more attentive to the essentials of written communication.

Upon reading the eighth part, the reader should be able to meet the following objectives:

1. Explain how children learn to recognize their own increased maturity and writing competence.
2. Describe certain variables that psychologists agree affect learning rate.
3. Name structural and semantic aspects of language, as declared by Walter Loban, that may be used by a teacher to appraise the writing of children.

It is difficult to write about the assets of a comprehensive approach to reading instruction and not be overly enthusiastic. Yet, each facet yields so bountifully that exuberance about it seems natural. Creative writing, above all other facets, prompts this kind of spirited reaction.

Creative writing both is and is not a good label for what really happens. Each pupil can invent and fashion and fabricate and thereby derive the joy and elation that redounds to a creator. Pride of authorship and the self-esteem it evokes manifests itself in increased self-respect and in increased interest in correctness and standards. Creative use of language in oral communication is apparent among children almost from the time they begin to speak. So, gratifyingly, children of school age have much experience in using language creatively (see Chapter 1). Now, though, they not only speak but their ideas are recorded in writing and each pupil can read and reread his own ideas. Over and over again, he can turn to his writings and know that he is their author. Then, when other pupils read his writings, sharing ideas, the pinnacle of authorship, is attained.

For the unschooled, creative writing often means "creating a plot or a story" and the preparation of junior Ernest Hemingways. Given the opportunity, an astonishing number of children can think up stories, but producing story-writers is only one side of creative writing. Most children, particularly in the beginning, are more productive when they create or, perhaps more precisely, recreate ideas in response to some firsthand experience. In other words, they give an account of something they have experienced rather than develop an imaginative plot.

Even though recounting experiences was dealt with in Chapter 2 reemphasis and clarification are made here to avoid or offset the new teacher or the inexperienced teacher's misconstruing this approach. Very effective first writings of children are sometimes reproved because of lack of understanding of the connotations of "creative."

In brief, then, creative writing may be defined as a composition that reflects a child's own choice of words, ideas, order, spelling, and punctuation. The content may be fiction or nonfiction, imaginative or documentary, expository or narrative. The stimulus may have been selected by a teacher or elected by a pupil and represent his own choice.

Creative writing includes certain other conditions, too. Obviously, a child, to write, must have some skill in handwriting, must know letters of the alphabet, must have some idea about letter order in words, and must show some knowledge of letter sounds in written orthography. How and when such capabilities are acquired can be puzzling to the inexperienced. Accordingly, it seems timely to elaborate on each.

Handwriting

Almost all educators agree that fundamental to the acquisition of skill in handwriting is the fostering of a favorable attitude toward handwriting. To achieve this, the very first steps in handwriting should be accomplished in a circumstance in which the children have a genuine purpose for writing. An ideal way to start, one abounding with personal pride and ego involvement, is to have first-graders write their own names.

After each child has made a drawing to accompany the first class story dictated, the teacher can show him how to put his name on the picture. It is now common practice in many schools for each pupil to have a copy of his name (usually in printing) on his desk top. Each can copy his name to the best of his ability, and he is started on the road to writing by producing words—whole words that are filled with meaning.

Some children have considerable manual dexterity and they produce letters legibly and easily. Others show clearly that they can produce some letters but have difficulty with certain others. The pupils who need help on certain letters should receive it; those who need no such help should be left to proceed to learning other skills. The advantage of this method is that each child works on his own needs and thus shows considerable willingness to put forth the effort to improve his own writing.

Practice on specific letter forms focuses attention on specific needs. Children are quick to recognize how functional this kind of training can be. They see the value of a letter model. Because practice is individualized to specific needs, it becomes very useful and productive in the fixing of legible writing habits.

From recording names on pictures to labeling pictures is an easy step. Transition from this to copying a notice or an announcement, a sentence in a class story, or an entire story follows readily. In a short time, some pupils are copying entire stories with astounding legibility.

Some school districts have developed their own manuscript alphabet and provide copies for each teacher and sometimes each pupil. This being the era of easy reproducing, many schools now provide each child with his own desk copy of the alphabet. In school districts that do not have their own form, almost any of the commercial forms can be used as a guide. For instance, the manuscript guide provided by the American

English Books series[1] combines the best recent modifications in older efficient styles of writing.

Of course, the teacher should plan instruction periods so that the children will have ample opportunity to acquire competence. They want not only to write legibly and with ease and speed; they are at the same time interested in producing neat and attractive papers.

Letters and Letter Order

Chapter 3 stressed the functional learning of sounds that letters represent and the names that identify letters. The key idea is functional learning. By now, the reader may have become keenly aware of how "functional learning" best describes the Language-Experience Approach to learning. The words "work," "operate," and "function" all mean "to act in the way that is natural or intended," but "work" suggests success or effectiveness, "operate" stresses efficient activity, while "function" always implies activity that accomplishes an end or goal. To know letter names must be to know the purpose that letters serve or how they function in communication and not just the ability to recite the alphabet by rote.

In speech, letters represent sounds. Children come to school for the first time possessing sizable speaking vocabularies and tremendous phonological facility. It remains for the school to make them articulate in the use of specific letters to represent specific sounds and the blending of sounds into words. This is why learning auditory discrimination takes precedence in the initial stages of learning letters.

Transition from knowing letter sounds to knowing letter names is readily accomplished, because, once sounds have been learned, the letter names serve a practical purpose. Furthermore, letters can be repeated orally as they appear in alphabetical order. Parroting the alphabet is an old-time show-off of early erudition; reciting any other list of twenty-six names in a fixed order is just as significant. To know the purpose of letters, the sounds they represent and their names, requires education that goes well beyond the parroting stage.

The order of letters within a word is what distinguishes one word from another. When the beginning reader goes beyond sight recognition of whole words, he becomes increasingly attentive to letter configuration and letter order as a means of recognition. Each act of auditory and auditory-

[1] Alvina T. Burrows, Russell G. Stauffer, Doris C. Jackson, and June D. Fere-bee (New York: Holt, Rinehart and Winston, 1960–1961).

visual discrimination requires a more precise distinguishing of letter features within words. As the reading vocabulary of children increases, they are required to note small differences of detail in order to distinguish one word from another.

By the time children reach the stage where they begin to try their hand at creative writing, they have acquired a sensitivity to letter order. In addition, each time they see a dictated story being written, they also see letters being formed and placed in certain order, even from the very beginning when the teacher records the first dictated class story. The children see each letter being made and see the letters arranged in different order in each word; they see too the small white space between letters and the larger white spaces between words.

When words from the word banks are arranged in sentences, attention is directed to some degree to letter order. When a word is needed to complete an idea, the pupil carefully observes the letter arrangement as the teacher writes the word. The same keen observation is made of the words reproduced by the teacher for a pupil's word bank. If a writing error or a typing error is made, the pupil sees how the teacher corrects the error so that the letter order or spelling will be correct. By the time pupils begin to write creatively, they have had considerable experience with letters and letter order in words. The first writing-spelling attempts are made with greater ease than might be thought.

Most important in all this is the phonic training the children have been receiving in consonant and vowel substitution. The more skilled they are at substituting letters and building new words in word families, the more apt they are to produce (or substitute) the right letter or letters when they are writing (that is, spelling) words. As a matter of fact, the spelling or producing of letters to represent a word is just about the best evidence a teacher can obtain of the effectiveness of her word-attack teaching. Each error may be indicative of the need for additional phonic teaching. That is to say, the phonological spelling attempts of individual pupils provide the best evidence of how successful the phonic program has been for the class.

Getting started

The discussion on creative word usage in Chapter 3 stated that children are most responsive to constructing sentences and building stories that they themselves create from the words in their word banks. They spend hours of scholarly time in creative construction, and it seems that each success results in increased effort.

Daily construction soon has children wanting to use words that are not in their word banks. At first, they turn to the teacher for needed words, and the semantic efficacy of this spelling and writing of new words is superior retention. These are the words the children remember best, it seems, because they have filled recognized needs.

The need to turn to the teacher for a gap-filling word proves to be too long a wait for some, once they have gained confidence in creating sentences. As a result, they try to write a missing word themselves and thus make their first attempts at creative writing and spelling. The thrill of being a producer stimulates them to even further efforts. Of course, the alert teacher begins to urge some pupils to try producing the words they need. She may ask a child not only how he thinks a word begins but to write the word as he thinks it should be written. One fellow needed the word *bright* to complete the sentence "The sun is —— today." So the teacher asked "How do you think the word 'bright' begins?" Ronald replied, "With the letter *b*." "What letter do you think comes next?" "Is it an *r*?" he asked. "Good," replied the teacher, confirming Ronald's association and decision. "Go ahead and finish the word as you think it is." Encouraged by the teacher and his success, Ronald returned to his seat and wrote *brite*. His spelling, or letter-sound association, was correct phonologically even though not morphologically. He was applying phonic knowledge correctly.

From these early writing-spelling attempts to complete an idea built on word-bank resources to writing an entire idea is an easy step. Any alert teacher can determine the timing of when to propose creative writing. Teachers should be cautioned, however, against either inadvertently or deliberately coercing children into creative-writing attempts before they are ready, resulting in futile first attempts.

Instructions to the children are simple and straightforward but require a teacher's integrity. Provide the children who are ready for creative writing with paper 12 × 18 inches in size. The top half of the paper should be unlined, providing space for drawing. The bottom half should have five lines with ¾-inch space between and should be divided by a dotted line. Between each two of the five lines is another line dividing the ¾-inch space into two spaces each ⅜ inch wide. This kind of paper allows ample space for writing, the widest lines for capitals, the narrow ones for lower-case letters. The space between the lines keeps the writing area open and uncluttered.

The children may be told to write about anything they wish or the teacher may suggest a topic or two. The story in the illustration on page 84 resulted from a teacher's suggestion; she had listed as topic possibilities "bright," "different," and "funny." Valerie chose to write about "bright."

Children should be expected to do their best writing. That this is a time to do good handwriting or letter and word formation should be made clear, but the teacher should be cautious about making them preoccupied with handwriting. Their preoccupation must be with the ideas they want to record.

The children should be told to spell the words as best they can. By now they have some idea of what "spelling" means. They have some idea about sounds and letters that represent sounds. Occasionally, some word will stop them completely and they will want help, and then they should feel free to turn to the teacher for help. They should not become so stymied that they neither write nor seek spelling help. If the teaching practices have promoted pupil-teacher rapport, encouragement from the teacher will hardly be needed. On the other hand, it may be wise to keep the children constantly alert to the teacher's readiness to help.

While the children are writing, the teacher can move about the room and offer aid as needed. Sometimes a child is uncertain about what to say next, and a question from the teacher such as "What will you say next?" may help him bring out his ideas as he explains them to her. Or, a pupil may need just one word to complete an idea and the teacher may say, "Is —— what you want?" If it is the needed word, the pupil will recognize it at once and acknowledge the help. Then, too, when a pupil struggles too long with a spelling need, the teacher can help move him along. She should be cautious, though, about creating the attitude that she is seeking a certain kind of adult perfection. What is wanted is a perfection of pupil expression unhampered by adult standards. Improved standards will follow automatically.

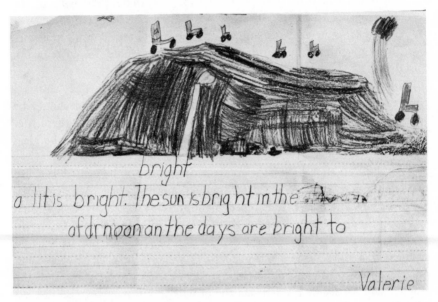

bright

a lit is bright. The sun is bright in the
afdrnoon an the days are bright to

Valerie

In Valerie's production, the title is placed appropriately, but *bright* does not start with a capital *B*. The second sentence begins with a capital but the first does not. The first sentence ends with a period but none of the rest do. Some letters are reversed, and some spellings do not conform to standard American orthography but are correct phonologically. All in all, Valerie's first attempt at creative writing is highly successful. She has a title, develops a series of ideas, separates words adequately, does excellent writing, and uses some punctuation and some capitalization. She is remarkably alert to written language, and her many achievements merit commendation.

Valerie's drawing deserves examination too. Notice the sky and the sun casting its rays on cars crossing the mountain. Across the mountain and in the darkness away from the sun, Valerie has a huge street light to illuminate the way for cars. On the whole, she has shown an astonishing sensitivity to the concept of brightness in the world about her. She recorded her understanding in a detailed and varied drawing and in language. Both symbol systems help tell a great deal about the kind of person Valerie is.

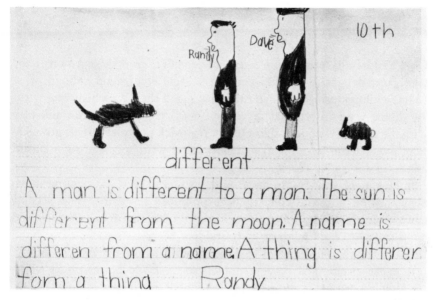

different

A man is different to a man. The sun is different from the moon. A name is differen from a name. A thing is differer form a thing   Randy

Now take a look at Randy's story about *different* and the wonderful ideas he has recorded and the excellent drawing. How "different" Randy's and Valerie's productions are from what occurs in the classroom where children are confined to reading preprimers and coloring in stenciled pictures.

The delight of a roomful of Randys and Valeries is immeasurable. Each child has a way of expressing himself that is fascinatingly unique and as much a means of identifying him as are his signature and fingerprints. The atmosphere that prevails is one of children eager to write and willing to do so all day. Writing has become not a task set by the teacher but a pedagogical privilege. The pride of authorship swells in each bosom. Each child produces his own version, and it is ever astounding how each pupil in one class produces an original interpretation of one idea.

Of course, all this takes time: first a brief stimulus time, then production time, and finally sharing time. Sharing seems always to reach an apex of achievement; children love to share what they have done. Various ways of sharing can be planned—whole class, group, buddy, display. Sharing may take place during spare waiting moments in the school day, set periods of time, or, preferably, by both.

Promoting creative writing

Once children have started to write, it becomes their preoccupation. They take great delight in writing and never seem able to do enough of it. (Some children arriving on an early bus spend their preschool time writing. Some want to write at recess and need to be told to run and play with the class.) Of course, the constant feedback provides instant gratification. Every letter, word, and sentence that is written is seen the moment it is done and can be shown to others.

Interestingly enough, drawings take on a new look and new meaning. Somehow, because the children have produced the story, they become more attentive to the illustration. Drawings become more detailed and more supportive of what is said. Children seem to sense a close bond between the two mediums of expression and, therefore, use them jointly.

A paper, pencil, and crayon supply center should be set up to which the children can go anytime during the school day. Paper is cheap. Pupils should not be allowed to waste it, but neither should they be restrained. Paper of different sizes (15 × 12, 8 × 11, 3 × 7, and so on) should be provided, as well as newsprint 18 × 12, as already described. This encourages children to be selective and to think about writing as serving different purposes.

Newsprint can be mounted on an easel or a chalkboard or corkboard or stretched out on the floor, but the easel seems to invite the greatest response. Short children need a small box to stand on to reach the top of the paper and still write legibly. The large size of the paper permits large letters, a long story, and a big picture. Newsprint seems to be popular also because the first writings they saw were written on it, early in September when the teacher recorded whole-class stories as described in Chapter 2. Children recall this early experience warmly and apparently enjoy writing on the same paper as the teacher.

The smaller sizes of paper can be used on desk tops and allows for accounts of various lengths. The children are responsive too to the demand to adapt letter writing to different paper size and line width. The smallest may be used for notes to say "thank you," extend an invitation, ask for help, keep a personal diary, take home, and so on.

Even though the children most likely will write, write, write and will find a multitude of things, places, and persons to write about, motivation from the teacher should be planned, too. Selected stimuli allow for the use of material within the curriculum—science activities and experiments (see Appendix A), health activities, social studies, and so on. Numerous opportunities are available that evoke marvelous pupil response. Children seem to be more candid when they write than when they talk; perhaps the aloneness of the writing act invites this. Stimuli selected by the teacher may use current events from newspapers, magazines, radio, and television. Children respond readily to writing articles for a class or school newspaper or a magazine. Here is a long list of topics most commonly written about.

animals	television	insects
pets	favorite food	parades
fish	picnics	school building
toys	swimming	school playground
Mother	public playground	school room
Father	neighbors	teacher
sisters	friends	desk
brothers	church	library
home	synagogue	school library
breakfast	uncles	librarian
dinner at home	aunts	picture books
barber	cousins	favorite books
beautician	grandparents	principal
dentist	best friend	principal's office
doctor	trips	snow man
illness	museum	snow balls
cars	post office	sledding
airplanes	dictionary	ice skating
airport	encyclopedia	roller skating
trains	favorite stories	birthdays
school secretary	fairy tales	Halloween
school nurse	folk tales	ghosts
school custodian	games adults play	auditorium
art teacher	games children play	other teachers
music teacher	city buses	other classes
physical education	school bus	rainy days
teacher	bus driver	snowy days
school cafeteria	leaves	hot days
school cook	trees	cold days

lazy days
Sunday
Saturday
weekend
classroom art corner
classroom listening post
classroom building corner
Washington's birthday
Easter
Memorial Day
May Day
rivers
oceans
mountains
caves
ice cream stand
hamburger stand
drug store
grocery store
shoe repair man
police
patrol cars
school patrol
lights
fairs

Labor Day
Father's job
Mother's job
family car
family camper
garden
flowers
lawn mowing
snow shoveling
Yom Kippur
Flag Day
Veterans Day
Election Day
first air flight
pilgrims
Thanksgiving
Indians
Columbus
John Smith
Martin Luther King
The President
winter
Christmas
Christmas trees
Christmas toys

Christmas gifts
Hanukkah
New Years Day
Valentine Day
Lincoln's birthday
Canada
Mexico
other countries
Miss America
Miss Teen-Age America
comic papers
magazines
trouble
help
guessing
detectives
mystery
Dad's speeding
science experiments
vacation
summer
spring
night

As was noted in the section on the motivation of experience stories, field trips should be thought of as only one means of motivation. Field trips have the danger of overwhelming of young minds with more new ideas than they can easily assimilate. Trips should focus on one or two aspects of an experience, and, before they are made, pupils should review what they already know or think they know about what they will see. For a trip to a zoo, for example, a talk or a list of animals that may be seen should be prepared. Particulars known about animals can be listed; pupils can speculate about the height of a giraffe, for example, and the length of his neck and legs and so on. Contrasts can be drawn by speculating about whether or not a giraffe could stand up in a classroom or in a gymnasium or walk under a freeway or expressway overpass. Field trips, to be useful, should be dealt with wisely.

Concept development

Concept development can be ardently pursued. Children love to play with words and the multiple meanings of words. Most everyone has completed the sentence "Happiness is ——" for such ideas as "Happiness is an ice cream cone," "Happiness is my baby brother," "Happiness is when the birds sing in the morning." Children can be invited to make this kind of response with many words and sentences.

Multiple meanings of words invite reaction, too: run—to go fast, run free, sail before a wind, race, melt as wax; snap—to close the jaws suddenly, a fish grasping at bait, to break a twig, talk back, snap fingers, crack a whip; stand—to be on your feet, take a position of firmness; a small place of business; comb—a device for adjusting the hair, the crest on a chicken or turkey, to search; double—twice as many, a double bed, to double over, a twin; dress—to put on clothes, a lady's garment, to put a room in order, arrange the hair, prepare a chicken for cooking.

Opposites evoke varied responses: hard-soft, big-little, ugly-pretty, high-low, sweet-sour, wet-dry. Noun-verb usages invite other reactions: foot, as feet and to go on foot; fill, as material used to fill a hole and to fill something; tie, as a necktie and to bind. Words like *help, play, different, funny*, and *nose* invite ready response. All a teacher need do is write *help* on the board and invite children to write "help" stories.

"How I feel about ——" is always a good starter for a story. This encourages children to reveal their own opinions and feelings and can have a rewarding effect as children discover how different pupils feel differently about milk, for instance, and why they feel as they do. Such topics as hate, love, honesty, safety patrol, war, and peace evoke interesting and sometimes startling responses.

Thus, in a refreshing, stimulating, and fruitful way, children's concepts, as a product of their thoughts, can be extended and refined by showing them how to notice the structure of concepts, both the perceptually obvious and the not too obvious, how to notice similarities and differences, relationships, novelty, levels, hierarchies, order, and so on. In addition, concepts in the content of daily living can be dealt with as concepts of space, time, number, people, humor.

The reading that children do from the very beginning, when they turn to the classroom library table to "see and read" illustrated story books or to locate words learned in the dictated stories, provides a vital source of concept development. By the time the children begin locating their word-bank words in books, newspapers, magazines, and funnies, they are adding a new, rich means of enlarging their concepts. Dictionaries, encyclopedias, and other similar sources provide maps, graphs, and illustrations that can help extend and refine ideas. Most important, however, is the fact that the actual reading that children do provides a ready source of ideas for creative writing. Pupils start writing stories similar to those they read. They write their own fairy tales, myths, mysteries, plays, reports, descriptions, experiment accounts, and so on.

Creative-writing examples

The following selections are typical of what may be expected from a first-grade class. They range from first writing attempts in October to writings done in April. The interest areas illustrate the multitude of persons, places, and things children write about. Some of the examples are reproduced photographically to show as authentically as possible how children write and create. Most of the examples show spelling, syntax, grammar, and diction just as the child authors produced them.

The school   10–15
is Big. I M in
school. School is
fun. I go on a BUS.
          Gale

Philip has a   10–14
Puampcinn. It is
big.
          Timmy

I walk to   10–12
school. Mommy
gos   nd Kis
my father.
     teResa

Stop and Go   10–19
Stop wen The
lite is red. I Go
wen The lite is green.
          Katy

Halloween   10–20
Halloween I Went Out
TricK or Treting
I see Evry Boody
That I No.
          Dawn

A careful examination of the creative-writing samples above, all produced in October, reveals many things. Examine them again.

HANDWRITING

A look at the handwriting shows the writing skill acquired by mid-October. Most of the letters are well formed, large, and open. The relationship between capitals and lower-case letters in most of them is excellent, as is the spacing between words.

SPELLING

The spelling shows that some of the words are spelled correctly according to American English spelling conventions. Most of the others are spelled correctly according to American English phonology. The freedom to spell "the best you can" produces letters to represent the sounds the pupils hear as distinct as well as blended together. This is precisely what phonics does in language—letters and letter combinations represent sounds and blend together to represent words. The phonological wealth that children possess is astounding, as is their ability to use this wealth when encouraged to do so.

The quality of the spelling displays other equally important conditions. The children know letters, the sounds the letters usually represent, and the shape of the letters when produced in manuscript. This knowledge was not acquired by rote memorization but by functional use. It was the purpose the letters—their shapes and their sounds—served that facilitated their retention and recall.

Even more remarkable is the ability of the children to use their knowledge of letters and sounds in so many new and different situations. The positive transfer of letter knowledge is in reality problem-solving learning. Letter knowledge is highly generalizable or transferable from word to word. Correct spellings, especially ones that are phonologically correct, represent abstractions from the products of responding and not the responses themselves. More simply, the capability of a pupil to spell a word phonologically is a measure of his ability to link letters and sounds and to solve new spelling problems. This is the test of successful learning. The pupils are successful not only with phonological but, frequently, with conventional spellings of words. This is evidence of positive transfer of learning from phonic training with known words to letter-sound production of unknown words—namely, successful problem solving. Application of phonological principles relevant to the sounding of words usually results in immediate transfer to spelling.

The spelling performance pupils exhibit when writing creatively represents basic conditions of meaningful learning. As a result of many

Betsey

I am a girl and I is
six. I brought some
book for the children
to read. I live in a house

10-16

I just had a shoort
har aot a wumin cot
it for me and I like
it shoort. the wumins
name was ine. Beth

the nedl. We
got a nedl. it
had four nedls.
the dotrs name is
dotr Rains.
Katy 11-2-65

Dale

I am a Boy. and I am
6 ers old. and I go
to school. and my
name is Dale. I am in
frst grade.

writing-spelling opportunities (repetition), pupils respond to sound-letter associations (practice) in order to meet the written-communication demands (stimulus) in the almost simultaneous occurrence of stimuli and response circumstance (contiguity). New improved behavior patterns are being acquired that result in permanent change. When a pupil reads back what he has written both immediately and at a later date, he is obtaining reinforcement as feedback. This recognition of achievement pays off with priceless self-reward. When others can read a pupil's material, reward and information have produced the highest order of reinforcement.

Each creative-writing opportunity provides the conditions of reinforcement: immediacy, frequency, and number of spelling opportunity reinforcers. Finally, the sound-letter generalizations that the pupils make circumvent the necessity to learn discrete spelling responses for each discrete spelling stimulus. Generalization, not rote memory, thus becomes an important aspect of spelling behavior.

Some people question permitting and encouraging children to spell phonologically while they write creatively. The explanation above should help allay this concern. Equally important, if not more, is the basic purpose of creative writing—to have children realize that they can communicate in writing much as they do aloud. Pupils write easily and readily, as well as creatively, to transmit ideas just as in talk. If early talking attempts of infants were stopped to correct each error of enunciation, syntax, and semantics, children would become confused and produce grave speech errors. The same results would occur if early writing attempts were corrected for purism in syntax, grammar, semantics, and spelling. It is vitally important, therefore, that teaching practices be geared to the learner's objectives—a favorable attitude toward the efficacy of written communication.

Changes in spelling practices come about in a natural way. When the children exchange their creative writings, some discover that they cannot read all that was written because of spelling deviations. This is when pupils ask each other what message the medium is to convey. When such questioning occurs, the pupil is made aware that something is wrong and that the something is the letters or the spelling used to represent the sounds. This is the beginning of a spelling conscience that is a teacher's delight and a scholar's boon. Pupils want to spell words so they can be read, and that is precisely why society developed written language with letters in a fixed order. Attempts at editing begin astonishingly early in the writing career of children. Spellings are changed and omitted words are inserted.

As indicated earlier, the letters that pupils use to represent sounds provide probably the best evidence of the effectiveness of a teacher's teaching of phonic and structural word-attack skills. In Beth's writing, there is much evidence of good teaching. Her spelling of *short* (*shoort*), of *hair* (*har*), and of *cut* (*cot*) shows her recognition of beginning and ending sounds and an alertness to vowel sounds. Her spelling of *women* (*wumin*) is typical of the astounding phonological skill children possess and will display when encouraged. Beth responded to both consonant and vowel middle sounds. The last word (*jne*) is her spelling of *Ginny*, a remarkable display. Many children have difficulty with *j* sounds or do not hear ending sounds such as *e* represents here. Notice, too, the consistency of the spelling—*shoort* is spelled the same way twice as are *wumin* and *cot*. Children seem to realize, perhaps more intuitively than articulately, the need for consistency in spelling.

Dale's spelling of *first* (*frst*) is another example of impressive facility. He grasped the initial single consonant *f*, the *st* blend at the end of the word, and, most amazing, the influence and location of the *r* sound.

Katy's spelling of *needle* is outstanding in that *nedl* is the phonological respelling for *needle* as it is used in dictionaries. Katy has no knowledge about syllabic *l* as such, but she has phonological knowledge about what the sound *l* represents as in *needle*. Katy is not a phonetician but she is highly skilled phonologically. Notice, too, how she produces *doctors* (*dotrs*) in one instance and *doctor* (*dotr*) in the next. Children's spellings often coincide with dictionary phonic respellings and show awareness of derivative and inflectional changes.

Notice, too, Gale's use of *M* for *am*, Timmy's *puampcinn* for *pumpkin*, Teresa's spelling of *gos* for *goes*, and Dawn's spelling of *Treting* for *treating* and *No* for *know*. Spellings used in creative writing abound with such phonological accuracies and simplified forms that advocates of simplified spelling should be excited by such performances.

SYNTAX, GRAMMAR, AND PUNCTUATION

A common comment about children's writing is that they use *and* to go from sentence to sentence rather than terminate sentences with periods. Take another look at the materials above and see how *and* was used in this way in only three instances. Now examine the sentences and the parts of speech. Notice the sensitivity to subject-predicate relationships and their role as the core of a sentence and how often verb-noun usage is in agreement. Notice the use of adjective qualifiers. Periods abound. Children know when to signify the end of a sentence by voice change when they are talking, and they soon display similar knowledge when they write. Remember that each illustration is a first attempt and that no teaching of syntax, grammar, or punctuation had been done.

SEQUENCE

Even at this early stage of creative writing, the order of ideas is excellent. Children are aware of sequence and they relate ideas in an orderly fashion. Each writing above is really a recounting of an experience rather than an imaginative story. No plot development was required. No punch line or novel ending had to be held in mind until the last. Order of ideas was required, and it was accomplished.

DRAWINGS

The four photographically reproduced stories show the illustrations the children prepared to accompany their compositions. Beth shows herself at a beauty parlor; the details are quite good as is her use of color. Betsy's picture would merit a favorable rating on the Goodenough-Harris Drawing Test. Dale depicts himself on the way to school and shows a car passing by. Katy provides excellent detail and composition.

Drawing reveals not only artistic ability but also self. The medium provides a means of expression, a way of projecting concepts by form symbolism rather than by words. Notice the use of detail, color, and plot setting. Notice, too, the degree to which space was used.

These compositions represent what can be expected of a program pursued much as the one described here. They are first attempts, but they reflect astounding word wealth, ingenuity, and resourcefulness. Given ample opportunity and encouragement, beginners will produce results that stand in sharp contrast to the output of first graders in situations where pedagogically blind suppression is practiced.

Writings through the year

The next story below was produced by Iris on November 1. At that time, Iris had over a hundred words in her word bank, arranged in alphabetical order. She was making excellent progress in recognition and retention of words. Her word-bank list already exceeded the count in most basic-reader series preprimers and almost equalled the number in primers. She was about ready for participation in group directed reading-thinking activities. Only a few of the words in her story appeared in her word bank. Thus, her creative writing was placing new demands on her speaking-meaning vocabulary and was adding new words to her word bank—*fall, leaves, orange, turn,* and *ground.* Words added to the bank were recorded by the teacher with correct spelling on word cards. Interestingly enough, this correct spelling was readily accepted and recognized.

fall levs   11–1
fall levs are fun to
plae in. Sumare brown.
and sumare orange. and
sum levs trn color. in fall
levs fall to the ground.
                    Iris

The following typical accounts were also written in November. Most were accompanied by a drawing.

I Rake LeVs   11–9
I Rake up my Nxt dr
nabrs. I get the LeVes
and Put the LeVesin
the Basket.
                    Tom

I playt with my friend.
We playt on Sunday. We like
to play. Ann likes to play with me.
We playt with a cat.
                    Monica

My Ded Cat   11–9
Ones I Hade a Cat.
He was white and yellow.
One night my father
come Fame my grandfathers
house. Wenn my Father
Come home Fame my
grandfathers house he said
Ruste is Ded.
                    David

We went to the book
Far. then we got som
books. Ther wer som
big and Little ones. I
bot som last night.
Then I took thm home.
Then I Read my book.
We will go to the far
agen.
                    Jody

The following accounts show the progress of Darrell over a period of months. His first creative writing attempt was made on November 1 and tells about his watching TV. A "translation" of it follows in parentheses.

I wds the wid wsdn   11–1   (I watch the wild western
wst on T Thn I wds   first on TV. Then I watched
OK Kobr   O.K. Cracker)

Big Red   12–3

Big Red was a dog.
Big Red won first pris.
And he plled a boy in
a pind. I like Big Red. And
he was on a Movie.

Are School Room   12–10

We wrok in are school
Room. We Read. We have a
tree in are Room and we
decorate it. It has Santa
Claus and Candy Cans
and staking on ar
Christmas tree and it has
Pretty balls and it has
Prasits.

I got a foot ball and a   1–6
walkie-talkie for Christmas.
And an record player.

Me   2–10

I am tall. I do good work.
I have blue eyes. I have brown
hair. I can count to 100
hundred. And I am seven year
old. And I am a boy. I am in
the first grade. The End.

Where I Like To Go   3–7

I Like to go to West Cheder
a lot becus it is one hundred
mils away frum here. I go
thaer becus it has a big hill.

The Three Bears   4–18

The Three bears live in the woods.
Thare was father bear and mother bear
and baby bear. Thare house was mad
out of wood. And thare was a girl named
Golde lox. She went to the three bears
house when the bears wer away from
the house because they wer wateing
for thare pareg to ceool. The End.

Darrell's writings are typical from a first grader. His first attempts reflect some sensitivity to letters and the sounds they represent as well as to letter order in words, word order in ideas, and idea order in an account. The spelling is mostly phonological. The titles vary considerably and show a wide range of interests. The quality of his sentences and his idea-order presentation shows constant improvement. His spelling according to standard orthography is increasingly more accurate. Whenever he meets a word or an idea that he cannot spell, he spells it phonologically and goes on with his story writing. Note how he spelled *Goldilocks* (*Golde lox*) and *porrideg to cool* (*pareg to ceool*).

Darrell's handwriting showed marked improvement through December, too. After that, his skill was such that all his writings were equally good. By April, he was using space more economically by making smaller letters and spacing words more compactly. Darrell's own style of handwriting was being acquired and refined.

The writings presented here are only a sample of all the writing Darrell did during the year. Once children start creative writing, they seem to do it almost constantly. They want to write at home, at lunch time, at recess, during milk break. Interestingly enough, most parents cooperate when the children write at home by not spelling for them or putting words in their mouths. Most of the home-written stories are just like the ones done in school.

The following represent the range of interests and skills of typical first-grade creative writing from the end of October through the middle of March. The writing by Dawn is from November 3, Robby's from November 15, Louise's from December 7.

I like a trl to
swim funny. Trl a
funny Shell is a Trls
house. ATrl is fun.

(trl = turtle)
                Dawn

The praed

yesterday i was in a
Praed. And i was in
Amdlis niaber A. 54. And
my papap was draving
The Amblis.
                Robby

(Amblis = ambulance; niaber = number)

Cismsy

I Horp It sts to snow.
Cismsy is olms hre. We get
sim toys. I like santo cls
and I am shr he likes me to.
My gil fan was sak.

Louise

In the classroom in which Louise was a pupil, her story about Christmas was typical. With a theme such as Christmas, one might think that a great deal of uniformity of writing and spelling might occur, but this was not true even with so dramatic a stimulus. On this particular day, December 7, eleven different spellings were used by the children in a class of thirty-one: *Cismsy, clsmis, Crsms, Crsmss, Cesmus, Csim, Maerry Cismsy, Crhrimise, Cismisy, Marry Casmiss,* and *Christmas.*

Children write their own ideas and do their own spelling when urged to do so. Timmy, the boy who had spelled Christmas correctly, explained that he had been using the word at home and that was why he knew how to write it. On December 22, Katy also spelled it correctly. The five stories following hers were all written in January.

O Tannenbaum

We sing O Tannenbaum. It is a
German song. A man named Luther
cut down a Christmas tree and
took it home and shoed his wif
and children how the stars shined
on it. O Tannenbaum is a folk
song. The Germans were the first
pepl to have a Christmas tree.

Katy

We were exspeermiting. We
put a pensl on the water and it
floted. We trieed some roocks and
all the roocks sank.

Erik

Bright Snow–White Snow

I like snow it is fun.
I like to make snowman. It is
fun too. You can make a snow
fort. It is fun too. And I like
to go down a hill.

Karen

When We Went to The Art Museum

My Daddy and my Mommy and me
went to the art museum. One man
drew a lot of pictures. I bote
five little baskets when we went
to the art museum. It was fun
at the art museum. We go to
stors sometimes. The mans name
was Andrew Wyeth. My sisters
and brother stay at my Mom-moms.

Anne

Second Billy Goat Gruff

Second Billy Goat Gruff is a
goat. He is a little bit tall. He has
a small beard. Second Billy goat
gruff has small black horns. He
has a brown fur. He has brown
huffs. He has a little brown tail.
His family is Big Billy goat gruff
and Little Billy goat gruff. I like
it because Second Billy goat gruff
got over the bridge and because
they got all the green grass
they wanted.

David

Hansel and Gretel

Hansel and Gretel and thair
father were very happy untill
thair father had to marry a
woman. And she was called a
Stepmother. She did't like children.
So that night the Stepmother
and thair father were taking.
And Hansel and Gretel were a
sleep. Thair Stepmother and
father made a loud noise and
woke them up.

Karen

This is a pretty boat.
It is all different colours.
It can carry lots of people.
It Travelseverywhere. It takes
many people to all different
coutrys.

                    Brigitte

These two were produced in February and March:

George Washington
George Washington Father was
name Frank. He was our first
Presudent. He choped down the
chery tree and George telled
the trth to his father. His Father
put the hatchit up in the closit.
He fought the British.

                    David

My Mommy
My Mommy is pretty.
She has blue eyes and brown
hair. Her name is Arinda. She
is thirty-one years old. She
is nice. She spanks me
sometimes because I need
it but when she is in a good
moond she doesnt spank
me. She is supertishesh
because when she drops a
comb she steps on it
before she picks it up.
She is silly. Yesturday she
went out side in the snow
with me. She looks like my
aunt. She is the most
wounderfulest mother I've
ever had.

                    Jean

Once children start writing, they do so whenever opportunity permits. However, special times should be devoted to such writing so that teacher guidance can be provided most effectively. Writing done at times other than those specifically planned are a special bonus.

One teacher introduced an idea that proved productive throughout the year. She made a 5-×-7-inch form with the heading "Write it. Don't say it," from which she could run off several blanks at a time. The children responded overwhelmingly. They could take a form from a stack in a box and write. They wrote memos to each other, to the teacher, to their parents, and to anyone else. Some used the memo forms to write reminder notes to themselves.

If pupils wish to have their stories typed, they must dictate their written accounts aloud to the typist (the teacher or a teacher's aid or a high-school student), for a number of reasons. Since the typist is not copying from an original, she is not bound to reproduce the spellings of the child, so now she can spell all words according to standard orthography. When a child reads his material aloud, he frequently discovers syntax and grammar errors. Sometimes preoccupation with writing results in errors that usually do not occur in talking. A child may discover that he failed to insert a verb or a conjunction or a preposition. He can repair this now when he reads to the typist. In addition, children thrill to the opportunity of reading their authored products aloud.

When the typed copy has been completed, the pupil can read both his original and the typed version. It is astonishing how often the correct spellings are recognized. At first, children seem to take little account of differences in spelling, but, after a number of opportunities like this, they begin to compare two versions and their spelling consciences become more acute.

At no time are the children asked to recopy their stories in order to correct their spelling. Some of the more sensitive children occasionally do so on their own. The teacher must be careful then that she does not create the impression that she wants all children to recopy and correct. What she wants is all children to write.

Even before some children start recopying entire stories, most do some correcting. Erasures are quite common; words are erased to produce them more accurately phonologically and orthographically. This is also part of the development of spelling conscience.

Punctuation and capitalization are corrected by the typist, and children respond to the adjusted versions. It must be remembered that failure to place periods is frequently an inadvertent result of the desire to get ideas down on paper. In their haste, children, just as adults, skip some of the communication essentials.

A primer-size typewriter allows children to type their own writings rather than write them by hand. Children love the typing privilege. It should be dealt with as a privilege, because this promotes respect for and

After School

After school I go home on bus thirteen. And when I get home I get dresst. And when I get dresst I go out and play. And I play in the farist. And I play in my fort. And today after school I am going to play with my dog. And after I play with my dog. I am going to play with my babby. And after I play with my babby. I am going to go to my freiend's house And when I get back from my freiend's house. I am going to play with my toys. And then I will eat my super And then I will woshst tv. Brian Smith March 22

Clowds

I like clowds. Clowds
give us rian sometimes.
When rian comes down
we have gray clowds. Clowd
help us. We shuld be glad
that God maked clowds.

Robin March 14

Our Voikswagon

We are going to get a Voikswagon.
It will be blue outside and the
inside will be white. Our
Grandady is going to give us it

The Voikswagon is up in
Washington. I am going to ride
back with Mommy. I like to
ride in the Voikswagon. My daddy can
go to the plant esyer. Mar 9 1967

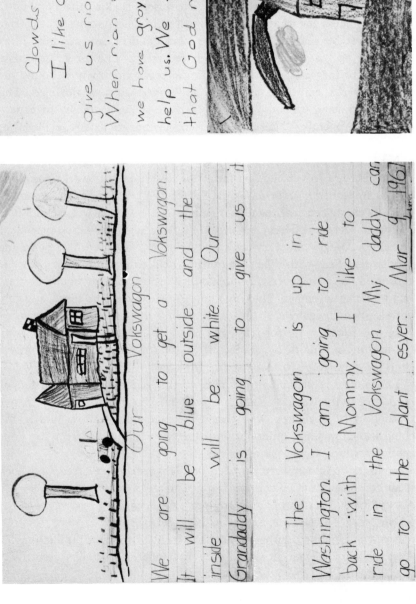

Lura

responsible use of the typewriter. They learn readily how to insert paper and line it up. If some pupils experience difficulty doing this, an able pupil assigned as typewriter aide can provide the needed help.

A reexamination of the stories reproduced in the preceding pages will reveal how language skills in written communication improve with usage. Notice how sentence length changes: The number of words per sentence becomes greater as the year progresses, as does the number of qualifying ideas incorporated into a sentence. The number of different words increases sharply. Early in the year, children tend to reuse ideas, seemingly because of the security this represents. The use of adjectives and adverbs increases, clearly reflecting a sensitivity to how nouns and subjects, verbs, and other adjectives and adverbs can be qualified. This more discriminate response results in a more acute examining of experiences. (In Appendix B, in the Stauffer and Hammond studies, evidence of the amount of such change is given from analysis of children's writings.)

Notice, too, how early spellings show considerable sensitivity to consonants but not to vowels. Consonant sounds are less variable. Consonants sounds are substituted for each other: *k* for *c* in *cut*, *s* for *c* in *city*, and so on. Vowels, on the other hand, are quite variable. One vowel can and does represent several different sounds. This is why dictionaries provide a vowel key, usually on every set of facing pages. Vowels are slippery, and people need help with them. Dictionaries seldom provide more than one consonant key, however. Children reflect these circumstances in their early writing attempts. They not only omit vowels but they substitute vowels phonologically: *cot* for *cut*, *frst* for *first*, *dotr* for *doctor*, *sum* for *some*, *nxt* for *next*, *far* for *fair*, *agen* for *again*, *plled* for *pulled*, *watering* for *waiting*, *trl* for *turtle*, *sts* for *starts*, *shr* for *sure*, *shoed* for *showed*, *pensl* for *pencil*, *bote* for *bought*, *trth* for *truth*.

This ability is phonologically noteworthy and represents tremendous sensitivity to the world of sounds and letters. The ability is an asset rather than a liability. Spelling power—that is, the recognition of how unorthodox conventional spellings differ—begins to show. Spellings "correct" by convention are increasingly used.

Similarly consonants are dropped or their order is reversed, and both silent consonants and vowels are dropped: *choped* for *chopped*, *chery* for *cherry*, *stors* for *stores*, *floted* for *floated*, *shoed* for *showed*, *pepl* for *people*, *becus* for *because*, *wrok* for *work*, *pris* for *prize*.

Again one might rightly ask how this kind of spelling production reflects spelling achievement as measured by standardized spelling tests based on conventional spellings. In Appendix B, reports of carefully documented studies indicate most convincingly that spelling achievement acquired this way is astoundingly high.

Other ideas about creative achievement

A first-grade boy, rereading in May some of the pieces he had written in November, looked up and said, with an amused expression on his face, "That's the way I wrote when I was little." This boy was most likely prompted to turn to his earlier writings in order to enjoy again some of his own creations and bask in the reflected glory of authorship. But his increased maturity and facility caused him to face up, through self-discovery, to his earlier shortcomings. Thus, the modesty and capability of a scholar, who knows the power of change and growth, were being acquired early. He was also awakened to a sense of the delight and excitement of learning about communication and the intellectual power to be derived from precise communication. It is this kinship with self-knowledge and creative power that "makes him seem worthy to himself and stimulates him to further effort" (3, p. 2).

All children want to write. This is what Alvina Burrows and her colleagues wrote about so convincingly in 1939 (3); conditions have not changed in the 30 years since they made their 4-year experiment. The creative use of language enables children to record what they think or feel is important and to communicate their experiences and imaginings. The Language-Experience Approach to initial reading instruction bears witness to this burgeoning use of language.

Though theoretical positions may vary, psychologists have concurred for many years that certain variables affect learning rate. Some are personal—age, sex, intelligence, creativity, curiosity, motivation, intent, and so on. Some relate to the material to be learned—meaningful or nonmeaningful, verbal or motor, serial items or paired associates, similar or dissimilar items. Others are concerned with situation or the general arrangements for practice of skills and abilities (7).

In contrast to the general agreement about effects on learning, there is little agreement about sequence and organization of practice. Short distributed practice sessions appear to be most effective for whole learning, rote verbal learning, and simple motor skills, but, when a task is complex, no general rule applies. On the other hand, it is known that active participation and understanding of the nature of the skills to be accomplished facilitate learning. Another principle of learning economy, accepted without much question, is that knowledge of results facilitates learning. Social psychologists have alerted us to the effects of group factors and social pressure on thinking and learning and to the potency of personal and social satisfaction. The gradual development of symbolic and cognitive behavior has shown not only that maturation influences development but also that children seem to have a built-in knowledge of relationships (2, 6).

The word "creativity" has become a magic term, recently (4). Creative thinking is distinguished by the fact that there is something novel about it and that it may or may not be tangibly expressed. Novel thinking, in which ideas are used in a new form or new connections, means transfer learning:

> From all this there comes, like a welcome breath of fresh air, a belief that children and others can be motivated by needs other than those of hunger, thirst, pain, and sex, that they can learn to know and to value the sweet taste of intellectual achievement. (4, p. 10)

Creative and divergent thinking are thought of as almost synonymous, as thinking that may proceed by a variety of paths to diverse ends. Abilities required are ideational, associational, and expressional fluency; spontaneous and adaptive flexibility; originality; and elaboration.

Thelma Thurstone, in reacting to J. P. Guilford's ideas, says that she, too, has experienced "better results than we had hoped for" in her attempts to teach children to transfer from a specific ability to generalized thinking. She also found enthusiasm: Children enjoy creating: "Perhaps if we did not do so much to keep children from being creative, they might like school better" (9, p. 39), she concludes.

Walter Loban, in his study (5) of the semantics and structure of language used by the same children from kindergarten through the sixth grade, related, to a solid base line, such diverse and significant aspects of language as the following. His list may serve as a guide to examination of the samples of children's writing in this chapter (5, p. 81).

1. flexibility of sentence pattern and of elements within the sentence pattern
2. proportion of organization and rambling
3. variations from conventional usage, grammar, and syntax

4. degree of coherence through subordination
5. diversity and range of vocabulary
6. extent to which generalizations occur
7. freedom from language tangles or false starts (mazes)
8. amount of language and length of units of communication
9. number of separate concepts presented
10. amount of concreteness and abstractness
11. use of affective verbs and other emotional language
12. use of figurative language (metaphor, simile, irony, hyperbole, personification)

The list, though not all-inclusive, presents elements certain to enter into any study of language proficiency. Furthermore, they apply equally to oral and written language.

Significant conclusions of Loban's study are that formal instruction in grammar seems to be an ineffective method of improving expression; pupils need many opportunities to deal with their own ideas in situations in which they want to communicate successfully with others; attempts to achieve flexibility within patterns other than basic sentence patterns should be the measure of proficiency; instruction in elementary school should have more to do with oral language.

Ruth Strickland studied children in primary grades for the relationship between their use of language and the development of silent- and oral-reading skill. She concluded (8) that at an early age children learn with reasonable thoroughness the basic structures of their language, that the oral language of the children she studied was far more advanced than the language of certain basic-readers she examined, and that children in the highest category of reading age, oral-reading interpretation, and listening comprehension also made more use of the common structural patterns in extended and elaborated form than did children who ranked low on these variables.

Reexamination of the samples in this chapter readily reveals their advanced language and how it differs from that commonly found in pre-primers and primers. The Language-Experience Approach did much for oral-language readiness and for extending and refining perceptual experiences as children had opportunities to see, hear, touch, manipulate, write, draw, and talk about it all. Active contact with things and ideas may be why these children learned to read much as they learned to talk. Perhaps this is why educators have urged repeatedly that children should be guided to see and understand that reading is no more than talk written down. (1, 4).

Conclusion

This chapter on creative writing describes in detail what creative writing is, how to get first graders started at it, and what achievement to expect throughout the year. Other related topics—handwriting, spelling, phonics, motivation, concept development, and creative thinking—are also discussed.

Children use language uniquely and functionally long before they start school. They acquire this creative-talking facility by talking with others and among themselves as they play! Talk's purpose is to communicate. Skill in creative writing is best acquired in much the same way. The purpose of writing is also to communicate: Just as with speech, children will write to and for each other and themselves.

Creative writing is defined as a child's writing for some personal or social purpose in his own language. Each pupil selects his own words, ideas, and order and writes with his own handwriting and spelling. First steps occur when children use words in their word banks to express ideas. When a word not in a word bank is needed to complete an idea, pupils try their hand at writing and spelling without being overwhelmed because they have already acquired confidence in their vocabularies. Handwriting has to be taught functionally; it must serve a purpose from the very beginning. Phonic instruction pays off as children spell words phonologically. A spelling conscience is developed early as children discover on rereading that sometimes their letters and order of letters does not convey an intended word to others or to themselves. They also notice that sometimes a letter order they have used has produced a word that can be read but does not agree with conventional letter order.

Numerous ways of motivating creative writing are described and illustrated in this chapter. Many writing samples were supplied and appraised. Growth in written syntax, grammar, and semantics power was discussed. Writing, being more exacting than talk, yields greater returns when children increase their reading vocabularies, and so their language usage in general grows more rapidly. Children love to write and share, to be authors as well as readers. Some are more creative than others, in oral and written language as well as in expression in the arts. But all children love to create.

Bibliography

1. Boney, C. DeWitt. "Teaching Children to Read as They Learned to Talk," *Elementary English Review*, vol. 16, no. 4 (April, 1939), pp. 139–141.
2. Bruner, Jerome. "The Course of Cognitive Growth," *American Psychologist*, vol. 19, no. 1 (January, 1964), pp. 1–15.
3. Burrows, Alvina T., Doris C. Jackson, and Dorothy O. Saunders. *They All Want to Write*. 3rd ed. New York: Holt, Rinehart and Winston, 1964.
4. Guilford, J. P., "Intellectual Factors in Productive Thinking." In *Productive Thinking in Education*, edited by Mary Jane Aschner and Charles E. Bish. Washington, D.C.: National Education Association, 1965.
5. Loban, Walter D. *The Language of Elementary School Children*. Champaign, Ill.: National Council of Teachers of English, 1963.
6. Piaget, Jean. *The Origins of Intelligence in Children*. New York: International Universities Press, 1952.
7. Smith, Karl U., and Margaret T. Smith. *Cybernetic Principles of Learning and Educational Design*. New York: Holt, Rinehart and Winston, 1966.
8. Strickland, Ruth B. *The Contribution of Structural Linguistics to the Teaching of Reading, Writing, and Grammar in the Elementary School*. Bulletin of the School of Education, Indiana University. Vol. 40, no. 1 (January, 1964), Bloomington, Ind.
9. Thurstone, Thelma Gwinn. "Commentaries." In *Productive Thinking in Education*, edited by Mary Jane Aschner and Charles E. Bish. Washington, D.C.: National Education Association, 1965.

The library

READER INQUIRY AND REGULATION

This chapter deals with what might be described as the physical aspect of the teaching-learning environment most essential to the effective use of the Language-Experience Approach. The desired outcome of all reading instruction is reading students. If this goal is to be accomplished, a library is of paramount importance.

Of the three parts of this chapter, the first deals with libraries in general and the urgent need for libraries. The second part describes the role of classroom libraries as indispensable teaching-reading aids. The third explains the need for libraries in elementary schools and their function in the Language-Experience Approach.

Read the following objectives and make educated guesses concerning the answers. Honesty in facing up to what you do and do not know is the beginning of wisdom. Educated guesses about answers provide scholarly commitment. Both will keep you on course and regulate your comprehension.

1. Explain how the Language-Experience Approach is pedagogically based on functional communication and how it is psychologically based on action.
2. Describe the influence of the information explosion of libraries.
3. Explain how a library is the resource or product center for teaching and learning, and how command of reading-thinking skills is the skill or process foundation.
4. Explain why Peggy Sullivan described the Knapp School Project as "a librarian's dream come true."

Upon reading the second part, the reader should be able to meet the following objectives:

1. Describe how a teacher can arrange a classroom library.
2. Tell about the housing of books in a classroom library.
3. Describe how children can use a classroom library.

Upon reading the third part, the reader should be able to answer the following questions.

1. How does Mary Gaver define a school library?
2. How has the role of libraries in learning gradually emerged over the past 400 years?
3. Why should no basic-reader program ever be thought of as *the* reading program?
4. What are the principles that should govern teacher-library relationships, as declared by the American Library Association's *Standards for School Library Programs?*
5. How can a child in first grade make independent library visits?
6. How do community as well as home libraries provide a ready source of learning materials?

The functional and psychological aspect of the Language-Experience Approach as defined and detailed in the preceding chapters is of such magnitude and potency that it is difficult to describe it phase by phase. The pedagogy is based on language usage for communication and abounds with teaching-learning procedures that are practical, timely, and utilitarian. Psychologically, the approach is one of action and accords true significance to intent and purpose.

We have already seen the degree to which language is linked with reality and with tangible usages that can be subjected by children to real action. Their language is supported by perception, experience, faith, and all the fundamental emotions that are linked to their activities. The single firm intention to communicate is an astounding regulator of interest, energy, and values. In addition, a strong feeling of mutual respect arises from cooperation among children in their school and social life.

All pedagogical and psychological aspects of the Language-Experience Approach operate from the very beginning in a functionally interrelated way. Increased reading power does somewhat evidence stages of progress. Individual physiological, intellectual, social, and cultural differences make stages of progress discernible. But, by and large, the functional use of language involves *all* aspects of communication at each stage.

A library is an integral part of the Language-Experience Approach. It was referred to in the account of the second day of dictated stories

(Chapter 2). Once a child learns to talk, he rattles on and on in monologues with himself, monologues and dialogues with his peers, and questions and answers with adults. Similarly, once a child learns to read, he wants to read to himself and with and to his peers and adults. To satisfy the zest for reading requires, in brief, a library.

Some reflections on school libraries

In a democratic society, education must serve all youth for person-social-cultural purposes. As long as every adult as a member of an electorate possesses the power of the ballot, the civic demand that schools possess the resources of teaching and learning must go unquestioned. Printed and audiovisual materials are the basic tools of effective teaching and learning, including "the development of the discipline of critical thinking, the teaching of reading" (3, p. 3). Clearly, educational objectives can be fully achieved only when the nation's schools have a full complement of library resources, personnel, and services.

Libraries as creative centers can render two unique services. They can help develop reading interests and tastes and help lift the dead weight of poverty and ignorance. They are indispensable in meeting the demands of the information explosion (5). In the schools of tomorrow, pupils may spend more than half their time in school libraries and laboratories. Learning and teaching will then depend upon the full utilization of the cognitive processes of questioning, problem solving, reflecting, inventing, and communicating. The intellectual and moral values gained will increase cultivated enjoyments, scholarly achievements, democratic commitments, and mutual respect.

The provision of a school library or a trained librarian does not ensure a measureable difference in an educational program. Other variables that must be present in the most effective program of library services are the teacher (of prime importance), the librarian (her qualifications), and the principal (his attitudes and cooperation) (4).

It is wise to conclude, therefore, that a school library is the resource center for teaching and learning and the command of the reading-thinking process is the foundation skill needed to use this resource. This means that skill in reading and library usage must be put at the top of educational objectives and that teaching and learning must be geared to it from the very beginning. This is precisely what is done in the Language-Experience Approach.

Early in the 1960s, Francis Keppel, as U.S. Commissioner of Education, reviewing statistics on libraries, said (5, p. 375),

This is a national disgrace. I call upon all of you, who know that a school without a library is a crippled school, to dramatize this shame of America—to carry your concern beyond your own councils to the American people.

The statistics Keppel referred to indicated that the number of central libraries in elementary schools was about 44 percent; the number of full-time librarians employed in schools with centralized libraries was only about 51 percent; about 25 percent of elementary teachers were served by school libraries with librarians; and the number of books per pupil in elementary school with centralized libraries was 5.8.

No one can disagree with Keppel's evaluation of our schools' libraries as "a national disgrace." Marked improvement has occurred in the years that have followed, but we still have a long way to go. Even more disgraceful is the way some school libraries, even some with full-time librarians, are being used. As long as librarians are viewed merely as custodians of books and libraries are visited only occasionally to find something to read in spare time, library services and, more particularly, the teaching of reading, are reflected on disgracefully.

Lack of a central library, or availability of a small and limited central library, and the availability of only a part-time librarian or no librarian at all will undoubtedly reduce the effectiveness of all reading approaches. It is claimed that their effectiveness is reduced proportionally as library facilities are lacking. A language-experience program, however, even crippled by library shortcomings, will yield better results than other programs similarly handicapped.

The studies reported in Appendix B were carried on in schools that in good part merited a "crippled" designation. The value placed by educators and parents on the need for a school-library resource center is the crucial question in moving a school and its board of directors to positive action. Projects like that at the Knapp School are helping the nation out of the library mire.

The Knapp Project planned a five-year three-phase establishment of centers up across the country with major emphasis on elementary-school libraries. This is as it should be, because library attitudes, habits, and skills are best acquired from the very beginning of formal instruction (2, p. 5). Project director Peggy Sullivan in a report entitled "A Librarian's Dream Come True" (10) tells about the expert library help made available through the project, but she is emphatic in stating that this alone did not bring success. Cooperation of all school personnel, particularly teachers, was essential. At one cooperating college, students majoring in elementary education were asked which of several kinds of assistance they would most like to have in their first-year teaching jobs. Overwhelmingly their first choice was a centralized library with a qualified librarian.

Hazel Adams, as reading consultant in the Plainview–Old Bethpage school district, which collaborated with the Knapp School Libraries Project, reported in "The Changing Role of the Elementary School Library" that she saw many positive changes (1, p. 566):

> In the child's mind the library is no longer merely a place where he goes once a week to change a book (or, even worse, get a book for a book report he must write). It is still a place where a child may on any day take out and return books, but it is also a center for information, a place for leisure time activities, for story hours, for discussion of books and a place to listen to music or view filmstrips.

The circumstances she described at the Central Park Road School in Plainview, New York, can be accomplished anywhere. All that is required is reasonable support and direction.

Classroom libraries

ARRANGING A LIBRARY

Every teacher does some arranging in her classroom to facilitate her program and to make the room inviting. Most schools nowadays provide six-year-olds with more space than other classes. Desks are adjusted to their size and are mobile. Chalkboard and corkboard space are plentiful at the writing- and eye-level of the children. One corner of the room is usually an art area with easels and such for painting, drawing, molding, shaping, cutting, and pasting. Another corner usually houses the classroom library, with built-in and mobile bookshelves at a practical height for six-year-olds. There is usually a table or two, one for exhibiting books, magazines, and papers and one for reading and writing. Both have chairs. Also available are a small rocking chair, a large two-seater rocking chair, a stool, and a two- or three-step library ladder. Present, too, is a listening post with as many as six sets of earphones, a record player, a tape recorder, an overhead projector, a slide projector, and other audio-visual aids. Not all classroom library quarters are as well equipped as this, of course, but the more they are like this the better. It is readily apparent, too, that this corner is not easily confined but extends into the room. Some library corners are equipped with a rug and, in one first grade visited, folks entering the library corner had to remove their shoes. This was a regulation of the pupils and was carefully enforced by them. It was not uncommon for children to lie on the rug to read or listen, and so they thought the rug should be kept very clean. Also "it looked better clean," as one youngster stated.

Classroom library corners reflect the personality of the teacher and her ingenuity in providing and arranging books, furniture, and equipment in unique and inviting ways. The trick is in arranging the area so that the children will want to go there. If the place is overarranged and artificial, the children may be concerned about messing it up, which obviously defeats the purpose. On the other hand, if the arrangement is uninviting or so much like the rest of the room that a visitor has to ask where the classroom library is located, that, too, defeats the purpose.

Children are quite responsive to a touch of something pretty. A small bouquet of fresh flowers, for example, adds charm and color. Children invariably respond to flowers in a pleased and proud way; they sense the respect the teacher has for them and what the flowers represent. Pupil-teacher regard becomes mutual. Artificial flowers will do when fresh-cut flowers are not available.

Caro Lane, Supervisor of Special Education in Louisiana early in the 1950s, told the story of a little girl on her way to school carrying a single flower that she had picked on the wayside. When Miss Lane asked the girl about the flower, she replied that she was taking it to school to put on "the pretty table." Further inquiry by Miss Lane revealed that this teacher in her one-room school had brought a small marble-top table to school, calling it their "pretty table." If a pupil brought something pretty to school, it could be placed on the "pretty table." Such a table can also be an exhibit place for a good book.

Since the purpose of reading instruction is to get children to read, the place where they go to read should be as inviting as possible. Children who read only when in a "reading class" are not being taught a love for reading. The best index of the success of reading instruction is the amount of reading done and the eagerness with which children approach it.

BOOKS FOR THE LIBRARY

The classroom library should be readied before school starts in the fall. Children entering the classroom, perhaps for the first time, will see the library as part of the total room environment. Because of its inviting appearance, pupils may pause there, survey the area, and perhaps examine a book or two or a newspaper or magazine. Accordingly, the materials there when school opens are as important as the atmosphere.

There should be an array of colorful picture books with perhaps black and white illustrations, too. Some may have nothing but pictures, but many more should combine pictures and story: The children come to school to learn to read and they want to see words. Story books should also be available, with a lot of print but only a few pictures, books that look like books that Father, Mother, and Older Sister or Brother might read. Of course, the readability level will vary, but this is a boon rather than a liability. Many attractive books are now available that meet these conditions (see Appendix D).

In addition, there may be a limited number of copies of basic-reader materials, for instance, any preprimer or primer. Even though thirty copies of a preprimer might be available, *never* more than two copies should be in the classroom library. If preprimers and primers in four and five different series are exhibited, just two copies of each along with a few first readers may soon require a considerable amount of space. Using space this way is as unwise as putting out thirty books of one kind. Pupils, quick to note that the books consume a lot of space, sense that perhaps they have special significance, but this is just the opposite of the desired effect. No one in this day and age of vigorous attention to all aspects of linguistics will want to over-expose children to sub-standard language usage; yet that is precisely what will occur unless the precautions here noted are observed. Almost every set of basic readers includes at least two preprimers, sometimes three. If two of each from three sets are displayed, eighteen books will be taking up valuable space. With primers and a few first readers added, the space consumed becomes inordinate.

Magazines are available (Appendix D) in considerable number. The current month's copy, along with one or two from last year, should be displayed. Comic magazines are attention-getting material. Newspapers, some structured for school use at different levels of readability, should be exhibited. Adult community newspapers and adult magazines should be made available. Many children see these in their homes, on newsstands, or at the town library, and they should be led to feel that they are a part of their world, too. They like to "see and read" these much as adults do; children love to imitate and play adult roles.

The listening post should have a variety of recorded or taped stories, with some recorded just as they appear in some of the books. This way a child can either listen to the oral reading only or listen and follow along in the book. Nursery rhymes can be taped for listening, and stories with a musical background or records with only music can be supplied. Listening to music is as comforting and relaxing for children as it is for adults.

Some books on the display tables may lie flat; others may stand partially open to attract attention. The number of books, other than the preprimers and primers, should be about two per child; in a room of thirty children, the number should be about sixty.

USING THE LIBRARY

As already stated, the classroom library should be so arranged that a child, entering the room for the first time on the first day of school, is attracted by its appearance and curious about its offerings. *First* impressions are important impressions and, frequently, lasting ones; hence, it should be readily apparent to each child that, in this room, this teacher is putting *first* things first.

High on the list of attitude-determiners is the teacher's interest in books. Almost anyone can arrange an attractive area to display books, but the way a teacher handles a book, turns its pages, uses a book mark, her tone when she speaks about books and the expression on her face and in her eyes, and especially the way she talks about books are all tell-tale signs of appreciation of books. Not only does she talk warmly and with enthusiasm about the books for the children but she also talks about what *she* is reading. Children just know she genuinely likes books: "Love for reading is not taught; it is created; not required, but inspired; not demanded, but exemplified; not exacted, but quickened; not solicited, but activated" (9, p. 4). On the first day of school, a tour of the room is in order, the children following the teacher to listen, see, and touch. At the library, how books are really man's best friend should be explained.

A dictated experience story, most likely not obtained until the second day, provides an excellent lead to reading: Recall the teacher's success (in Chapter 2) with a copy of *Snow White* that she had placed on the library table, along with other books using the words <u>snow</u> or <u>white</u> and some preprimers in which some of the children's names appeared. The class gathered in the classroom library even though they spilled out. The children loved the coziness much as some adults love the coziness of an easy chair.

Next the teacher picked up the copy of *Snow White* and had different children point to the words and read them. Then she opened the book and invited children to find the words on different pages. On one page they counted seven appearances of "Snow White." She selected other books containing the words *snow* and *white*. One girl found *snow* in *snowman* and identified it for the class. One boy found *snow* in *snowy*. He exclaimed that he had found *snow* but that it had, as he put it, "a funny tail on the end."

Once the children caught the idea, she gave copies of different books to several children and designated them as leaders and then directed other children to gather with a leader and find words they could read. To Bill, for instance, she gave a copy of Snow White and had three other children join him at some other spot in the room. In a short time, there were eight groups scattered about the room buzzing like bees over the honey they were finding. The teacher moved from group to group to enjoy and endorse their findings and to be sure that all had a chance to "read." Pupils like Bill and Nancy found any number of words they recognized on sight. A few recognized only *snow* or *white* or both and their names.

After the children had located words for about 5 minutes, the teacher interrupted and had a short sharing session. Different pupils read aloud words they knew. One rule was imposed even though the pupil's enthusiasm made it difficult to enforce. Whenever a pupil read aloud, the others had to close their books and listen. It was easy to show the children how to keep a page place by placing a finger in the book.

On another day she showed the children how they could find words they knew in magazines and newspapers. Visiting the library corner was now a reading pleasure. Children were busy locating words they could read as well as enjoying flipping through an entire book, magazine, or newspaper.

The teacher did not make an issue over the fact that some of the words were all capital letters, others all lower case letters, and some both. No point was made about the different print sizes and shapes. One day, when Nancy pointed out that her name was printed three different ways, the teacher listed all three (for everyone to see): all capitals, a capital N with lower case, and italic.

Even though much has been said about how to enlarge a word bank (see Chapter 3) and how to promote transfer of recognition to different print sizes and shapes, and to different print media (see Chapter 2), little has been said about word cut-outs. In the library corner, or perhaps the art area, there should be a stack of old magazines such as *Life, Time, Good*

Housekeeping, Instructor, and *Grade Teacher* to which the children may turn not only to locate words but also to cut them out and keep a file of known words. The children are very responsive to this activity and for a while engage in it ardently.

The best readers do some cutting out but more selectively. They are challenged by such approaches as finding the same word in different sizes and shapes and assembling the list for ready comparison, or they look for a known word in a phrase context and cut out the phrase. This is helpful in enlarging and refining sensitivity to different verbs, adjective and adverb qualifiers, and so on. It is not that these words are referred to as parts of speech or labeled that way but that they understand how a word like *pretty* can qualify dress, flower, picture, and other words and how *run* can be *homerun, run away, run to the store,* and so on. On the other hand, the child making slower progress will spend much satisfying time searching for and cutting out the few words he can read. Lack of cutting dexterity may cause the young scholar to mutilate some of the words he cuts out, but, since he is not filled with fears and anxieties, he is undaunted and searches for additional words. It is interesting how much behavior, employing cognitive sensorimotor activity, provides an energizing dynamism that prolongs interest. This is due in good part to the fact that what they are doing is linked to a socialized action—others are doing it too— and because knowing some words and recognizing them in contexts printed for adults stimulates self-esteem. As Jean Piaget puts it, interest is a regulator of energy "and it suffices for work to be interesting in order for it to appear easy and for fatigue to diminish" (6, p. 34).

So by many ways and acts, the classroom library becomes a place to visit to do things—to read, listen, read to each other, locate words, cut out words and assemble a second word bank, and more. It is a place to which any pupil may go at any time as long as he does so in a quiet and orderly manner. A mutual respect between teacher and pupils and among pupils develops, and the children sense that they are dealing with shared values of mutual integrity.

The library area provides a good setting for many of the occasions when the teacher reads to the children. She may sit in the big rocker to read while the childern sprawl at her feet, or she may sit on the floor while the children sit on chairs, rockers, or stool. This kind of mobility helps these energy-packed six-year-olds use some of their energy and keeps the room from becoming a static and sterile place of the kind that breeds discontent. Reading aloud by the teacher should be almost a daily ritual. It is a marvelous way to interest children in books, stories, and poetry. It exposes them to acceptable and, sometimes, rich language patterns. It sets the tone for sharing.

In brief, the classroom library is the keystone of the reading, learning, communication arch. It will be the Mecca to which all pupils will turn if it is treated that way.

The school library

The best way to illustrate the change that has occurred in libraries during the latter part of the 1960s is to compare new elementary-school buildings with those erected early in the 1960s and before. In the earlier buildings, the school cafeteria was somewhere in the center—a large, roomy, inviting place from which all morning the most enticing odors emanated. Any child in almost any part of the building could tell how the lunch was faring by the way his gastronomic juices were responding.

In the schools of the late 1960s, however, architects have placed the library in the center of the school, so that now all classrooms have ready access to it. On occasion, the cafeteria in the rear of the building can be identified by faint odors. Food for the body is still essential, but, since a school's chief objective is learning, food for the mind is given priority.

The school library should have a status similar to that of the classroom library. It should be the most readily seen, the most strikingly furnished, the best equipped, and the most invitingly designed part of the building complex. Where it is, a new attitude about the library prevails: Children use it, they are proud of it, and they treat it with the regard that man's best friend merits.

Mary Gaver draws a sharp distinction between a classroom library and a school library as the centralized collection. She describes a library as an organized central collection of books and other materials, broad in variety and content, appropriately housed for the ready use by children and teachers and under the direction of a full time librarian (4). The best statement about school libraries is that of the American Association of School Librarians (3, p. 3):

> In the education of all youth, from the slowest learner in kindergarten to the most intelligent senior in high school, an abundance of printed and audiovisual materials is essential. These resources are the basic tools needed for the purpose of effective teaching and learning. . . . This

fact holds true for the multitrack curriculum, ability groupings in subject areas, the expanded and intensified science program, the toughening of the intellectual content in all courses, advanced placement and accelerated programs, the development of the disciplines of critical thinking, the teaching of reading, the provision of a challenging education for superior students, the meeting of needs of all students no matter what their abilities may be, ungraded elementary school classes, and similar practices and proposals.

Add to this the following lines from the same publication and the picture is complete (3, p. 11):

> The school library, in addition to doing its vital work of individual reading guidance and development of the school curriculum, should serve the school as a center for instructional materials. Instructional materials include books—the literature of children, young people, and adults—other printed materials, films, recordings, and newer media developed to aid learning.

Skill in library usage must be near the top of the list of scholarly reading skills. Learning and teaching will then fully utilize the cognitive processes of questioning, solving, inventing, and communicating. Students must learn how to select, analyze, evaluate, and organize information from all sources of communication.

From Thomas Petyt's *ABC* (1538), an abbreviated Latin primer to Domenius' *Orbis Pictus* (1658) with its pictures and names to *New England Primer* (1727) with its rhymes and riddles and fables to the McGuffey readers (1840) with their graded selections of fiction and nonfiction and their pictures, illustrations, and instructions to the libraries of the 1960s is a record of over 400 years of gradual emergence of the role of materials in learning. It cannot be said that books have not been available for children. By 1710, books for children were in such abundance that "guides" were needed to identify the best ones, an evident change from Caxton's first printing of *Reynard the Fox* (1481) and *The Fables of Aesop* (1484) to Francis Seager's *The Schools of Vertue* (1557) and John Bunyan's *Pilgrim's Progress* (1678). The need for guides is obvious from then on merely by the multitude of such stories as Daniel Defoe's *Robinson Crusoe* (1719), Jonathan Swift's *Gulliver's Travels* (1726), Hans Christian Andersen's *Fairy Tales* (1846), Edward Lear's *Book of Nonsense* (1846), Lewis Carroll's *Alice in Wonderland* (1865), Louisa May Alcott's *Little Women* (1868), Mark Twain's *Tom Sawyer* (1876), Robert Louis Stevenson's *Kidnapped* (1886), Kenneth Grahame's *The Wind in the Willows* (1908), Eric Knight's *Lassie Come Home* (1940), E. B. White's

Charlotte's Web (1952), and Sheila Burnford's *The Incredible Journey* (1961).

Nonfiction for children has sometimes been overlooked by historians of children's books. In early times the scriptures were taught through catechisms and books of advice and exhortation: Simon Patrick's *A Book for Beginners* (1662), for example, and John Quick's *The Young Men's Claim* (1691) (7, p. 49). From James Boswell's *Life of Samuel Johnson* (1791) to Carl Sandburg's *Abe Lincoln Grows Up* (1928), biographies and autobiographies have been popular with children, lured by human drama. Informational and hobby books have always been in special demand, too.

Graded readers can never substitute for the wealth of materials in a library. The seven books in the McGuffey series were no more a substitute than are the fifteen books of some modern series. Most authors and publishers of graded readers would be quick to deny that they intend to substitute for a library, but they cannot deny that the voluminous teaching practices recommended in their manuals, if followed even with little vigor, do not allow time for instruction in materials other than the readers.

A wide range of materials has been available for centuries and could have been abundantly supplied in the classrooms. Why have they not? Why, when in the twentieth century books are being published at astonishing rates (28,762 titles in 1967 alone) is reading instruction limited at the grade level to the use of basic readers? As long as reading is dealt with as a subject rather than a process, this stultifying practice is apt to persist. As long as reading instruction is paced largely by teacher questions about literal facts only, the material used for instruction is apt to be limited to graded readers because, once the teachers know the stories, they can use the same questions year after year. As long as reading comprehension is measured by a child's ability to parrot story facts, reading instruction is apt to be limited to graded readers. As long as reading instruction is viewed as primarily a sounding of words, reading for meaning will continue to be of secondary importance. As long as normative rather than individual standards measure achievement, reading instruction will remain primitive.

Librarians as well as teachers must aid the reading-learning-living process in such a way that pupils learn to take initiative. They must know when and why to seek the help of a librarian, just as they learn when and why to seek the teacher's help. One librarian, commenting on work habits nurtured by the Language-Experience Approach, said, "These children know what they want and why, and their behavior as scholars is astounding, even among the first graders." Availability of materials, important in the preparation of scholars at all levels, is not enough. Children must be taught how to set reading goals and find personal and social answers in the facts they seek.

The American Library Association's *Standards for School Library Programs* declares general principles that should govern teacher-library relationships (3, pp. 65–67):

1. The teacher makes the library meaningful and useful to his students through his knowledge of the library's program and resources. . . .
2. The teacher motivates his students to make extensive use of library resources for classroom work and for purposes not connected with class assignments.
3. The teacher participates in the formulation of school library policies by serving on or communicating with the faculty library committee.
4. The teacher utilizes every opportunity to help the library in his school reach standards of excellence.
5. The teacher participates in the selection of materials for the school library and in the evaluation of the library's collection in his specialized field. . . .
6. The librarian provides teachers with many services related to materials that are helpful to them in connection with their teaching program. . . .
7. Using research skills successfully, satisfying curiosities through fact-finding, developing an interest in and liking for independent reading, and finding enjoyment in books, recordings, and other materials are important elements in the education of children and young people. . . .
8. The teacher brings his class groups to the library, sends small groups or individuals from the classroom to the library or its conference rooms to read, to learn library skills, or to do reference or research work, and makes collections of materials from the school library available in his classroom. . . .
9. The teacher keeps the school librarian informed about curricular changes and gives advance information about class assignments, so that resources are available in the library. . . .
10. The teacher becomes familiar with other libraries in the community. . . .

The librarian, on the other hand, renders the following services (3, p. 66):

1. builds systematically the collections of the school library so that materials are readily available for the curricular needs of students . . .
2. provides a variety of professional materials for teachers
3. acquires appropriate materials recommended for the library by teachers, as promptly as possible

4. assists teachers in the development of effective techniques for using the resources of the library and teaching library skills
5. keeps teachers informed about new materials that have been added to the library
6. helps teachers in the preparation of bibliographies and reading lists
7. locates information and performs other reference and searching services for teachers
8. serves as a resource consultant on curriculum and other school committees involving library materials . . .
9. provides informal in-service training for teachers about library resources, sources of information for printed and audio-visual materials, the evaluation of materials, and related topics

For the individual student, the library and librarian should supply a continuity of service that provides for cumulative growth in library skills and reading, listening, and viewing abilities and tastes from kindergarten to high school. The library should be a laboratory where students learn to research and study alone and in groups under teacher and librarian guidance. Guidance should be implicit, varied, and effective in every contact the student has with the librarian. Thus, the library should become closely identified with a student's recreational reading as well as his academic pursuits. The library is the most important aspect of a reading-to-learn program. How and why the library serves this purpose must be stated emphatically and clearly. (An even more detailed account of the role of the library can be found in chapter 8 of "Libraries and Reading Instruction" in *Directing Reading Maturity as a Cognitive Process* (8).)

ACTING ON THINGS

Sometime during the second week in school—the first week if it can be arranged—each first-grade class should visit the school library. Many of the children may already know where the library is, have seen how busy a place it is, and have peeked in and watched. The library, as the marketplace of the school, has the potential to capture interest both directly and subliminally. Pupils sense its active yet disciplined and dignified participation in the mental universe of dynamic inquiry and reason. The decisive criterion of a library of worth is its critical and empirical yet humanistic activity.

The librarian should be prepared to receive the first-graders and the children should be prepared, too. The librarian knows six-year-olds, how they act, how to hold their attention, arouse their curiosity, stimulate their interest, and make them comfortable and welcome. The pupils' expectancies, if the visit has been anticipated, should not be overstimulated but eager and excited. If the classroom library is a yardstick, then its simulation can foster only the warmest attitudes.

Before going to the library, questions like "What do you think the library will be like?" "Why do you think the school has a library?" "Why do you think the library is so busy a place?" should be discussed. Reaction will vary according to the pupils' background and experience and should be expected, accepted, and used to advantage.

Many a carefully planned visit has been lost in the welter of too many things to see. Just like traveling on the same road a number of times, repeated visits make for familiarity and comfort. The first time, a general view of the library will do, with a brief reference to the check-out desk and a see-and-feel visit to the books for young readers (children must feel a book or two) and then a story session. Every librarian is a story teller; she loves children, books, and stories, in that order. If each class is permitted to take back to their room five or six books especially selected for this occasion, the magic circle will have been closed. One or two of the children, allowed to carry the books, will expand with pride at the privilege. Then watch with what eagerness the books will be looked at, read, and thrilled to back in the classroom.

Thereafter, in weekly visits, the various aspects of the library can be examined so that the children will become acquainted with its resources. "Variety" and "library" become almost synonymous. The children come not only to select books to take out but to listen at story hours, poetry sessions, and panel discussions, for research, and for many other activities.

On a special visit, early in October, each child may select a book to bring to the classroom library. "Any book I like?" Asked one little fellow. "Yes, any book you like," replied the teacher, "but one that you think the others might like, too" This added suggestion is not too binding or restricting and creates a number of positive conditions: First was "my like" and second was what "others might like." This may lead to more careful reflection over a book's interest and difficulty. On the same visit, some of the books in the classroom are returned to the library; others in the school may want to see them, too.

Of growing importance in the past decade has been the steady increase in the number and size of community libraries. Not only federal and state aid but also citizen committees have been ardent and active supporters of public libraries. Community libraries invariably have a sizable unit devoted entirely to children, with library hours scheduled to accommodate them. Children love to visit community libraries as a source of special pride. They can go there evenings and weekends and summers. Visits require a certain degree of maturity and children rise to the challenge.

Interlibrary loans make additional sources available. One young fellow was truly astounded when he learned that the material he sought would be sent to his community library from a nearby city library. Age six is a marvelous age at which to learn that such resources are available.

Many families have libraries of their own, and giving books at Christmas and birthdays is common practice among many people. Book clubs for children and their subscribers are increasing, too. Children who have libraries in their homes love to share their books with classmates.

WHY READ?

Children read for self-enjoyment or to satisfy personal curiosities but also to share. There are people, of course, who read just to escape or to fill a friendless void but they are the exception. The majority of people are social and want to share, and it is this spirit that is to be cultivated as desirable in a classroom.

Children share ideas as they dictate whole-class stories and group stories. When they dictate individual stories, they share their versions with a group or the class. The spirit of sharing permeates the classroom. Even before the select-a-book October visit to the library, the children have shared reactions to books in the classroom library: Why I liked this book, this story, this page, this picture, this sentence, this idea, this word, provide the impetus for sharing. Varied sessions provide change of pace, fill voids, stem from spontaneous eagerness to share immediately or border on outburst. Other sharing times can be carefully planned as a specific part of the school day.

A child may have very specific personal reasons for his choice of a book to bring to class from the school library and he will want to tell others about it. At least, he must be given the opportunity to do so. A good procedure is to provide a small lectern as a physical base for the book and a psychological base for the child. He may feel more secure behind the "wall" that a lectern provides. Some children are very verbal and secure, over-confident in fact, while others are just the opposite. The teacher should help in all instances. The shy children, still pretty much in private worlds, may do no more than stand up and show their selections, but they are up, and that is important.

Ideas gained through books are an excellent source for dictated stories. Or the books may provide ideas for sentences assembled on word-card holders and adding words to the word banks. Sharing a book may take many forms. (Chapter 7 indicates more.)

INDEPENDENT LIBRARY VISITS

All first-grade children have school-library time for book exchanges, stories, exhibits, and the like. When they reach a certain level of progress in reading and word recognition, though, and qualify for group directed reading-thinking activities, then they have earned a special privilege. Library visits can be made individually for as long as half an hour at a time, but usually only once a week, to read at leisure.

The reading performance required for this privilege is ability to read orally and silently and comprehend material at the basic-reader primer level. This does not mean that a pupil has been led through a particular basic-reader series but that because of his skills and experience at reading he can pick up almost any primer or its equivalent and read it. Many children reach this level of performance early in December, others not until January or February, and some still later.

Once a child has the skills needed to go to the library alone then, of course, he requires additional instruction on library use. Usually, five or six pupils in a room have advanced equally so the librarian is not taxed with special instruction. Location skills and use of the card catalogue are taught. A child soon learns how to enter a library quietly and go about his business. Purposes for going to the library are examined just as are purposes for reading in a directed reading-thinking activity.

An independent library user is granted another special privilege about once a month. Because he is reading widely and has more opportunity to deal with books that he thinks others in his class might enjoy, he may on certain occasions select two books to take to his classroom. They are issued in his name, demanding certain responsibilities. He is given an opportunity to tell the class why he selected the books, and he must check on their whereabouts to return them at the end of the loan period.

Conclusion

This chapter describes how a classroom library, school, community, and home libraries are an integral part of the Language-Experience Approach. Once a child has learned to read, he wants to read, and this requires materials.

The provision of the best of library facilities does not ensure measureable differences in reading programs. Other variables are the experience and attitudes of the teacher, the librarian, and the principal.

Considerable progress has been made toward changing the condition of school libraries since the early 1960s. Nevertheless, we still have a long way to go, not only in making libraries available but also in their proper utilization. Full-time librarians are needed. Projects like the Knapp School Project are helping us see more clearly how and why better libraries are needed.

A classroom library is a major contributor to the success of the Language-Experience Approach. Such a library can be the center of a room, physically and pedagogically. Teachers can be as creative as possible in their arranging and use of a classroom library and will find that their ingenuity will pay huge dividends. Their own interest in books and reading will be mirrored by the children. Enthusiasm need never be quarantined.

The library is rapidly replacing the cafeteria as the physical hub of the school. Food for the mind is as important as food for the body. Much leadership has been provided by the American Library Association, especially through its *Standards for School Library Programs*.

Books for children have long been available. By 1710, they were so abundant that guides to the best ones were needed. Today many guides, catalogues, and bibliographies group books by subject, by category, by title. A library can be abundantly supplied with books.

Class and group visits to a library are described. In addition, much emphasis is given to independent visits of children to the school and community libraries. Reference is made also to the value of home libraries.

Bibliography

1. Adams, Hazel. "The Changing Role of the Elementary School Library," *The Reading Teacher*, vol. 19, no. 7 (April, 1965), pp. 563–566.
2. American Association of School Librarians. *A Proposal to the Knapp Foundation to Demonstrate the Educational Value of a Full Program of School Library Services*. Chicago, Ill.: American Library Association, 1962.
3. American Association of School Librarians, *Standards for School Library Programs*. Chicago, Ill.: American Library Association, 1960.

4. Gaver, Mary V. *Effectiveness of Centralized Library Service in Elementary Schools.* 2nd ed. New Brunswick, N.J.: Rutgers University Press, 1963.
5. Keppel, Francis. "The Unlimited Future of Libraries," *School and Society*, vol. 92 (December 12, 1964), pp. 374–376.
6. Piaget, Jean. *Six Psychological Studies.* Edited by David Elkind. New York: Random House, 1967.
7. Sloane, William. *Children's Books in England and America in the Seventeenth Century.* New York: King's Crown Press (Columbia University Press), 1955.
8. Stauffer, Russell G. "Libraries and Reading Instruction," *Directing Reading Maturity as a Cognitive Process.* New York: Harper & Row, 1969.
9. Stauffer, Russell G. "The Role of the Teacher," *Reading for Meaning.* In Proceedings of the 34th Annual Education Conference, vol. 3. Newark, Del.: University of Delaware, 1952.
10. Sullivan, Peggy. *A Librarian's Dream Come True.* Chicago, Ill.: Knapp School Libraries Project, 1964.

6

Group instruction by directed reading-thinking activities

It is in the dynamics of group interaction that the self-regulation skills of critical and creative reading are fashioned and honed. It is the purpose of this chapter to make known explicitly how and why this is and why it must be initiated as early as possible in the life of a reader.

This chapter is divided into four major parts. The first part presents a plan or sketch for Directed Reading-Thinking Activities (DRTA). The second part details how the three basic steps of the plan function and how they parallel problem-solving practices. The third part explains when and how to organize a group of first-graders for Directed Reading-Thinking Activities. The fourth part is the longest part of the chapter, because it contains an account of a Directed Reading-Thinking Activity actually accomplished.

The reader is urged to read the following objectives and make educated guesses about the answers. He will gain understanding to the degree that he makes them his objectives. This process results in a personal and intellectual commitment that helps regulate his thinking and keeps him on course.

1. Explain the distinction between group instruction and individualized instruction.
2. Explain the two distinguishing features of a group DRTA.
3. Describe the five basic principles in a DRTA.

Upon reading the second part, the reader should be able to meet the following objectives:

1. Tell why developing purposes for reading is the key skill in a reader's repertoire and how this skill is acquired.

2. Explain why and how reading is reasoning.
3. Explain why reading is in reality the testing of predictions and allows for instant feedback.
4. Tell why the PRP (Predict-Read-Prove) of reading is pedagogically and psychologically sound.

Upon reading the third part, the reader should be able to meet the following objectives:

1. Describe how a teacher determines that children are sufficiently advanced in reading ability to warrant organizing group instruction.
2. Tell why the amount of reading being done is probably the best indicator of achievement and progress.

Upon reading the third part, the reader should be able to meet the following objectives:

1. Describe how a pupil can become aware of his own conceptual resources and limitations.
2. Explain why material used for DRTA instruction should be well constructed.
3. Tell why words and pictures should be integrated so as to carry a plot forward and avoid picture-word duplication.
4. Describe what a pupil does when he meets a word he does not recognize at sight and why he follows the steps defined.
5. Explain how teaching children to deal with varying amounts of information is to teach them to be reading detectives.
6. Explain why proving predictions is so important and how doing so develops listening skills.
7. Tell why "on with the story" is an appropriate motto for DRTA circumstances.

In the previous chapter, brief reference was made to that time in a beginning reader's progress when he has advanced enough to be introduced to Directed Reading-Thinking Activities in groups. A distinction between group and individualized instruction by Directed Reading-Thinking Activities is that a pupil moves as a reader-scholar toward efficient reading practices by learning to think clearly and consistently in the medium of a group, refining a systematic approach to reading, so that he can use it while on his own.

Growth toward reading maturity must have an early start and an aim. Just as John Dewey referred to democracy as the best form of social cooperation, so group Directed Reading-Thinking Activities provide the best form of pedagogical and intellectual cooperation. In the actions of a group, sound intellectual and emotional dispositions are acquired and ease, economy, and efficiency of reading increase. The intellectual habit of reading for meaning must not only be developed early but it must also be adjusted to varied and elastic use and continued growth. By reading for meaning, the reader may avoid premature crystallization of ideas by putting faith in inquiry and direction. Without these qualities, reading and thinking become a vagrant use of energy and incline one toward dogma and cant.

If this all sounds challenging and awe-inspiring, then it serves its purpose well. The teaching of reading and thinking is a serious business. It must be dealt with as such if children are to learn how to participate in a mental universe in which they can find self-respect and social respect.

The directed reading-thinking activity plan

A group Directed Reading-Thinking Activity has two distinguishing features: All members of a group read with about the same competence and all read the same material at the same time. The primary objective is to develop skill in reading critically. A critical-reading performance requires each reader to become skilled at determining purposes for reading. The reader either declares his own purposes or adopts the purposes of others and makes certain he knows how and why he is doing so. He also speculates about the nature and complexity of the answers he is seeking by using his experience and knowledge to the fullest. Then he reads to test his purposes and assumptions. As a result, he may (1) find the answers he is seeking literally and completely stated, (2) find only partial answers or implied answers and face the need either to restate his purposes in light of the new information or to suspend judgment until more reading has been done, (3) need to declare completely new purposes.

This problem-solving approach to reading may be used with both fiction and nonfiction. The purpose in either circumstance will vary according to the reader's ability to perform critically, creatively, and maturely. His reading rate will vary according to the purposes declared and the nature and difficulty of the material.

Proof that answers have been found either in part or completely may be presented to the group by means of oral reading or written reporting. Both means of providing proof should be used.

The group size considered most acceptable for good teaching ranges from eight to twelve members. Groups of limited size permit pupils to compare and contrast their thinking with that of others in the dynamics of interacting minds. Each can observe how others use evidence, make assumptions or educated guesses, adapt rate, provide proof, and perform creatively.

Certain principles underlie the effective development of a group Directed Reading-Thinking Activity. They may be listed as follows:

I. Identifying purposes for reading
    A. Individual pupil's purposes determined by
        1. Pupil experience, intelligence, and language facility
        2. Pupil interests, needs, and goals
        3. Group interests, needs, and goals
        4. Influence of the teacher
        5. Influence of the content
            a. Nature and difficulty of the material
            b. Title, subtitles, and the like
            c. Pictures, maps, graphs, charts
            d. Linguistic clues
    B. Group purposes determined by
        1. Experience, language facility, and intelligence of each member of the group
        2. Interests, needs, and goals of each member of the group
        3. Consensus of the group or subgroups
        4. Influence of the teacher
        5. Influence of the content
II. Adjusting rate of reading to the purposes declared and to the nature and difficulty of the material. This adjustment is made to
    A. Survey—to overview a selection or text
    B. Skim—to read swiftly and lightly for single points
    C. Scan—to read carefully from point to point
    D. Read critically or to study: read, reread, and reflect so as to pass judgment
III. Observing the reading
    A. Noting abilities to adjust rate to purpose and materials
    B. Recognizing comprehension needs and providing help by clarifying
        1. Purposes
        2. Concepts
        3. Need for rereading

C. Acknowledging requests for help in word recognition by providing immediate help in the use of
   1. Context, or meaning, clues
   2. Phonetic, or sound, clues
   3. Structural, or sight, clues
   4. Glossary, or meaning, sound, and sight, clues
IV. Developing comprehension
   A. Checking on individual and group purposes
   B. Staying with or redefining purposes
   C. Recognizing the need for other source material
   D. Developing concepts
V. Fundamental skill training activities of discussion, further reading, additional study, writing
   A. Increasing powers of observation, or directed attention
   B. Increasing powers of reflection by
      1. Abstracting or reorganizing old ideas, conceiving new ideas, distinguishing between ideas, generalizing about ideas, and making inductions and analyses
      2. Judgment or formulating and assessing propositions
      3. Reasoning or inferring, demonstrating, and systematizing knowledge deductively
   C. Mastering the skills of word recognition in picture and language context analysis, phonetic and structural analysis, and dictionary usage
   D. Developing vocabulary or pronunciation, word meaning, semantic dimension, analogous words, contrasted words, word histories, new words
   E. Developing adeptness in conceptualization and cognitive functioning or making and testing inferences; making particulars, classes, and categories; understanding, reversibility, mobile equilibrium, and conservation
   F. Mastering the skills of oral reading or voice, enunciation, and expression, reading to prove a point or to present information, reading prose and poetry to entertain, choral reading.

Three basic steps

The basic steps in effective development of a group Directed Reading-Thinking Activity (DRTA) can be used whenever a group of children are dealing with the same material at the same time under a teacher's guidance. The plan is especially useful when basic readers are used but any textbooks may be employed.

DEVELOPING PURPOSES FOR READING

The key step in a Directed Reading-Thinking Activity is developing purposes for reading. They are the directional and motivating influences that get a reader started, keep him on course, and produce the vigor and potency and push to carry him through to the end (3, pp. 12, 24-35). The versatile reader adjusts his reading rate to his purposes and to the nature and difficulty of the material being read. By focusing on purposes from the very beginning of formal reading instruction, the reader learns to appreciate their use and value. The young reader will not be too articulate about what he is doing, but with experience and maturity, he will begin to see how to be deliberate. Of all the reading skills, the one that authorities and teachers and readers bemoan as most lacking is versatility. It is my conviction that the fact that students can complete high school and college without accomplishing this high skill reflects inappropriate methodology from the very beginning of reading instruction.

Three essentials to directed reading-thinking instruction are the teacher, the group and the material. The teacher and the material determine to a large degree the nature of the skills acquired by the pupils.

The teacher must avoid being the instrument of authoritarian indoctrination. Her teaching must be such that the group is never intimidated by the tyranny of a right *teacher* answer—one that the group dare not question.

If a teacher is to direct a reading activity so that the pupils' thinking is both required and honored, she will, in a very important sense, be emotionally removed from the give and take of the reading-thinking process. Her role is <u>agitator</u>, as one second-grade boy described it, an intellectual agitator. In this capacity, she asks and asks again: *"What do you think?"* *"Why do you think so?"* and *"Read the line that proves it."* These directives are sufficiently specific to stir the minds of all school children. When the pupils state what they think, express their opinions, and listen to the ideas voiced by others in the group, then they will be reading to see who in the group is right or wrong or partially right or partially wrong and why.

In these circumstances the pupils will not be reading to find an answer to a question asked by the teacher. They will not fear being wrong and rousing signs of displeasure in the teacher. Neither will they be preoccupied with currying the teacher's favor. If they fail to find an answer, the blame of failure will not be projected onto the teacher, since it was not her question. This is how the teacher is emotionally freed from asserting the tyranny of right answers.

In turn, all members of the group are involved in the act of creating hypotheses, conjectures, purposes, using them to guide their reading, and reading to test their significance. It is in the context of the group that the adequacy of reading and meaning is tested. It is the group that demands that individual predictions, to be acknowledged, must be warranted by available evidence. The group sits as auditor, authorized to examine the evidence, verify the questions and answers, and state the results.

Stories, on the other hand, must be well-written and reflect conflicts, issues, incidents, eventualities. These maintain and propel a reader's interest and carry him on to the end. The ever present human interest provides the motivation that facilitates the reader's grasp of the social relationship of the story heroes as he follows their problems. This is what permits readers to grasp a story and reduce human behavior to its elements. In short, because a story makes sense, it keeps the motto "on with the story" uppermost in the mind of each reader. Events that lead from the beginning to the end of a plot unfold in gripping sequence and hold the reader's attention, not to be released until the climax has been reached.

Pictures vital to the telling of a story must be built into the presentation of a plot. They must be planned to help carry a plot forward; to aid the reader by strengthening, reinforcing, and developing visual images; to establish and develop concepts; and to heighten drama and interest. At no time must the pictures reveal what is intended to be told by the story. In other words, pictures as well as words provide the medium for telling a story. If it is allowed that a good picture is worth a thousand words, then it must be agreed that picture and story should not repeat the same thousand words.

DEVELOPING HABITS OF REASONING

This then leads to a second aspect of a Directed Reading-Thinking Activity: reasoning while reading. Interestingly enough, the word "reason" is derived from the word "ratio" and a ratio means a balance. What is it that a reader balances while he is reading? He balances his experience and his knowledge and the yardsticks provided by society that he has learned to use, because they are socially and culturally acceptable, against those of the authors. To the degree that he has examined carefully the experiences and knowledge that he uses, he can be a critical reader. In other words, critical reading can be initiated at the first-reader level.

While reading a story entitled "The Paper Umbrellas," pupil predictions indicated the degree to which children can use evidence to reason about story outcomes. After examining the pictures on the first two pages, the children thought that the boy would help the lady pick up some pictures. They also thought that a strong gust of wind might blow the pictures so far away that it would be difficult to locate them. On the next two pages of the story, they discovered that the boy had to move very fast to prevent one of the pictures from being blown down an open manhole. He did manage to save the picture. However, when he looked about he saw people approaching a bus holding newspapers over their heads. Now he was concerned about his own newspapers, and the source of the papers that the people were carrying.

The children put to work the information they had acquired. Some predicted that the newspapers being used as umbrellas had been taken from the boy's stand. Others thought that the people had carried the newspapers with them from their offices or places of work. Still other children felt that, if the people had taken the newspapers, they had also paid for them. One lad thought that, since the boy was gathering the pictures, perhaps the old lady stood by his newspapers and took care of them.

DEVELOPING HABITS OF TESTING PREDICTIONS

In the instance above, children used evidence to reason and predict, leading to the third step in a Directed Reading-Thinking Activity: testing to find out whether predictions made or hypotheses declared are right or wrong. Testing is done by reading silently and then orally particular lines in a story to prove to the group that predictions were either right or wrong. Under these conditions there is immediate feedback, the data processing is continuous and guided by the pupils' directives. Most strategic is the instant and constant testing that is done as the reader either substantiates or denies his hypothesis and is required to prove to the group what he has found.

These three steps—predicting, reading, proving—are the PRP of a Directed Reading-Thinking Activity. The PRP process is repeated each time a pause is made in the reading. Stops can be made at different points in a story so as to require readers to put ideas to work. The demands are different at each stop. With little information available, as with the use of a title only, many conjectures are possible or, in other words, divergent thinking can occur. If three-fourths of a story has been read, then predictions should be limited because the story outcome is now in sight. In other words, convergent thinking is now being done.

Organizing a group

In directing a class through the different phases of the Language-Experience Approach, quite an intimate knowledge of pupil progress is obtained. The dictated-experience phase, the creative use of word-bank cards, the creative writing, the reading of library books, the location of known words in different contexts, the facility with word-attack skills—all provide evidence of achievement and progress. Even so, it is desirable to identify specific critera and weigh their significance.

An early sign of progress is a pupil's ability to recognize and remember words used in a whole-class or group dictated experience story. Some will do as Bill did in Chapter 2, when he recognized and remembered thirty-five of the thirty-seven different words. Some will remember only a word or two. Most children will range between these two levels.

When the children have progressed to the dictation of individual stories, the number of words they recognize and the ease with which they are recognized increases. This is especially true of average and above-average children; they may add as many as eight to ten new words per story. The slow learner may continue at his one-to-three-word-per-story pace but will remember the words.

As they acquire word-attack skills, children show increasing ability to attack and recognize their own dictated words. This is a significant early sign, since it provides evidence of resourcefulness in the use of word-attack skill, essential to participation in a group DRTA.

The number of known words that children identify in newspapers and the like is also a good yardstick. Ease of transfer of recognition skill to different contexts and different print shapes shows flexibility as well as mobility.

By the time a pupil's word bank totals 150 words or more, his prowess will be well established. Some pupils may "memorize" this many words, but this seldom occurs. The words will have been learned functionally in a communication context and will be recognized and remembered because of their utility as well as their configuration.

Usually, too, by the time vocabulary is this large, creative writing will be well under way and the word bank may no longer contain a copy of each known word. The maintenance of a word bank may begin to be a liability. It takes time to add the words and, since some are seldom used again, the bank begins to lose its utility. This is the time to introduce a selective entry of words. Now only words of special significance are added—unusual words like *gigantic* and *Nanticoke;* special words like *settlers* and *cogwheel;* names like *Christopher Columbus* and *Pinocchio;* lovely words like *colorful* and *glossy.*

One of the most significant indicators of progress is the amount of reading being done. It is not so much the number of books that is important as it is the evidence that a favorable attitude toward books has been fostered and that the children are reading. Not only will pupils be reading book after book but they will also be reading to and with each other. Teaming up promotes smooth and expressive oral reading and facilitates the use of word-attack skills.

In brief, then, pupils are ready for group instruction when their word-bank words total about 150 or more, when they read orally with considerable ease, when they love to read and turn to books readily, and when they show facility in attacking a word they do not recognize immediately at sight. A formal check can be made in each of these areas if a teacher feels insecure about her knowledge of a pupil, but the check should be made in such a way that it will not reflect on the pupil or stifle his interest in reading.

It must be remembered that a pupil may not perform equally in each of these aspects. Nevertheless, if he participates in group instruction where all read and react to the same story at the same time, he will do so with eagerness and confidence.

A directed reading-thinking activity illustration

The aims in a Directed Reading-Thinking Activity (DRTA) in a group situation are twofold. The first aim is to teach children the skill of extracting information of predictive value from a given context of either fiction or nonfiction. The information each pupil extracts depends on how it fits into his store of experience and knowledge. At times, the ideas or assumptions called into use interact with each other freely, at others more rigidly. The likelihood of extracting information of good predictive value is increased if the ideas and assumptions relate flexibly to each other. Thus, various combinations can be examined and their usefulness tested as material is read.

To accomplish effective utilization of this skill in different content areas DRTA training must use both fiction and nonfiction. The transfer of this skill from fiction to other materials is not necessarily automatic. Pupils must see the relevance of the reading-thinking process in all areas. This way, they can continuously relate what is learned in reading class to the job of being a student and to the practical reading tasks of everyday life.

The second aim is to provide, through the group, ways of behaving as a thinking reader that will be useful to pupils when reading on their own. In a group in which the pupils' thinking is uppermost, each pupil's fund of experience and knowledge, either relevant to what is being read or hindering him in calling up ideas and making assumptions of predictive value, can become clearer. What a pupil sees in a story or article, a title or subtitle, or a picture or illustration depends on how he has perceived and organized previous information, how things are alike in some respects and different in others.

If the information received earlier is too generalized, too close to being nonverbal, too dependent on haphazard concrete-perceptual experiences, the pupil may become aware of these inadequacies in the group situation. Otherwise, left on his own or educated in nonthinking, parrot-like circumstances, he may never learn to question the validity of his ideas and concepts. He operates using his loosely structured concepts inappropriately and therefore fails to extract information of predictive value; hence, he continues to perpetuate his blunders and shortcomings. Persistent and intelligent effort is required; otherwise, the new constructs a pupil makes will be at the same low level as the constructs he has previously made.

PUPIL AWARENESS OF CONCEPTUAL RESOURCES

How can a student become aware of his own conceptual resources and limitations in a group-directed reading situation? The role of the group can provide a milieu conducive to sound mental construction rather than compounding wrong concepts. The favorable conditions are these:

1. All in the group examine the same material.
2. Each pupil reacts in terms of his own private stock of experience and knowledge.
3. Because pupils share ideas and the spirit is competitive and fosters the will to do, it *motivates.*
4. The information extracted and the assumptions made are compared and contrasted and likenesses and differences are noted.
5. The activity itself provides the means for the creative use of ideas.
6. Each pupil's personal integrity is at stake.
7. Each pupil's educated guesses must be defended, proved or disproved.

8. Available evidence must be presented to the group for acceptance or rejection. The group is the auditor, jury, and judge.

9. Pupils learn to have the strength of their convictions and not to be dominated by loud verbalizers.

10. Pupils learn to respect the thinking of others, to study how they examine evidence and how they prove points.

11. Pupils learn to temper their emotions in the crucible of group interaction, to be enthusiastic without being obnoxious, to rejoice without being offensive, to accept mistakes without being stifled.

12. All this is done under the direction of a prepared teacher. She knows the content, the important concepts to be attained, and how to promote thinking in others without putting words in their mouths. She knows the desired *effect*.

By so arranging the conditions of intellectual interaction, children can investigate the hidden processes of their own and other people's thinking. Then they can avoid being docile, unimaginative, and stereotyped in their own thinking. Furthermore, authority and dependency are oriented toward the textbook and the group rather than the teacher. Abercrombie says on free group discussions (1, p. 75):

> Perhaps from the educational point of view the most important feature is the wide range of behavior which is useful; in different ways it is as useful to listen as to talk; to agree as to disagree; to criticize as to approve. The topics covered are so varied that no one person can for long retain a dominant position as the most knowledgeable or the most clearheaded. Sooner or later even the cleverest finds himself in a web of confusion out of which he is helped maybe by the most inarticulate. Often indeed it is the academically weak student who can offer a direct common-sense way out of the maze in which they all are stuck. Any one student may be at one moment the teacher, at another the pupil, and the tact, patience, and skill which students severally or jointly may command when they undertake to teach another are worth seeing.

Those who are skilled in the business of teacher education will recognize at once that the pursuit of such purposes is primarily a matter of outlook and philosophy. The ends described can be accomplished in almost any kind of learning situation. The child acquires from repeated experience the attitude that he can think and that he can find out what he wants to know. He acquires craftsmanship and artistry. The wonder of knowledge becomes as intriguing as a great adventure.

A DRTA ACCOUNT

The outline of a Directed Reading-Thinking Activity has been presented and certain basic principles and assumptions underlying the development of an effective group DRTA have been declared. Practices in each of the five basic steps were briefly outlined. It was pointed out that, in essence, a DRTA has two parts—a process and a product. The first four steps, identifying purposes, guiding adjustment of rate to purposes and materials, observing the reading, and developing comprehension, comprise a process cycle. Each step of a DRTA sets the cycle in motion: check comprehension, reset purposes, adjust rate, read. In fact, it might be shown that each time a reader stops to reflect, even in the middle of a sentence, he sets a similar cycle in motion—he pauses to check his understanding, decides to proceed with the same or different purposes, quickly adjusts rate, and then reads on. The product of the DRTA is the extension and refining. This is the time when, by direct attack, an attempt is made to increase powers of observation, reflection, and conceptualization.

Basic readers are adaptable to the fundamental purposes of a DRTA in a group situation. Controls of vocabulary, concept, interest, illustration, and story length make this true. The rate of introduction of new words and new concepts is controlled and permits pupils to try newly learned comprehension skills without being frustrated. At the primary level in particular, stories are about events or ideas within the scope of most children's experience. Gradually, the content reaches out beyond their experiences—socially, historically, numerically, geographically, esthetically, scientifically, and humorously—but at a pace that should not overwhelm them. The length of the selections is such that the material can easily be read in the time limits imposed by the demands of the total curriculum.

"A One-Time Magic Garden" (3, pp. 101–106) is one of a series of first-reader stories prepared to develop reading-thinking skills by means of a well-contrived plot and paced vocabulary. The plot moves forward steadily from the first page, the plot-introduction page, through a series of related episodes to the climax. The title is bound to the story and helps orient the reader toward the main idea of the plot. The answer to "A One-Time Magic Garden" is not provided until the very end. Curiosity about its meaning helps the reader speculate and stay on course.

A One-Time Magic Garden

"This must be magic," said Bill.
"Dad just put it in this morning.
Then it was little, but see it now."

"I can see it go," said Cooky.
"It is going up as fast as a bird.
I wish I could go up on it."

"You can," said one of the twins.
"I will show you how."

101

(Illustration) Along the entire left margin of the page is shown a huge cornstalk, and the children, as well as the dog, are climbing the stalk.

Ted jumped on and said
it was fun.
Next Bill and Red
jumped on, too.
Soon all but one of the twins were going up.
Ned just looked at the children.

He thought, "They are going up
faster and faster.
When will they stop?
How will they get down?"

Then the girls called to him.
At last he jumped on, and
away they all went,
up . . . up . . . up . . .
102

(Illustration) The group is standing in the presence of a friendly green giant. In the background are trees bearing toys instead of fruit.

"Good morning," said the man.
"My name is Uncle Green, and
this is my magic garden.
I just give things away.
Take all you want."

"All we want!" said Cooky
"I want so many things.
I will take balls, bats, and skates."

"I want new skates, too," said Ned.
Then away he ran to get them.
103

(Illustration) The green giant is presenting a coat made of corn husks to the youngest girl in the group.

Susan sat down to talk
with Uncle Green.
Soon she said, "It is cold up here.
Can you give me a coat?"

"I have just the coat for you,"
said Uncle Green.
"It is good at all times.
Put it on when you are cold and
when you are hot.
Put it on when it rains, but
do not get it on upside down."

Susan put on the funny-looking coat
and went for a walk.

104

(Illustration) The green giant is seated on a chair-shaped tree stump and is watching the children picking different toys from the trees in the garden.

All the children were happy.
They were laughing and playing
in the garden.
Uncle Green sat down alone to see the fun.

Then Ted said, "I do not see Ned.
Help me look for my twin brother."

"I do not see Susan," said Nancy.
"We must look for her, too."

"I can find them," said Uncle Green.
"No one can hide in my garden."

105

(Illustration) Two of the children are looking down a huge cornstalk through an opening in the clouds. The green giant and the other children are approaching the sky opening. Far below a village can be seen.

"Here we are," called Ned.
"Susan and I know how to get down."

Uncle Green laughed and said,
"You are looking down my magic hole.
You can go down there like a fireman."

Ted said, "We will go now,
but we will come up in the morning."

"No, no," said Uncle Green.
"This is a one-time magic garden.
No one can come up two times."

106

MEETING NEW WORDS IN CONTEXT

The frequency with which words are met is vital for retention. As any experienced first-grade teacher can confirm, and any new teacher soon learns, one or two contacts with a word are not enough to effect retention, even among bright children. Teachers can also confirm that presenting words in isolation by rote drill in order to get needed recontact with a word seldom does the trick. Flash cards misused are the shackle of the learner, the despair of the naïve teacher, and the frustration of the well-meaning parent.

Analysis of vocabulary usage shows that from strictly a "mechanics of reading" point of view, the repetition of old and new words within a story is good. The psychology of learning has for years been clear about the efficacy of meaningful repetition or recontact with what is to be learned. Each new word is used a minimum of four times in "A One-Time Magic Garden." J. B. Stroud puts it this way (5, p. 373):

> The two great expediencies used to insure retention are thorough initial learning and subsequent practice or review. No matter how thorough the initial learning is, forgetting is to be expected in time unless subsequent practice is engaged in. Such practice may take several forms, as in rereading material previously studied, using the material in different contexts, engaging in symbolical practice by direct recall, class discussion.

Far more important, though, is the meaningful and appropriate introduction of words according to the natural communication demands of the context and concepts of language and pictures. Thus, each page of the magic-garden story can provide the basis for many examples of the semantic-concept triangle. The picture provides <u>experience</u>, one of the ingredients for meaning. The story provides the <u>language</u>, another in-

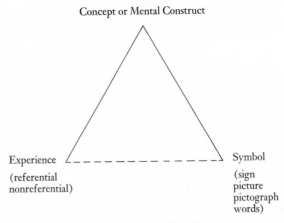

Concept or Mental Construct

Experience
(referential
nonreferential)

Symbol
(sign
picture
pictograph
words)

Semantic-Concept Triangle

gredient. This is the base of the semantic triangle and provides the foundations for meaning. When the two ingredients are joined in the mind of the reader, a <u>concept</u>, or idea, is fashioned. This is the apex of the triangle and represents the peak attainment of conceptualization.

Since the words in "A One-Time Magic Garden" are used in a conventional way, agreed upon and accepted by our society, the children who read this story should meet these words in the story context. *The words should not be presented prior to the reading and in isolation.* Because of the appropriate and timely use of the words and because the children will be intent on reading for meaning, the likelihood of their recognizing the words on their own is high. When the pupils are talking, no one needs to stand by and prompt or tell the words. The words and their meanings are quite common. Similarly, while they are reading, no one need stand by when the children meet these words, because they are used appropriately in a meaningful setting.

If the efficacy of context is not enough, the pupils have the opportunity of using, on their own, the phonetic and structure clues they have been taught.

When a teacher writes all new words on the chalkboard and tells the children what the words are, or helps them analyze the words before they meet them in context, the pupils do not have an opportunity to use the skills they have been taught. The teacher short-circuits their learning.

It is commonly thought that experience is the best teacher. But this is only half the story: the other half is "particularly if it is second-hand." How true this is! Life is filled with second-hand experiences. In fact, much of what we learn is gained through second-hand experiences. One need not jump off a bridge to understand the danger of doing so nor touch a burning match nor fall on ice nor lose a dog to find out what these mean. Reading is a rich, indispensable, and dynamically vital source of experience. It is paramount, therefore, that from the very beginning children be taught to read in such a way that they acquire this attitude about reading. As early as possible, children must become sensitive to the fact that reading can give them new ideas and change old ones. Most important in all this is that the teacher's attitude toward reading be such that it will foster a reading-to-learn attitude.

DATA PROCESSING, FEEDBACK, AND TESTING

One way to program the reading of a selection is to permit the reader to process certain amounts of data, or evidence, and speculate about events to follow. In the case of "A One-Time Magic Garden," because of the nature of the title it is suggested that speculation be invited in response only to the title at first. The predicting (weighing of evidence), data processing (reading), testing (selecting relevant data), and evaluating (confirming or rejecting hypothesis) will occur in four steps:

1. prediction from title clues only
2. prediction from first-page clues
3. prediction from the first three pages of clues or evidence from half the story
4. prediction from five-sixths of the story or the first five pages. Now the reader uses all information except the climax page.

If this kind of segmented treatment were given to every six-page story, one would soon defeat the purpose of a DRTA. It would soon become as stultifying as what is still the recommended practice in so many other instances: readiness (teacher tells, teacher asks questions), guided silent reading (teacher watches pupils read), comprehension check (pupils answer teacher's questions and tell back the story), oral reading (pupils read a page orally, taking turns and following in the book to detect pupil errors), readiness, and so on as the cycle is repeated. It is important, therefore, that the teacher vary the amount of material (information) to be processed from story to story. In a DRTA procedure, the purpose of dealing with various amounts of information is to teach children to be reading detectives. Throughout the instruction time, pupils must discover for themselves the predictive value of clues in one-sixth, one-fourth, one-half, two-thirds, and five-sixths of a story. That this kind of thinking-reading performance can be initiated in the first grade is easy to prove.

Title Clues, Step 1. Have the pupils find the name of the story in the table of contents. Note, please, that this is *not* to be done with each story; it would be ridiculous. A title carefully chosen not only to name a story but also to be useful in developing reading-thinking skills serves many purposes. It can be the equivalent of a central theme. In this case, the title is highly suggestive as to a possible outcome of the story: "A One-Time Magic Garden" has special meaning. The trained reader will keep this in mind throughout. All clues, all items of information, are oriented around this idea. The title gives direction and focus. In this respect, it represents an all-embracing set of clues.

The title permits and encourages <u>divergent</u> thinking. This means, as J. P. Guilford has said (2, pp. 176–182), the producing of a diversity of ideas that are logically probable. The ideas are reasonable or credible within the limitations of the facts available. Divergent thinking prompts creative thinking. E. Paul Torrance says (6, pp. 62–63):

> The creative reader sensitizes himself to problems, gaps in knowledge, missing elements, something incorrect. This calls for the formation of new relationships and combinations, synthesizing relatively unrelated elements in a coherent whole, redefining or transforming certain elements to discover new uses, and building onto what is known. In this search for solutions, there is the operation of ideational fluency (the production of a large number of possibilities).

After the pupils have read the title in the table of contents, the teacher asks them to close their books so that full attention can be given to predicting from the title. Pupils will not be distracted by picture clues or other titles in the table of contents.

Here are some of the predictions made by one group of ten six-year-olds. The teacher initiated the purpose-setting session by asking them: "What do *you think* a story with a title like this may be about?" This question is usually enough to get things going. Occasionally, though, particularly in the earlier DRTA sessions, it may be helpful to rephrase the question and ask: "What do you think might happen in this story?"

"It may be a trick garden," said one boy. "Maybe it grows only one time and then the people have no food," was another response. "This could be a make-believe garden with only fairies and princesses." "Maybe they have the biggest tomatoes. My dad did one year." Each of these conjectures reflects a use of ideas suggested by the title. Notice how each varies and is revealing about the child and his experiences and language.

How ridiculous it would have been to have urged this teacher to *tell* the children that this is a story about a giant cornstalk and a giant's garden that grows toys. Such betrayal would yield little. Children know about gardens and magic. They know what it means to grow things and how magic might help.

Four of the children made conjectures, this is an excellent number. At times, all in a group may offer a different conjecture. At other times, only one conjecture may be heard. At all times, the teacher must be ready and willing to accept the responses that develop. If only one response is made or even no response, the occasion demands a good deal of restraint by the teacher. It is tempting to step in and offer ideas, and this might be done on rare occasions. But it is far better to continue and discover what kinds of information are needed to arouse responses and to find out later why the title clues did not set them responding. If this kind of reserve is exercised and alertness to additional clues is maintained, the children will gain in thinking power and assurance. They are the ones who must experience and discover what to do with difficulty. This is certainly not the time for barricades against learning.

Before going on, the teacher questioned the others in the group by asking which one of the four ideas they thought would be the likely one. Three thought the trick-garden idea was good, one thought it would be about tomatoes, and two thought it would be about fairies and princesses. So, all had done some thinking; all had made a decision. There had been no coercion.

"How can we find out who is right?" asked the teacher. She received a quick reply: "Read!" They knew what it meant to read to find out.

"Read to the bottom of page 101 and then close your books," said the teacher.

Children asked to be independent, asked to recognize a need and know what to do about it, must be trained. Just before a first reading is done, pupils need to review briefly from time to time what to do if they come to a word they do not know. The steps are:

1. Read to the end of the sentence.
2. Look for picture clues.
3. Sound it out.
4. Ask for the teacher's help.

To know that they do not know a particular word, the children will first have to see it. Visual discrimination is their first reaction—noting likenesses and differences of structure. Undoubtedly, too, they will then try to sound it out. Still failing to recognize it, they will use context clues. In reviewing these steps for the children, context, or meaning clues should always be listed first. The potency of meaning is so great and the idea of reading for meaning is so important that meaning should always take precedence. Also, once pupils have an idea as to what a word might be, the skills of phonic and structural analysis become more functional.

As soon as the group knew how far they were to read, they "took off." The first picture had helped focus on the nature of the plot and its direction. All knew that children were involved and that the corn was growing tall.

The teacher observed the silent reading and thought of it as the most important time in the entire word-recognition training program. All reading teachers are agreed that the object of instruction is to develop self-reliant, independent, discriminating readers. All are agreed, too, that it is the teacher who sets the climate of a DRTA by words, tone of voice, manner, and skill-training facility. If children are to be self-reliant in their use of word-attack skills, it is the teacher who must direct experiences that will foster such an attitude.

A first step on the road to word-recognition independence is to foster an attitude of "try it yourself first and then get help if you need it." One of the advantages of structured basic-reader material is that, by controlling the number of new words on a page, the ratio of new words to running words, or previously learned words, and the relationship of new words to picture content, new words can be so presented as to encourage the reader to try the word on his own before seeking help. This is only half of the process, however. If the child is to try out his fund of word-attack skills, he *must* be given the *opportunity*. The best opportunity for the child who is learning to read is to meet new words for the first time in a story context. It follows from this that the teacher *must not* present the new words in isolation, in a mistaken notion that she is preparing the child to read. All that happens then is that the child is prepared for a kind of mental servitude in which he lacks the freedom and the ability to determine his own word-recognition skill.

Next in importance is the pupil's willingness to ask for help. Teachers sometimes say that children will not ask for help. This is true in a situation where they have been deprived of the healthy give-and-take of discovery learning. Teachers who find that children do not ask for help should examine their own behavior in relation to the learning environment: Where it is open, accepting, scholarly, and understanding, pupils will know that they do not know and will ask for help when they need it. When a pupil asks for help with an unknown word, such questions as "What do you think the word might be?" or "What have you already done to find out what the word could be?" are often all the help that is needed. If not, more direct guidance can then be given.

After the first page has been read and all books have been closed, the comprehension check can be started by a number of questions from the teacher. She might ask, as she did before, "What do you think now?" or "Were you right?" or "What do you think will happen next?" Each question serves a particular purpose.

"What do you think now?" and "What do you think will happen next?" set similar lines of thought in motion. The latter question focuses more sharply on "what next" ideas. It invites anticipation and speculation about events to come and calls into play the use of ideas garnered thus far. To make educated guesses, pupils must screen and evaluate ideas and make decisions about events to come in light of events that have occurred. The first question elicits almost the same responses but lets the pupils decide for themselves that "what next" ideas are called for. In other words, "What do you think now?" is somewhat less directive than "What do you think will happen next?"

"Were you right?" focuses on the reading purposes and an evaluation of *right, wrong,* and *partially right.* This is a good approach that meets with favorable response. The pupils know whether what they had predicted actually occurred. They know, too, that the test of their decision will be to read the lines that prove or disprove or partially support. The question "Were you right?" focuses on proof. Pupils schooled in the processes of a DRTA will hardly wait to be asked a question. They know that, when all books are closed, comprehension will be checked and evaluated.

In this instance, the teacher asked, "Well, were any of you right?" to which the boy who had spoken about tomatoes replied immediately, "I wasn't right about the tomato but this may be a magic cornstalk!"

Now the teacher said, "Read the lines that gave you this idea."

The boy opened his book and read eagerly: "This must be magic," said Bill. "Dad just put it in this morning. Then it was little, but see it now."

The oral *rereading* to prove a point was done with considerable smoothness and expression. This boy was out to prove a point and this was his preoccupation—not the saying of words. He did not read monotonously word by word or with a sing-song high-pitched voice. The reason is obvious: He was providing evidence in defense of a point, not evidence that he could say words.

The oral rereading was not motivated by purposes different from the purposes that motivated the original reading. Such notions apply only in situations where the pupils reread a story aloud after it has been read silently. Even then the purposes are usually trumped up, fabricated teacher-purposes that neither motivate the children nor deceive them. They soon realize that all that is wanted is a routinized pronouncing of the words. In a DRTA circumstance, the oral rereading is motivated by the purposes that initiated the silent reading. This is as it should be. Now is the time to read to prove or disprove.

When the lines were read orally, the other members of the group kept their books closed. This required them to listen discriminately to the lines being read. They had to decide whether the lines being read were correct and proved the point being defended. This kind of training in listening is of a high order because it requires discerning attentiveness.

"I think I was right, too," said one of the girls. "I believe it is a trick garden. The story said it was going up as fast as a bird." Then she read aloud the lines that supported her reply.

The pupils who found that their predictions were wrong were not distressed. They had thought well. They readjusted their thinking to accord to the new information. They knew from experience that circumstances like these required flexibility. They were developing emotional stability and maturity as well.

First-Page Clues, Step 2. "What do you think will happen next?" asked the teacher.

"I think they will crawl up on the stalk," said one, "and find some magic."

"I think this stalk isn't strong enough to hold them," said another.

"I think they will grow a lot of magic corn and have the best popcorn in the country!" said a third.

"Read pages 102 and 103 and see who is right," said the teacher.

The teacher might have probed for more conjectures, but she sensed that all were sufficiently questioning in attitude to go on. A most important skill for teachers to grasp in such situations is to know when to have the pupils read on. No one can spell out all such circumstances nor would one want to. Each situation varies so that the teacher must play by ear.

This time the teacher did not realert the children about how to handle word-recognition needs. They knew what to do. More important, they knew that they could ask for help and receive it without sensing a cool air of dissatisfaction on the part of the teacher or being scoffed at by the group. The learning climate was good. To know that you know that you do not know may be the beginning of wisdom, but the next step is equally important: to know what to do about what you do not know.

Throughout this silent reading session, the teacher stayed alert not only for requests for help but also to observe the pupils' reading performances. She watched for reading posture, lip movement, finger pointing, facial reactions to plot development, reading rate, and so on. Not all pupils finished and closed their books at the same time, so she took advantage of these seconds by carrying on a private conversation with a pupil or two who finished early. She asked, in a low whisper, "Did you find out what the magic garden is?" Children respond especially well to such sessions. They welcome the personal attention. Furthermore, this serves as a double comprehension check. A pupil reluctant to speak up in the group may be drawn into active participation this way.

After all books had been closed, the comprehension check started at once. All the teacher said was: "Well?" as an invitation to respond. In rapid order, now, they read aloud lines to prove points about the garden and Uncle Green.

One-Half of Story, Step 3.   Speculation about what might follow was so ripe that all the teacher needed to do was listen.

"I think the green giant will keep them in the garden," said one, "and they can't go home. That's why they call it one-time."

"I think they will get home again but they can't take the toys along," said another.

"Uncle Green looks very friendly. I think he will help them get home again with all kinds of toys."

The pupils were of course responsible for reading both the pictures and the text as they went on to the next two pages. The most obvious source of information is the two pictures. At this stage of reading progress, pupils should be schooled turning first to the pictures. Notice, too, how throughout this story the pictures have helped carry the plot forward. In this instance, the pupils were primed to see how the children return home. Neither picture provides evidence. Furthermore, both provide information but raise questions such as What is Uncle Green giving Susan? Why do Ned and Nancy look worried? Answers can be found only in the text.

Notice, too, how the facing pages (104 and 105) help carry the plot forward. The ideas presented are not what the children had expected. Yet they are plausible and fit the plot. The content does not sound contrived. The surprise in the plot holds the reader's attention and keeps him involved in unraveling the story. This is as it should be. A good deal of careful planning, writing, and arranging is required to set up a series of stories that will be useful in the teaching of reading as a thinking process.

Again the teacher observed reading performance. Again she made short but timely person-to-person visits. These check-up sessions keep the reader focused on meaning. Attention had of course been given to recognizing words, but words are recognized so that the plot can be comprehended.

After all books were closed, the comprehension-check session got under way at once. "The children didn't go home," said one lad with a certain amount of concern. "Why do you think they didn't?" asked the teacher.

"Maybe this is a trick garden and they are trapped," was the reply. "Yes," said a girl. "Uncle Green looks too happy. I believe he tricked them."

Five-Sixths of Story, Step 4. "How many think the children are caught?" asked the teacher. Almost all hands went up. Two children felt sure they would get home again, but were not sure how. One boy thought the "one-time" idea meant that they could go home but never come back. "Read on and find out," said the teacher.

All too often the last picture in a story designed for this level gives away the ending, leaving no need to read on. This last picture did not give away the ending and it proved to be puzzling. The pupils had to read to find out, and the teacher knew this.

Almost before the teacher could look around, the books were closed again. It was obvious by the "ohs" and "ahs" that the pupils had reached the end. All knew what "one-time magic garden" meant. During the discussion that followed, the teacher asked a girl to read the line that proved the "one-time" point.

Before dismissing the group, the teacher printed the new words introduced in this story on the chalkboard. Then she asked different pupils to pronounce a word. Reading the new words in isolation is a good test. The words were first met and dealt with in context. If a child does not afterward recognize a word in isolation, the teacher might ask him to turn to the story and use the context clues to help him.

Conclusion

This chapter is concerned with the fact that reading-thinking skills must be taught as early as possible in children's reading-to-learn and learning-to-read program. A major advantage of introducing children to directed reading instruction by means of the comprehensive Language-Experience Approach is that they learn the rudiments of reading in functional communication. They learn to read much as they learned to talk.

Learning to read differs from learning to talk, though, in that it is planned and directed and aimed at acquiring skills that are to be used deliberately and purposefully to acquire knowledge. Accordingly, as soon as children have advanced a certain distance in learning to read, they need to be taught how their new skills can be used, refined, and extended for high utility.

The outline for a Directed Reading-Thinking Activity, or a problem-solving approach to reading, presents five basic steps. The first four are very similar to the steps usually associated with reflective thinking. This is thinking and acting that enables a reader to direct, act, know, and convert. It frees him from merely impulsive and unregulated reading, which may be largely imaginative, to reading that is concerned with critical and creative ends. The steps outlined show that reading is not a single unitary activity but a process that can be adapted to the purpose of the reader and the nature and difficulty of the material.

How children acquire critical and creative ability almost from the beginning of their school careers depends to a large degree on how the teacher directs reading instruction. She must so direct it that pupils' thinking is required, honored, and refined. She must oversee the PRP process and foster in each pupil the attitude of *predicting* or setting purposes, *reading* or reasoning, and *proving* or testing the ideas read in the light of the purposes declared.

Pupils in a language-experience program evidence certain readily recognized signs of achievement and readiness for group instruction. The best evidence, of course, is the amount of reading they do and enjoy. Other signs are the size of their reading vocabularies; the rate of growth of their vocabularies as well as their range and complexity; the quality of oral reading; the nature and quantity of creative writing; the ability to use sound or phonetic knowledge and sight, or word-structure knowledge as well as meaning or context knowledge in decoding a word; and their attitude toward reading.

The most essential teaching variable is the teacher. It is her attitude toward reading and thinking and instruction that makes the difference. She must be dedicated to the proposition that reading is a mental process and that efficient reading-thinking skills must be taught.

Bibliography

1. Abercrombie, M. L. Johnson. *The Anatomy of Judgment*. New York: Basic Books, 1960.
2. Guilford, J. P. "Frontiers in Thinking That Teachers Should Know About," *The Reading Teacher*, vol. 13, no. 3 (February, 1960), pp. 176–182.
3. Stauffer, Russell G. *Teaching Reading as a Thinking Process*. New York: Harper & Row, 1969.

4. Stauffer, Russell G., *et al. Away We Go.* New York: Holt, Rinehart and Winston, 1960.
5. Stroud, J. B. "The Role of Practice in Learning." In *The Psychology of Learning.* Forty-first Yearbook of the National Society for the Study of Education, Part II. Chicago, Ill.: University of Chicago Press, 1942.
6. Torrance, E. Paul. "Developing Creative Readers." In *Dimensions of Critical Reading,* compiled by Russell G. Stauffer. Proceedings of the Annual Education and Reading Conferences, 1963–1964. Newark, Del.: University of Delaware, 1964.

7

Individualized directed reading-thinking activities

In this chapter a distinction is made between group Directed Reading-Thinking Activities, in which all pupils read the same material at the same time, and a Directed Reading-Thinking Activity that is individualized. The first provides readiness in many ways for the second. The key ideas in the individualized circumstances are self-selection, teacher pacing, and sharing.

The chapter is in four parts. The first part explains how instruction is alternated between the group plan and the individualized plan. The second part describes the characteristics of individualized directing reading-thinking activities. The third part gives what might be considered the ultimate goal of both reading and language-arts instruction: sharing. The fourth part explains how the individualized program is an action program.

The reader is asked to read the following objectives and hypothesize concerning the answers. He will increase his comprehension of the chapter to the degree that he makes these objectives his own. This results in a personal and intellectual commitment that helps him regulate his reading and thinking and keeps him on course.

1. Define a Directed Reading-Thinking Activity that is individualized.
2. Describe how, during a group DRTA, some instruction is individualized and how during individualized DRTA, some grouping occurs.
3. Explain how the discipline of accuracy and the hope of discovery provide the motivation for scholarly reading.
4. Describe why and how teaching time is divided between group and individualized DRTA's and why each period should run for at least 3 consecutive weeks.

Upon reading the second part, the reader should be able to meet the following objectives:

1. What is the basic principle of individualized instruction?
2. Explain how pupils get to know each other's achievement levels.
3. Describe the materials for individualized instruction.
4. Explain J. Richard Suchman's cognitive-control dimension and David P. Ausubel's concept of progressive differentiation.

Upon reading the third part, the reader should be able to meet the following objectives:

1. Explain how a pupil plans for self-selection.
2. Tell how a pupil develops word-attack resourcefulness.
3. Describe ways of sharing and how they are used effectively.
4. Discuss pupil records and how they are maintained.
5. Describe how self-regulation becomes a hallmark of a good reader.

Upon reading the fourth part, the reader should be able to meet the following objectives:

1. Explain how the reading program becomes in all respects a language-arts program.
2. Describe how pupils learn by listening.
3. Tell why this program is best labeled an action program.

The first five chapters of this book were devoted to how individual pupils learn to read. Teachers were urged to move away from whole-class dictated stories and group dictation to individual dictation by early October. Much of the account told about how pupils dictated their own ideas and used their own vocabularies and experiences. The words they first learned were self-identified. The sentences that they assembled on their word-card holders from words in their own word banks were of their own creation. The creative writing was their own and reflected their ideas and experiences as well as their handwriting. The books they selected in the classroom library and in the school library were of their own choosing. The ideas they chose to share with their classmates were of their own choosing. In fact, each phase of the teaching-learning circumstance was predominantly individual.

It was equally apparent that each pupil and each activity were group and class based. Each child was a member of a class and of groups that varied according to purposes, interests, and needs. Stimuli to evoke interest and response were in most instances presented to the entire class. Reactions used each child's individual sensory pathways but also required and inspired him to share ideas with his peers. Oral language was used to share reactions and exchange ideas. Dictated stories, word-bank idea creations, and creative stories were shared with the class. Books were read, enjoyed, and shared. Library visits were whole-class visits.

In brief, communication of ideas constituted the principal crystallization of school life—intellectually, affectively, socially, and individually. Interests, values, sympathies, and respect developed mutually. When the children worked by themselves, their conduct was marked by individual concentration and, when they were in a group, by effective collaboration. The children were learning to see other points of view and to coordinate them. They were acquiring new coordinations in the development of intelligence and affectivity.

The account of the why and how of directed group reading, in which each member reacted to the same material, described teaching-learning experiences quite different from the earlier ones. Now children were being introduced to the practices and procedures of a disciplined scholar. The practices were introduced as soon as the children's reading ability permitted, so that they could begin early to acquire sound habits and skills through repeated reinforcement. In a sense, the group DRTA provides the setting for pupils to learn to deal with logic. Jean Piaget puts it this way in one of his discussions about the progress of seven-year-olds (4, p. 41):

> With respect to intelligence, we are now dealing with the beginnings of the construction of logic itself. Logic constitutes the system of relationships which permit the coordination of points of view corresponding to different individuals, as well as those which correspond to the successive percepts or intuitions of the same individual . . . the mental instruments which will facilitate logical and moral coordination are the operation in the field of intelligence and the will in the field of affectivity.

In a way, then, this chapter on directing the reading-thinking activities of individuals is a reflection of the practices and procedures described earlier. On the other hand, as it describes the further growth and development in the educational lives of scholars it is quite different. Repeated experiences in the challenging interchanges of DRTAs result in a better understanding of personal interests and tastes. Reading choices become more selective, sharing sessions more sophisticated. So, even though a group in a sense is reverting from group to individualized instruction, the conditions are different.

An alternating plan

A question teachers ask the moment group DRTA's are introduced is, "How many days or weeks do we devote to group DRTA's?" It is a timely question. The children are so absorbed by the challenge of reading together that the question would not occur to them. Furthermore, as far as they are concerned, they never give up creative writing, dictating, library reading, and the like. All they do is add a new dimension. For the teacher, though, adding this new dimension makes different demands on her time and her need to be alert to the skills and disciplines the pupils are to acquire. So, she asks the question.

A satisfactory answer, one that will hold for the rest of the first year, is that, since basic readers are probably used for the group DRTA sessions, a good time to stop group DRTA's is at the end of a reader unit. A unit usually consists of eight or ten stories, which can be read in a DRTA in 2 to 3 weeks. This allows time for work in word recognition and some follow-up activities on concepts. At the end of a basic-reader unit, the books are put aside for a period of time equal to that devoted to the group sessions, perhaps 3 weeks.

The principal pedagogical difference between the two teaching-learning sessions is the distinction between group instruction and individualized instruction. This is not to imply that there is no individualization of instruction during the group time. There is, as has been shown again and again. Neither is it true that there is no group instruction during the individualized time. There is, as was also pointed out repeatedly. The skills and abilities acquired in both instances are also interrelated, but the point of pedagogical emphasis varies. On the one hand, in group DRTA's the formalized skills of a scholar are acquired and refined in the crucible of group interaction. The conditions require immediate justification and defense of a position taken and judgments made. It is through group interaction that pupils acquire the *humility* of scholars as well as a glorification of *will* and intensification of *action*. Here is where falsely directed self-will, pride, and sophistication are tempered so that pupils can become as realistic and truly rational as possible. Speculation or educated guesses or predictions make for free inquiry and for the empirical test of proof. The creative character of productive intuition or hypothesizing is decisively different from that of unproductive guesswork: Pupils engaged in hypothesizing want to prove their points; the others are afraid to do so.

These cognitive skills are acquired and refined not in a day or a week or a year but across the years and through the disciplines of accuracy and the hope of discovery. As children grow physically and intellectually and their interests and tastes are expanded and refined, as they meet with the increasing demands of the nature and depth of a spiraling curriculum, they refine the cognitive reading skills of a scholar. They acquire the art of noble detachment—minds disciplined and dignified, competent and productive, vigilant and independent.

A scholar learns to be self-reliant, enduring, open-minded, stable, humane, organized, confident yet humble. The skills and abilities acquired in group DRTA's are to be applied, extended, and refined by the child when he is on his own. He must learn to grasp the Socratic challenge to be and to know oneself, and for this the individualized DRTA sessions provide excellent training. The child learns to pursue his own interests, to refine interests into tastes, and to test his knowledge against the dimension of a class that is essentially honest and critical.

Accordingly, time, at least throughout the rest of the year in first grade, is divided equally between group and individual DRTA sessions. By February most children are capable of participating in group DRTA's. As has been explained before, some are ready in December, some not until March or April, but most are ready by February. Because the group sessions introduce a discipline different from anything experienced before, the influence on the individualized sessions is considerable. Pupils are, in a sense, returning to practices acquired over the first 4 months, but their return is different because they are different.

Common characteristics of individualized DRTA's

Every teacher knows that children are different, that the differences exist before the children come to school, and that good teaching increases pupil differences. Some teachers know that the range of differences among six-year-olds or entering first-graders is a spread of about 4 to 5 years and that, by fourth grade, the spread is about 8 years (2, pp. 346–347). In addition, intrapupil variances can be greater than interpupil differences.

Every teacher knows that some pupils learn at a faster rate than others. The rate of intake is influenced considerably by the student's capacity to learn; but attitude, motivation, and social-cultural factors also play a part. Every teacher can conclude that the purpose of individualized instruction is to improve the efficiency of each pupil.

If teaching is geared to the level of each pupil and regulated by his interests, tastes, experiences, and capacity to make decisions about what he selects to read, and, if it is paced by the teacher's knowledge of each pupil and the materials, then each pupil will achieve at his best level (3, pp. 3–10). It is not a question of the slow learner or the gifted or the average or the retarded. In fact, a basic principle of individualized instruction and pacing is to adjust expectancy in keeping with the best estimate of pupil capacity.

Accordingly, expectancies for the slow and the gifted must be adjusted. Acquisition of skills must be paced at each pupil's rate of intake. The fast learner will need fewer repetitions, less obvious presentations because of his ability to put two and two together, more material to aid him in his search for more refined meanings, and perhaps less guidance. The slow learner will need programmed step-by-step presentations, many repetitions, material at his reading and thinking level, and perhaps more guidance. His purposes may be simpler and more factual than complex and hypothetical, and his findings will be geared accordingly.

Step into any classroom in which reading instruction is effectively individualized and ask a child who is the best reader in the room, and he can quickly name the pupil. Similarly, ask for the name of the poorest reader in the class, and the slowest is readily named. Pupils know each other, their levels and potentials. As a matter of fact, there is less deception in this regard than in a regimented group situation. Pupils work together in different groups, many of which are spontaneously formed. Interest groups, skill groups, friendship groups, special-ability groups, and teams all result in a shifting and reshifting of pupils and in pupils getting to know each other better.

What is reflected, of course, is the wise use of basic readers for group instruction in reading-thinking skills. So-called grade norms no longer interfere with the flexible thinking and planning of teachers. Also reflected through the individualized instruction is the increased understanding among pupils—the spirit of working together, the lend-a-helping-hand spirit, and, of course, the better acceptance of pupils by each other. In addition, the steady diet of success breeds success. Pupils work harder, are friendlier, more cooperative, and more appreciative of small successes.

They see more clearly how to win friends and influence people by playing up each other's assets and working cooperatively to overcome each other's liabilities. Team spirit permeates the air.

The materials for individualized reading instruction are books (the literature of children, young people, and adults), other printed materials (periodicals, newspapers, encyclopedias, almanacs, atlases, indexes, dictionaries, readers' guides), films, recordings, and newer media developed to aid learning. The materials for individualized reading instruction—to be housed effectively for easy availability to pupils—require a library that will serve as a center. Whatever a reader, a student, or a scholar needs to do to locate ideas and information in order to answer the questions, problems, or needs that he has, is what a library should be able to furnish. The school curriculum provides the opportunities to develop the child's intellectual interests and capabilities. The dimensions of cognition or the conceptual world (concepts of time, place, number, people, morals, humor, politics, and so on) will ensure his becoming a responsible member of society. No phase of a reading program is in a more strategic position to foster self-learning, self-control, and self-charity and to bring meaning and understanding to a pupil's social efficiency and his ever widening world community.

In an individualized DRTA all the pupils are directed to select the material they need. The self-selection practice is a basic tenet of the approach, and it makes multivaried materials essential. To make selections, the pupil must first have made decisions about *why* he is reading. This makes the purpose-setting aspect of a group DRTA of paramount importance. It provides learning opportunities in a situation where decisions about materials to read are eliminated, so that attention can be sharply focused on the reading-thinking process. Now during the individualized DRTA period he can focus sharply on materials. He must know what is available and how to select and use most efficiently what is available.

Versatility is required. From what is available, the pupil must select material that he can understand and that gives him the best answers. This is like the cognitive-control dimension defined by J. Richard Suchman—the ability to handle and manipulate data (5, pp. 105–108). Readability assumes some importance, but a child who is free to decide and asked only to be honest can readily tell whether something is too difficult for him.

Of equal importance is the pupil's ability to go from generals to specifics. David P. Ausubel's progressive differentiation is an adaptation required of each reader. He must differentiate in terms of detail and specificity (1). What particulars does he want and to what degree does he want them? He does not want to deal with ideas in rote but wants to adapt, and he does not want to become a victim of the particular. Each reader becomes his own curriculum maker. He wants to use the concepts and principles that have the widest explanatory power and that serve best as a base for new learning and problem solving.

The training in inquiry of individualized DRTA's must meet three conditions. The children need some kind of focus for their attention—purposes. They need physical freedom to select data and information and intellectual freedom to process the data so as to satisfy their cognitive needs. They need an environment—a library or materials center—where, when they seek data, they find some and do not return empty handed.

The motivation for this kind of reading is cognitive and personal. The desire to close the gap between what the child thought might be the answer and the right answer—no matter how great the discrepancy—is considerable. When this is coupled with the pupil's desire to go on, even after reasonable closure has been obtained, the motivation is tremendous. The children gain in stature from the sense of power and confidence that results from all this.

Undoubtedly, too, the role of the teacher is different from those situations in which she takes the lead and the children look for rewards from her and the situation. The role of the librarian is different; she, too, becomes a director of the reading-thinking process. She must arrange materials so that the actions required can be carried out by the pupil himself. In addition, she must aid library usage in such a way that the student learns to take needed actions with less and less direct support.

Sharing ideas, the cosmic view

When the group sessions end and the children return to self-selection, they do so with a new zest and an interesting degree of levity. It is as though they sense a difference and are aware of the degrees of freedom the self-selection allows. Even though they had selected books before and had been reading and sharing, the continuity is interrupted and the perspective changes.

INTERESTS

Pupils are much more apt to pause and reflect over what to do and what to read when a group DRTA session ends. In 3 weeks, they have become accustomed to the group DRTA routine and its provocative orderliness;

such reaction is desirable and comforting. The thing to do when the change is made is to take advantage of their momentary pause.

This is a good time to introduce a plan for the individualized DRTA sessions. How does one plan for self-selection? Obviously, by examining one's likes or interests or tastes. A what-I-might-read sharing session can be held. Some pupil is sure to respond almost immediately by naming a book he wants to read and, thus, set others thinking and responding. Or, if the question is qualified to what I might read about, attention is focused on interests or topics. It is almost like the distinction between interest as a value and interests as the values to which ever more complex goals to action are assigned (4, p. 35). Interest involves a value judgment, and interests suggest the forming of values.

The "interests" mentioned by the children might be listed on the board so that they can be examined. If this procedure is too formalized, some children may turn away because they find it difficult to make such self-analysis and to project likes and dislikes in so formal a way. One must therefore proceed with caution and keep within the projection range of the children. Even a small list is a start. Self-examination and decision making about actions to take in the absence of books and the library and the stimulus they provide are not easy.

Interestingly enough, there will be more reading of nonfiction during the rest of the school year. This shift seems to be prompted by a number of conditions. The number and variety of stimuli that promote creative writing and dictated materials are so varied that they stimulate curiosity. As has already been indicated in earlier chapters, the topics range all the way from safety pins to battle ships to orbiting spacecraft. The rest of the school curriculum proves a fruitful source of ideas. Science and health activities yield a large return. Social studies and current events are also very productive of inquisitiveness. Of course, the omnipresent television is a ready source of ideas as are newspapers, magazines, and radio.

WORD RECOGNITION

Now that specific steps have been declared, describing what to do when a reader encounters a word he does not recognize instantly in the group DRTA situation, the same rules are reviewed for self-selection reading purposes. Obviously, a pupil may encounter more words he does not recognize while reading a book he has selected than when reading the stories in a basic reader that his teacher has selected. He may also experience a greater desire to unlock more unknown words. Most likely he will be making more attempts at word recognition than before the group DRTA sessions. Accordingly, it is wise to review the steps and post a chart listing them.

First, the reader always reads to the end of the sentence in which the unrecognized word appears. He does this because getting the idea proves to be effective. It keeps attention focused on comprehension and that is what reading is all about. In addition, he may study the picture for meaning clues.

Second, he tries to sound the word and pronounce it. Chances are good that, if he pronounces it correctly, he will recognize the word because it is already in his speaking-meaning vocabulary.

Third, he turns to the teacher for help. The mark of a scholar is that he realizes that when he has tried all the skills at his command he must turn to someone more skilled. The important decision is the full recognition that he does not know and needs help.

Throughout the self-selection reading period, word-attack skills are taught as they are throughout the group DRTA period. A group can be called together from time to time to discuss words they attacked success-fully and to tell how they did it. This kind of sharing of knowledge about words and about word-attack skills is particularly beneficial.

Some of the words so identified may be added to the selective word bank. In addition, some of the words may show up in creative writing. If this happens, it is evidence of the highest order that the children are functionally using the words they have learned.

WAYS

Prior to this time, sharing was done in a number of practical and partially spontaneous ways. A pupil might have found a page in a book that he wanted to read to the class. If when he approached the teacher it seemed not too disruptive to ask the class to listen, she invited them to do so. Then it might be discovered that three or four others had something to share: a new word learned, a way they unlocked a word, a picture, a funny sentence, a creative story.

Sharing time might be scheduled daily. Pupils may request some of the sharing time by listing their names on the daily scheduling board. Of course, the teacher stays alert to all the pupils and makes certain that all who want to participate do. Sharing time may also be used to fill waiting minutes; so many of these seem to occur in the life of first-graders. They await the milk break, the television program, their turn to go to the auditorium, recess, lunch, and so on. Waiting and sharing can become almost synonymous and make waiting a pleasant experience.

Sharing time is best scheduled for longer terms, though, either once a week (good at first) or twice in 3 weeks. Some of the most important reasons pedagogically for fixed times are:

1. If a pupil wants to share something with the class and wants the class to give its undivided attention, he should <u>plan</u> what he wants to share. This is not to imply that some planning was not done for the first kinds of sharing but to say that now deliberate effort is made to plan. The teacher and pupils talk about how to plan different presentations: oral reading, new words, a monologue, a team skit, a puppet show, and so on.

2. When pupils have planned what they want to share, they must give thought to <u>different</u> <u>ways</u> of sharing that are unique and will hold the attention of the class. A pupil may want to share something about George Washington, for instance, and make a tricornered hat to wear, or about April showers and wear a raincoat and hat, or about skiing and show ski shoes, or about words and prepare an illustration or a mural for a set of sequences in a story. Some of the sharing may be written, but most of it will be oral.

3. Some pupils are quite original about how to share, but others are not and become concerned. So it is quite helpful to prepare a <u>ways-to-share</u> <u>poster</u>. Each sharing idea can be written on a 3-×-5-inch card. The cards can then be arranged on a card holder, by pinning them on the corkboard, by keeping an orderly pile in a box, or by tying them together with a rubber band. This permits a pupil to reexamine ideas and select one that he thinks will serve him best. Some will need help in decision making, so the teacher is always available and observant.

4. After a pupil has planned what and how he will share, he needs to <u>rehearse</u> his presentation. This is truly a key aspect of sharing. To be effective and to ask others to be attentive, one must be prepared. There is not much difference between staging a play and staging a sharing session. Accordingly, pupils have to learn how to rehearse, privately, without disturbing the class. Pupils are unbelievably ingenious at both quietness and secretiveness.

5. Thought must be given to <u>personnel</u>. A pupil must decide if he is going to do the sharing alone or if he needs help. Thus, monologues, dialogues, teams, and casts are planned and scheduled. Partners vary from session to session and purpose to purpose and much interaction results.

6. Some thought can also be given to the <u>time</u> needed for a presentation.

This may prove challenging to some, but, if the idea is not carried too far, all can give at least an approximation: a very short time, a little time, pretty much time, and the like.

RECORDS

Now that the approach to reading instruction resembles that of individualized self-selection, some form of record keeping is in order. The best procedure is to have the pupils keep accounts. This is all a part of the self-regulatory aspect of being a scholar—to know one's interests, to convert interests to tastes, to pursue one's interests, to share one's interests, and to keep an account.

This, then, is the time to introduce book-record cards. Cards 3 × 5 or 5 × 8 inches provide just the right amount of space. Most pupils prefer the 3 × 5 index card, but some do better with larger ones. Index cards are excellent for the purpose; they are lined and durable. They are readily filed, too, in various types of container. Commercial file boxes are made especially for different sizes of index cards; shoe boxes and the like also serve adequately.

Records must be simple enough that the children can keep them and, at the same time, must be effective enough to serve the purpose of a record. One procedure practical enough to meet all purposes is as follows:

1. For every book a child reads, a card is prepared.
2. On the first line or two of the card the book title is copied.
3. A line is skipped and then the author's name is copied.
4. Another line is skipped and a double entry is made on the next line: (a) first the number of pages in the book is listed, (b) then the number of pages read is listed. A card might read: "36, 36," or "36, all," or "36, 10." The first two are entries that show that the entire book was read. The third shows that 10 of the 36 pages were read.
5. A typical card might be:

> *Lucy and Red*
>
> Micha Trimor
>
> 44   44

By the time record keeping is introduced, each pupil will have done a considerable amount of creative writing and will have enough handwriting skill to keep records. Even so, checks by the teacher are always in order to help maintain readable and accurate accounts.

When record keeping is first introduced, it tends to set off a wave of entries. Quantity seems to have high priority. Let the competition run its course. It will not last. This is especially true when the children with many cards discover that the number of cards does not seem to excite the teacher. She seems just as enthusiastic about Jim's ten cards as Myra's thirty.

Notice that the children are *not* asked to add a *comment* about the book. Comments, at this stage particularly, become almost a stereotyped redundancy. Let it be known, though, that if they wish to say something about the book they may. Discretion must then be exercised so that children will not get the notion that the teacher really wants a comment. If this happens, then it is better either to drop the idea entirely or require all to say something. Usually, though, when comments are voluntary, they evoke more and better responses than otherwise.

Above all, make it clear that a pupil does not need to read an entire book. Just as adults do, some pupils discover that a certain book is not interesting and they put it down after reading some of it. Or, because of the nature of their interest, they did not want or need to read the entire book to obtain what they wished. This kind of scholarly discipline promotes selective reading. A child may read an article in an encyclopedia, for example, and wish to make a record card.

The teacher should examine the book entries periodically. This is a good time to discuss books with children. A recent or an old entry may be discussed. If properly handled, children are pleased to share with the teacher and to have their cards examined.

When children have read the same books and kept similar entries, a stimulating procedure is to have a round-table discussion.

DIRECTOR

By this time the reader may be curious as to why this chapter has been labeled Individualized Directed Reading-Thinking Activities. It is true that the activities engaged in during the fall of the year and in the first phases of the program were directed by the teacher. Now, though, the contrast between group and individualized reading-thinking activities sharpens the dimensions of each. In addition, more of the activities are now being directed toward developing pupils who can deliberately bring to bear specific actions of a scholarly nature on a self-selected reading goal.

True adaptation to his peers comes about gradually as the budding scholar learns to present his ideas and make them understood. He learns to subordinate himself to the ideas he is presenting and to his audience. He learns to cooperate with others in the presentation of ideas and to show increasing appreciation for the points of view of others. He begins to seek justification or proof, not only in group DRTA situations but in all situations. He appreciates the need for regulated and conclusive discussion. He learns to think before acting, to plan, to anticipate responses and questions, to be ready—in other words, he is learning to be deliberate and to reflect; Piaget refers to reflection as "internalized social discussion" (4, p. 40). The pupil begins to see the value of actively pursuing a goal consistently and in a disciplined way. He avoids being offensive, ridiculing or scoffing or being overly critical. He shows appreciation for the flow of ideas and the amenities that accompany the interchange of ideas.

Above all, he learns to examine his own interests and tastes and gains increasing appreciation for the depth and seriousness of the questions he raises. Somehow he begins to sense that values reside not so much in the answers we give as in the questions we raise. Thereby, he uncovers the elemental motivation to learning and to thinking—the power of intellectual commitment.

All this requires careful direction by the teacher as she sets a course toward the true goal of education, to prepare thinking, reflecting, responsible scholars. We cannot wait until children are in high school to set progress toward these objectives in motion, but we must do so from the very beginning of formal instruction. In a reading-instruction world harassed by materialistic publishers and prejudiced, corrupt, and dogmatic extremists, we cannot afford for one minute to withdraw to a corner of mental timidity and emotional cowardice and extend the nonreading void in which so many children are caught. We must strive militantly to provide reading-thinking direction as defined here, and we must do so in the name of scholarship.

An action program

For the rest of the school year, the reading program is in all respects a language-arts program, a communications program. Reading serves a purpose. It is a means to pleasure in relaxation or entertainment as well as a means to pleasure through the learning of new ideas. Reading can be silent and, on occasion, oral. Oral reading is meant to prove a point in both the group and the individualized DRTA sessions. In the latter, oral reading is also for sharing a story or an idea. Entire books or parts of books are read. Encyclopedias are used, as are dictionaries and other similar sources. Newspapers and magazines are read. Books are read in science, health, history, music.

Much listening is done, too. Pupils listen to the dictated stories of their peers. Sometimes they hear eight or ten very different versions of the same episode, and they begin to sense that each person views things just a bit differently from his neighbor. Pupils listen to creative-writing accounts. They attend sharing sessions, and, almost every day, they hear the teacher read aloud. This is a delightful time of the day, and they never tire of it. Fiction and nonfiction as well as poetry are read, and the teacher's reading of poetry is really beautiful. So they are learning much by reading and by listening. Many new ideas are being taken in and many old ones are enriched.

Much opportunity to talk has been provided from the very beginning. Not only did the children dictate stories to the teacher and have a chance to say things their way, but they also had a chance to read their dictated stories to others. They read their creative-writing stories, too. In the sharing sessions, they helped stage different kinds of presentations and had many opportunities to talk. They appeared in front of their classmates on many occasions and in many ways—sometimes screened from them, as in puppet shows, sometimes wearing masks or costumes, sometimes behind a lectern or a table or a stand, sometimes next to a map or a chart or a picture, sometimes in a semidarkened room showing slides or overhead-projector transparencies, sometimes in a play or a skit. These opportunities help develop poise, confidence, and ease and they make the presenting person sensitive to his audience.

Almost since the first copying of his name, the child has been writing. He occasionally added a word to his word bank, being very careful to form each letter correctly. He wrote many, many creative stories and accounts. He kept his own reading records. Writing served him in many ways, and he learned that, if you wanted someone else to read your writing, you had to write letters and words clearly.

This is an action program based on the active use of language. As one first-grade girl said, "We are on the go all the time." They are always doing something—reading, writing, listening, speaking, planning, going to the library, making visits in and around the school and the community. This is truly a first grade on the go.

Conclusion

Much individualized instruction occurred prior to the initiation of group Directed Reading-Thinking Activities, but now a new slant is given to such instruction, because the training in the group situation helps the young scholar-reader to be more self-reliant and resourceful as a reader-thinker. He sees more clearly how to set purposes for reading, how to attack words, how to search for meaning, and how to be a versatile reading detective.

Individualized instruction helps the reader learn about himself, his interests, his tastes, his ambitions, his perseverance, his judgment. He learns how to select material that both answers his purposes and is readable. He sees the classroom, school, and community libraries as true resource centers.

How to examine one's interests and select from among them one or two to be ardently pursued becomes a crucial matter and requires direction by the teacher. Equally important, though, is how to share interests and knowledge with one's peers. If classmates are to listen and be attentive, presentations must be made in such a way as to hold their attention. This means that, to share, one must plan and rehearse so that the sharing is done with the ease of a professional stage presentation. To do this, the pupils and the teacher may help in planning, rehearsing, and staging. Props may be required. Time needed should be determined, so that a class schedule can be prepared. All this requires a considerable amount of resourcefulness and dedication.

In all respects, accomplishing all these features makes the language-experience program an all-embracing language-arts program. Required for success are ability to declare interests, to locate materials, to use materials, to plan ways of sharing, and to share. In other words children read, write, talk, listen, and think, in functional communication.

Bibliography

1. Ausubel, David P. "Cognitive Structure and the Facilitation of Meaningful Verbal Learning." Paper presented at a symposium of the division of Educational Psychology, American Psychological Association. St. Louis, Mo. (September, 1962).

2. Goodlad, John I., and Robert H. Anderson. *The Nongraded Elementary School.* New York: Harcourt, Brace & World, 1959.
3. Olson, Willard C. "Seeking, Self-Selection, and Pacing in the Use of Books by Children," *The Packet,* vol. 7 (Spring, 1952), pp. 3–10.
4. Piaget, Jean. *Six Psychological Studies.* Edited by David Elkind. New York: Random House, 1967.
5. Suchman, J. Richard. "The Illinois Studies in Inquiry Training." In *Piaget Rediscovered,* edited by Richard E. Ripple and Verne N. Rockcastle. (A Report of the Conference on Cognitive Studies and Curriculum Development, March, 1964.) Ithaca, N.Y.: School of Education, Cornell University, 1964.

8

Word recognition

The ability to unlock a word not recognized at sight is an auxiliary aid in the quest for comprehension. At no time should the teaching of word-attack skills take precedence over the teaching of reading for meaning. At no time should word-attack skills be taught in isolation, either from a semantic context or from a morpheme context. At no time should the teaching of word-attack skills, including dictionary usage, be ignored. Skills must be taught from the beginning of reading instruction and be maintained throughout. The roots of word-recognition training must be deeply embedded in functional action.

This chapter is divided into nine parts. The first part defines word recognition. The second part raises a provocative question about the word-attack skills needed by a resourceful reader. Parts three through eight discuss the six basic skills that embrace the entire word-recognition program. They start with phonics, the foundation skill, and terminate with the most practical lifetime skill, dictionary usage. The ninth part states why the roots of learning must be firmly embedded in psychological and pedagogical action.

The reader is asked to read the following objectives and hypothesize concerning the answers. He must understand that he will comprehend the principles and practices presented to the degree that he makes these objectives his own. This results in a personal and intellectual commitment that helps regulate his thinking and keeps him on course.

1. Define word recognition.
2. Explain why meaning or context clues should take precedence over other kinds of clues.

Upon reading the second part, the reader should be able to meet the following objectives:

1. Describe how some preschool children develop a reliable word-attack system.

2. Why can one conclude that the best way to introduce children to functional word-attack skills is by means of their own speaking-meaning vocabularies?

Upon reading the third part, the reader should be able to meet the following objectives:

1. Define auditory discrimination and tell why it is the foundation to unlocking words in a reader's speaking-meaning vocabulary.
2. Explain why children's ability to recognize and deal with sounds in words is truly remarkable.
3. Tell how to teach auditory discrimination.

Upon reading the fourth part, the reader should be able to meet the following objectives:

1. Distinguish between auditory discrimination and auditory-visual discrimination.
2. Explain how, because language use is discursive, communication influences word learning.
3. Explain why it is that auditory-visual discrimination can occur as soon as a child can read one word and need not be postponed until he can read fifty or more words.
4. Describe how auditory-visual discrimination is handled pedagogically and psychologically.
5. Tell about the value of a phonic booth.

Upon reading the fifth part, the reader should be able to meet the following objectives:

1. Describe word families and tell how the family idea is taught.
2. Explain why keys can be helpful in developing word families.

Upon reading the sixth part, the reader should be able to answer the following objectives:

1. Explain why the need to teach one skill after another can imply a discreteness that can lead to misunderstandings about systematic and intensive teaching.

2. Describe how a vowel key is developed and how it serves a reader.
3. How can a vowel key be both an asset and a liability in creative writing?

Upon reading the seventh part, the reader should be able to meet the following objectives:

1. Explain how it is that children use derivative and inflectional variations when they talk and can do so equally well when they read.
2. Describe how creative writing positively influences the recognition and use of structural changes.

Upon reading the eighth part, the reader should be able to meet the following objectives:

1. Describe six ways that word-bank usage influences dictionary usage.
2. Tell why it would be helpful for each first-grader to have a desk dictionary.
3. Explain how the building of consonant and vowel keys influences dictionary usage.

Upon reading the ninth part, the reader should be able to meet the following objectives:

1. Explain how printed language, like spoken language, is influenced by interpersonal exchange and cooperation.
2. Tell why the communication of ideas provides the best teaching vehicle for developing word-attack competence.
3. Discuss the eight generalizations about word-attack skills and phonics and tell why they are timely and relevant.

The reader is urged to review what has been said about developing word-attack skills in the earlier chapters. Special attention should be given to the first half of Chapter 3, on word banks. Notice again how skills are taught in functional situations with emphasis on pupils' usage. The cardinal principal observed in each circumstance is that the pupils recognized a need. The need for a skill to unlock a word should result from an encounter in which reading progress has been blocked. In other words, pupils should meet unrecognized words in a context, when they are reading for meaning and the demand for meaning is paramount. Skills should not be created in artificial conditions. Need for a particular skill should not be in isolation but in a communication context. Utilitarianism in word-attack learning makes skills that much more utilitarian. A skill is acquired not to impress an adult but to serve the reader.

In this chapter, practices and procedures concerned with word-recognition skill acquisition already described will be reviewed and placed in a comprehensive setting with other skill-acquisition procedures. All word-attack skills are to help the reader comprehend. He must learn how to use the skills in a self-regulatory way. Word recognition is an auxiliary aid to comprehension and should always be treated as such.

Word recognition defined

What does a child do, or what does any individual do for that matter, when he stops at a word he does not recognize at first sight? Obviously he *sees* the word first or, in other words, he uses visual perception. But seeing the word is not enough or the word would have been recognized. Next, he tries to sound the word with first visual clues and then sound clues. He analyzes the word to discover letter clues to the sounds that they may represent in this particular word context. Then he blends the sounds together so that, with the appropriate intonation, he can say the word. All this may not be sufficient, because meaning clues also determine phoneme sounds and intonation, so he may have to read on to find the meaning.

Word recognition, then, involves the ability to use context or meaning clues, phonetic or sound clues, and structure or sight clues. If this makes learning to read seem most difficult, how is it that year after year many children learn to read on their own? Their success implies three things. First, the skills of word recognition cannot be too complex or else these preschoolers would not be able to work out their own reliable systems. Second, there must be some pattern to the development of these skills or else the children would develop as many different systems as the well-meaning adult phoneticians have done. Third, there must be a latent power that facilitates recognition residing in meaning and communication or else the words would remain unknown.

Compare a reading performance in which immediate word recognition fails with one in which no difficulty is encountered. Recognition becomes the act of simultaneously seeing the word and identifying its meaning. Meaning directs the entire process.

Since meaning plays a dominant role in both situations—dealing with words that are not immediately recognized at sight and words that are—it is apparently the most functional key to word recognition. This is the position taken throughout this book, because it emphasizes *communication*, to which all other aids are subordinate. One deals with the phonetic elements not merely to say a word but as an aid in grasping its meaning. The same is true of the use of structural aids.

A puzzling circumstance

Acquiring facility at word attack cannot be too complex, for, if it were, children would not acquire it on their own. Year after year, teachers take professional courses in reading instruction and always show much concern about word-attack teaching. Year after year, tests to determine teacher knowledge of word-attack skills show astounding ignorance. All this is partly because the neophyte, unaware of the complex word-attack skill programs of authors and publishers, proceeds functionally to the heart of the problem and acquires simple yet effective methods, whereas, teachers, all of whom can read with considerable skill, do not use the word-attack skills of the neophyte and find it difficult to memorize the complex programs being published.

The children are right. There are only a few procedures needed to read almost any word that is already in their speaking vocabularies. The skills they use and the order in which they learned them are most likely: auditory discrimination, auditory-visual discrimination, consonant substitution, vowel variability, structural variation, and dictionary usage.

It puzzles some people and escapes others why word attack is taught in grades one, two, and three and then is forgotten in grades four, five, six, and beyond. The reason is simple. The child learning to read has a large functional speaking vocabulary. If a word he is trying to read is in his speaking-meaning vocabulary and he can decode the word so as to speak it, he then recognizes its meaning or use. Thus, speaking-meaning recognition functionally embraces reading recognition. This makes the following conclusion obvious. The best way to introduce children to skills that are functional is to use words they have selected from their own individual speaking-meaning vocabularies. This closes the circle described above (nonrecognition to recognition) in communication or in a situation where language is serving its purpose.

Auditory discrimination

Audition is hearing sound, and "The study of oral sounds used in communication is known as phonetics" (4, p. 3). The study of sounds as they are related to reading is called phonics (1, p. vii). The fact that phonetics and phonics are often used interchangeably does not alter their original meanings. Since language is a tool of society, it is important to know how the two terms are interchanged.

Discrimination means noting likenesses and differences. Auditory discrimination means noting likenesses and differences among sounds one hears. In brief, because auditory means sound and sound means phonetics (or phonics), auditory discrimination is in essence phonetic (or phonic) discrimination.

A question teachers and parents frequently ask is "When should instruction in phonics begin?" The most acceptable answer is: "From the very beginning of a child's school career."

In Chapter 1, much was said about the phonological wealth of children entering school. The children who can speak give, almost regardless of other circumstances, ample evidence that they have an ear for sound. A child displays an astounding blending of auditory-speech-meaning capabilities when, as so often happens, he hears a word new to him spoken only once and then, maybe a day or so later, uses it, speaking it correctly and in a right context without having heard it meantime. This feat occurs again and again in the preschool years. It prompted Otto Jespersen to say that, in his whole life, man achieves nothing so great as when he learns to talk (2, p. 103).

It is truly remarkable how well children observe sounds, how they learn to correct their own speech errors and those of others, and how they constantly add to their word wealth. The sound wealth children bring with them to school is fabulous. Even the poorest is wealthy.

Auditory-discrimination instruction capitalizes on this wealth and proceeds to make the children articulate about it, how to mine and refine it and use it deliberately. The way to start is to use words they know and to keep the decisions they must make simple and within their power.

Some training can be initiated on the very first day of school. Use a pupil's name, particularly one that has distinct ending sounds like Bill, Jane, Tom, or Ann. Say to the whole class, "I am going to say a word and you tell me if it sounds like Bill or if it does not." Then ask Bill to stand up so that all eyes and ears will be focused on Bill and say, but without distortion, the word *hill*. Some youngster will always recognize that *Bill* and *hill* sound very much alike and will say so. This gives the teacher an excellent opportunity so say, "Yes, *Bill* and *hill* sound alike."

This can be repeated with other words: *pill, fill, book, will, door, mill*, and so on. Notice that the first two words are like *Bill* but that the third is sharply different. Then the next word is like *Bill*, and so the sounds go, back and forth from like to different, with only one discrimination decision to be made.

The next day, another pupil's name can be used in the same way. Auditory training has thus been started, and it can be continued at a pace in keeping with the children's responses. The decision making has been kept simple: "*Yes*, it is" and "*No*, it is not."

A way to increase the challenge and the number of decisions is to present two words at a time. The key word may be *Ann*. Two other words spoken by the teacher may be *can* and *sit*. The decision that must be made is how to select the word that sounds like *Ann*. This type of activity can be repeated as frequently as desired or needed.

In each instance, the words that sound alike are rhyme words, with direct auditory attention to the vowel sounds. To implement this training, reading poetry aloud is most advisable; some reading can be done every day. In addition, the reading and repeating of common nursery rhymes helps sharpen the ear.

Auditory-visual discrimination

The functional use of language to relate an experience and dictate a story, such as described in Chapter 2, creates a circumstance in which communication prevents discrete introduction to phonic skills. Letters are not divorced from the service they render as *units* to represent sounds in a word; words are not isolated but represent *classes* as they function in a semantic or sentence context; the *relations* of words, as they are joined by syntactical rules, serve functionally in continuous communication.

Even though language usage is discursive and does not allow diverse events to be presented in their coincidence, our thinking processes allow for astounding coincidence and, as a result, analyzing them sequentially as first, second, third, is fallacious. While knowledge of sounds and the letters that represent them is helpful, analysis by breaking up coherent wholes or semantic units into so-called phonetic elements divorces the value of words and sounds from their communication purpose. So it is not astounding at all that so-called phonic systems and so-called linguistic systems show lack of agreement. The processes they are trying to analyze are those in which sounds communicate meaning and should not be interpreted to be those in which sounds are broken into incoherent units. Effective teaching of phonics, therefore, must avoid artificial phonic analysis of the word-learning process and keep teaching-learning focused on discursive communication and semantics.

Accordingly, one does not develop a sight vocabulary by using words in isolation, one at a time, or by illogical repetition of words with the idea that frequency of contact is an aid to retention ("Run, Dick, run, run, run"), or by warped discursive and semantic elements assembled in the name of linguistic uniformity ("Can Dan fan Pan?") Quite the contrary, words whose sounds and usages are known by children are used by them to present semantically functional ideas. From a communication context, words become identifiable in print, because of their primacy in context (*Snow White*), their attributes as parts of speech (*White* noun, *run* action verb, *pretty* qualifying adjective), their position in context (title, last word in story), their functional repetition (four different uses of *Snow White*), their discursive usage to communicate (declarative, imperative, interrogative), or the general semantics of denotation and connotation (*snow, Snow White, snowy*).

One does not first teach sounds or letter names or a sight vocabulary in isolation. One does not teach all the possible auditory-discrimination skills first, either, and then, weeks later, try to link them with a sight vocabulary acquired in isolation. Quite the contrary, auditory discrimination can be linked with visual discrimination from the very beginning of the reading-to-learn learning-to-read program. (This point is also made in Chapter 2.)

In brief, as soon as one word is recognized in print, as soon as it becomes a sight word, it can be used for auditory-visual discrimination training. If all or many of the children recognize *snow* at sight, the word can be written on the chalkboard. Now, while all eyes focus on the word, the teacher proceeds to audition by saying a word like *throw* and asking the class or a member of the class to decide whether it sounds like *snow*. *Eyes* are *focused* on a printed word and *ears* are *tuned* to a spoken word. In the all-auditory approach, it was suggested that a pupil's name be used and that he stand so that all eyes could focus on him. The parallel here may readily be seen.

As more words are learned by sight recognition, they become available for auditory-visual discrimination exercises. From the "Snow White" story, *cage* and *table* were recognized readily by many. Then in other reading, words like *turtle, fort, race, funny, slow*, and, of course, the names of the children were recognized. It is not necessary to wait until fifty or more words have been learned, as was recommended once upon a time.

Every day, some training in auditory discrimination and in auditory-visual discrimination *must* be done. The more proficient the children become, the more apt they are to transfer the skill and unlock more words in their individually dictated stories to add them to their word banks and reading finesse. They unlock these words because they know they are their words, facilitating recognition and escalating the number of words learned.

It is a simple psychological matter to increase the complexity of sound-letter learning. If two words are used, pupils must be increasingly more attentive. For instance, *snow* and *turtle* can be written on the chalkboard and the children can be asked to select the one that agrees with *slow*, with *myrtle*, and so on. Then three and four words can be used, sharply increasing the complexity of the task.

By this time, pupils will be ready to shift attention from the total word, or its rhyming vowel element, to the beginning sounds and the letters that represent them. Again a start is made with one word on an auditory basis. This time, though, the start is made with words that begin with a single consonant—*table, turtle, race*, and so on. The children must always hear the sound discriminately. Then, as soon as possible, attention must be shifted to auditory-visual training by proceeding in the same manner as described for word endings.

Write the word *table* on the chalkboard. Then say, "Does the word I say begin like table or does it not? *Take*." Then use words like *talk, town, boy, time, run, taste*. Next, write two words on the chalkboard or have the children select two words from their file boxes. Either way, use two words such as *table* and *ball*. Now say words like *take, boy, book, toy, big, ten*. Notice that the first sound in each spoken word agrees with one or the other of the two test words. Much practice of this kind should be done daily.

A good next step, after two or three known words have been set up in a column for selection and discrimination, is to ask the children to underline the letter that represents the beginning sound. The words *turtle, fort,* and *race* may appear in a column with a word like *town* the auditory stimulus word:

town	*fun*	*table*	*ring*
<u>t</u>urtle	turtle	<u>t</u>urtle	turtle
fort	<u>f</u>ort	fort	fort
race	race	race	<u>r</u>ace

Now the children are identifying a sound-letter combination while the letter remains in a semantic sound unit, a word. The letter *t* remained in the sound context with the five other letters and all six represented *turtle,* but only *t* represented the beginning sound. If the children have not as yet learned the names of the letters, now is a superb time to do so without confusing the letter names with the sounds they represent.

Words that begin with blends may also be used. It is wise in the beginning to use all words with blends and not mix blends and single-letter beginnings in one exercise. In blends, of course, the children underline two letters. For instance:

stay	*tree*	*spin*	*bring*
snow	slow	<u>sp</u>ots	plenty
<u>st</u>ick	<u>tr</u>ouble	blows	green
Alice	Spotty	play	<u>br</u>own

Always be sure that <u>auditory</u> <u>training</u> is done *first* and frequently thereafter. The children must be able to hear the sounds selectively if they are to apply discriminate sound knowledge to words and letters.

Diagraphs occur with considerable frequency. Children ask about them or use them incorrectly if they are not dealt with:

wheel	*change*	*that*
<u>wh</u>ite	<u>ch</u>imney	shoot
she	shop	church
thing	this	<u>th</u>ere

Another good activity is to ask what letter begins a word the teacher speaks. The teacher may say *boy* and the child should respond "The name of the letter is *b*," or he might write the letter or do both. This kind of response may seem a bit awkward but it helps fix the name-of-the-letter idea and avoids confusing the name with the sound.

An excellent variation of this is to say a word such as *boy* and ask all the children to find a word in their word banks that begins in the same way. Children love this. By the end of September, everyone has words in his word bank. Be sure that the word banks include names of children in the room. Slow learners are especially responsive to this and can soon have a considerable number of names—words—in their boxes. A child does not add another's name to his word bank unless he really knows it, though. Just to add names and stuff the box defeats its purpose.

Another step to take is to ask the children to supply a word that begins with the same letter as a spoken word. This proves to be rather demanding for some, and it must be used with caution. As is readily apparent, selecting a word from memory is like using a skill very much akin to spelling a word.

Once children have had experience with such activities, they soon learn to engage in them on their own. They do this by selecting partners or by forming small groups.

PHONIC BOOTH

If a phonic booth has not been set up by this time, by all means it should be now. A phonic booth or phonic corner requires some privacy for both the participants and the class. One teacher set up a wooden box she had obtained in a nearby store (screens can be used, too). The box was about 1 ½ feet by 4 feet on the base and 4 feet high. One end and one side were removed. Two chairs were placed in the box on the base with a small table between them in the middle. The space was big enough for children to get in and out with ease and small enough to be cozy and offer some privacy. The box was decorated with a false window on the outside; on the inside, where the children sat, the walls were covered with words and with a letter or letters underlined, such as boy, tree, chair, and three, scattered all over the wall in different positions and different colors. This booth proved to be a boon to the phonic training program, especially for the slower children. Phonic "teachers" were designated for the booth and were available if someone wanted help, and all did. The pupils chosen as "teachers" were the ones best with these skills. Any pupil could approach a "teacher" with his word bank and suggest they use the booth for phonic help. Of course, the "teachers" also sought out pupils. The booth was popular throughout the year and most helpful.

SUMMARY

It is apparent that by this time much practical sound training has been given. By starting with the rhyme of words or word endings, attention was focused on vowels, and this was helpful because they represent the predominant sound carrier. Auditory vowel readiness was being established.

When the switch was made to the beginning sounds and alliteration (*t*ip, *t*ap, *t*oe), attention was directed to consonants. When a person attacks a word he does not recognize at sight, he invariably does so from left to right in American English. This means he deals with beginning sounds first and, since most of the beginning sounds are represented by consonants, the approach being taught is in keeping with the demands of most of the word circumstances.

It is evident by now, too, that there is an order for teaching sound knowledge and for combining it with sight knowledge. The order for teaching is a pragmatic functional arrangement of sounds. The system for teaching is based on a practical application of the psychology of learning, which requires action and decision making on the part of the learner.

Letter substitution, or word families

The old game of building word families is just as captivating and beneficial today as it was a century and more ago. The label "word families" seems more appropriate and arouses more emotional warmth than any other label such as "letter substitution," "consonant substitution," or "linguistic substitution." Whatever you call it, the practice has tremendous utility and promotes a great deal of interest. One of the best summations of it was made by a six-year-old who said, "Gee, I got eight words from one word." Thereafter, in that room the children would talk about a five-word word or a nine-word word and so on and were constantly making words. One stimulus, for example, might be *r*un, from which can be derived *s*un, *f*un, *b*un, *g*un, *n*un, *p*un.

The procedure is simple and puts psychological learning principles to work. The words are always placed in columns and each word can readily be compared with a word above or below it. Transfer of knowledge occurs. Skill in blending sounds is enhanced. Letter order or spelling consciousness is fostered. Nonsense words are made from time to time, and they require a more independent sound-blending skill and are a bigger challenge.

Start with a common word, such as *Bill*:

Bill	*boy*	*make*	*go*	*like*
hill	toy	take	so	bike
will	joy	lake	no	Mike
mill	Roy	rake		tike
pill		sake		

One should not be hesitant about changes in word endings. They also fit the comprehensive-family plan. When the children show some proficiency with beginning-consonant substitution, switch to consonants on the ends of words:

can	*sat*	*his*	*big*
cat	sad	him	bit
car	Sam	hit	bid
cap	sap	hip	bin
			Bill

One should also not be hesitant about blends and diagraphs as they fit the family situation:

stick	*snap*	*brown*
trick	trap	clown
chick	flap	frown
sick	tap	crown
Dick	cap	town

When blends are used, pupils soon discover the need for a list of letter combinations. This provides an excellent opportunity to do two things. First, return to single-letter substitution and show children how they can proceed with orderly use of the consonants in the alphabet. As a matter of fact, it is advisable to give each child a consonant *key* by providing him with a 3-×-5-inch card on which the consonants are written in alphabetical order. The teacher should write or type the letters so that they are distinct and uniform:

```
b c d f g h j k l m n
p q r s t v w x y z
```

Now return to a word like *Bill* and let them see how this orderly help works:

Bill	kill	sill
dill	lill	till
fill	mill	vill
gill	nill	will
hill	pill	zill
jill	rill	

By proceeding this way, the children get more words, do more blending, and occasionally come up with a "word" they have never heard—*lill, rill, vill, zill*. This is excellent: If they can blend these sounds together and pronounce such "words" correctly, then one can feel quite confident that they have grasped the basic principle. This ability will be helpful when they need to deal with polysyllabic words. However, be sure the children don't just make lists of words without having an opportunity to use the words by reading them to each other or the teacher.

On the same card the teacher can add common blends and digraphs much as follows:

b	c	d	f	g	h	j	k	l m
n	p	q	r	s	t	v	w	x y z
bl	cr	fr	ph	sh	sn	sw	wh	
br	dr	gl	pl	sk	sp	th		
ch	dw	gr	pr	sl	st	tr		
cl	fl	kn	sc	sm	str	tw		

Making words through word families is a useful activity for the rest of the year. It does many things for the child, and it proves particularly helpful when creative writing blossoms and spelling becomes more demanding. Many a word can be spelled by means of the family-association plan.

Now the phonic booth increases in popularity. So many people want to use it that the demand exceeds the accommodation. So pupils can get together elsewhere, two or three desks may be moved together or a small table may serve. Space and place need not in any way slow down progress.

One group of four boys, buzzing away around a table, when asked what they were busy at, answered that they were in "the manufacturing business." "Oh? How is that?" they were asked. "We are manufacturing words," they replied almost in unison, and they were. They had their consonant keys and were making words. Word manufacturing is a very profitable business to be in when one is in first grade.

Vowel keys

All the activities described thus far have proven so useful almost simultaneously that it is regrettable that they cannot all be presented at one time. Spreading skill activities could imply a discreteness that does not exist in actual language use. In addition to the spread imposed by space and order is the fact that some children move rapidly and some do not. This program does not harness any child. Children may learn as they can and at their own rates of assimilation and accommodation. Because all are invited and encouraged to be active participants, all tend to make better progress than they would otherwise.

By the time children have progressed to the vowel-key stage, they will have had much experience with words, with letters and how they represent sounds, with word families, with blending sounds, and with attacking the words in their dictated stories that they do not recognize at sight. All this provides superb readiness for another step and another skill in the word-attack armory.

In the recognition and use of consonants, the idea of consonant substitution is paramount. Not only can word families be enlarged by substituting consonants but also some consonants are substituted to represent different sounds, as *k* in *cat* and *s* in *city* and so on. Accordingly the concept of consonant substitution takes on long-term utility, as will become apparent in the section on dictionary usage. In a similar way, a major understanding about <u>vowels</u> is their <u>variability</u>. One vowel represents several different sounds. The concepts of <u>consonant substitution</u> and <u>vowel variability</u> are constantly reinforced because of their utility.

One procedure that allows for small increments of progress in the right direction is to return to the word-family game. One way is to make words by changing a word beginning and then by changing endings:

cat	let	black	boy
fat	met	track	toy
fan	men	tram	ton
man	mew	tray	tot

Or the children can make a freewheeling substitution in much the same pattern:

cat	bath	fable	match	jar
can	math	Mable	catch	jail
man	maple	mantle	car	Jane
tan	table			

Another way is to keep the medial vowel constant and change both ends:

cat	net	tin	not	hut
man	new	sit	rod	bud
far	ten	him	bow	pun
lad	beg	did	log	sum

This causes children to focus on vowels as well as consonants and shows them how medial vowel sounds sometimes change depending on the accompanying letters.

From this step, changing the medial vowels follows rather readily. First, list the five vowels as a guide: a e i o u. Then the words can be made:

not	ten	hut	far	beg
net	tan	hit	for	big
nut	tin	hat	fur	bag
nit	ton	hot	fer	bug
nat	tun	het	fir	bog

From this to the construction of a vowel key is a ready transition. Start with a one-syllable word containing a long $\bar{a}$ sound such as *āte*. The best plan is to use the key word used in dictionary keys. By so doing the alphabet-card key and the key in the dictionaries the children use will be in agreement. The practicality of the key is readily apparent, first in auditory discrimination: "Does the vowel heard in *day* have the same sound as the vowel heard in *ate?*" Then try such words as *make, big, late, car, cake, cane, sit.* Do this until the decision can be made readily and, of course, correctly.

The teacher can start each pupil's vowel key by writing on a 3-×-5-inch card the five vowels and then a key word for long $\bar{a}$: *āte*. Be sure to use the correct diacritical mark.

a	e	i	o	u
āte				

Next add a word like *căt*, with the short *ă* sound. Again do auditory exercises first with words with short *ă* and then with words using another short vowel. Next put *āte* and *căt* together and do sound-discriminating exercises again. First, use words that have either a short *ă* or a long *ā*. Then use words that have different vowels so that the pupil must decide that the vowel heard represents neither a long *ā* or a short *ă*. Thus, *vowel variability* is introduced.

Proceed in the same way with each of the five vowels. Each time, add the key word to the vowel key. Vowel variability is now brought into sharper focus, both visually and phonically. A key may appear as follows:

a	e	i	o	u
āte	mē	īce	nō	ūse
căt	gĕt	sit	nŏt	cŭt

This accomplished, add the *r*-influenced vowels one at a time. Words like *cär, hër, sïr, nör, für* serve as good key words. Be sure always to start with auditory-discrimination training.

Not all children will build vowel keys at the same time. But once the construction of keys starts in a room, other pupils become interested and attentive and frequently exceed teacher expectations.

Vowel keys can become an iron curtain for poor teaching. Supervisors, principals, and visitors are duly impressed when they see vowel keys on desk tops of first-graders. But the keys can be almost completely non-functional if they are foisted on the children. This when it happens is a terrible loss, because the attitudes of the children are influenced as well as their failure to acquire an essential skill. Vowel keys should not become a decorative front.

When does a vowel key serve pupils? Before a key is built in any classroom, the teacher should be sure that she can answer this question with conviction.

A vowel key helps children attack words in their experience stories. Because the words represent the words that the children speak and that already have sound value for them, the pupils' chances of unlocking, or sounding out a word are increased if they can use vowels as well as consonants.

A key is useful in unlocking words that occur in sources other than a pupil's or his classmates' dictation. He may be attacking a word in a library book or a newspaper or an encyclopedia.

A key is especially helpful in creative writing, too. As was shown in Chapter 4, pupils at first tend to leave off vowels in words in which consonant sounds seem to predominate, as in *hf* for *half*, *dfrrt* for *different*, *crmms* for *Christmas*. But as they continue with creative writing and increasingly develop a spelling conscience, they look for help with vowels. Then they turn to their vowel keys.

A word of caution is in order about how easily use of a vowel key for writing can defeat both purposes. The children may begin to feel guilty about their spelling and curb their writing; in that case, the vowel key becomes a whip rather than a tool. It should be pointed out to them occasionally that they might use their vowel keys for help with a word, or, better yet, when they ask for help with the spelling of a word, they can be shown how their vowel keys might be used. The concept of vowel variability thus becomes firmly established. Its long-term utility will become increasingly apparent in the next section.

Structural variations

When children talk, they correctly use such meaning changes as *run-runs-running*, *ball-balls*, *paint-painted-paints-painting*, *slow-slowly*, *rain-rainy-raining*. (A reexamination of the dictated stories in Chapter 2 show this to be true.) They appreciate the functional uses of inflectional and derivative changes.

When they reread their dictated stories, they learn to read such words without confusion. They see how *run, runs, running*, are different, and they add a card to their word banks for each word change. Some teachers reinforce visual recognition by making direct comparisons of words in columns:

run	paint	rain
runs	painted	rainy
running	painting	raining

Taught this way, the children experience little trouble in dealing with such changes. As a matter of fact, they soon become proficient at changing words deliberately. Motivation for this runs high, because children can display a new skill and they can add words to their word banks. Knowing words like *snow, call, walk, pull, fish, watch,* and *go* leads to ready change to and recognition of *snowing, snowed, calling, called,* and so on.

Success with such changes influences creative writing. After the first flurry of writing, children begin to be attentive to word endings and spell words much as required. (Another look at Chapter 4 on creative writing will provide evidence of this.)

When creative writing is daily and the stories become longer and longer, another very interesting sensitivity appears. The more children write, the more they face the demands of spelling and the more resourceful they become. Much of their spelling is phonological. When a polysyllabic word like *Halloween* is spelled, it may very well be done by phonological parts or syllables and be produced as *hal O en, needle* may be spelled *ned l, doctor* as *dot r, pumpkin* as *puanp cinn.* Another interesting variation at about this stage of progress is the capitalization of the first letter of each syllable. *Decorate* would be written *DeCorAte, West Chester* as *West ChesTer, Christmas* as *CisMas, Tannenbaum* as *Ten N Bam, Museum* as *Mu See Um,* and so on. This is more apt to occur when words appear in a title and so may reflect sensitivity to capital letters in titles.

Numerous opportunities to use and produce language leads to a seemingly natural way of dealing with variations. At such times, as the pupils begin to respond, more teaching opportunities become available and the teacher can capitalize on the alertness evidenced by systematic teaching of discrimination. For instance, some children delight in locating a polysyllabic word in a dictionary and seeing that they have syllabized it correctly on their own.

Dictionary usage

In Chapter 2, an early use of the dictionary was made in reference to word banks. As soon as pupils accumulate so many sight words that locating a word they want becomes cumbersome and time-consuming, the orderly arrangement of a word bank takes on significance. The moment an alphabetical system is introduced, the children recognize its merits. They delight in taking their twenty-five or more words and alphabetizing them.

Organizing the word bank yields a number of practical learning opportunities:

1. The children recognize the value and purpose of the orderly arrangement of letters alphabetically.
2. The letter order is now known functionally and not by rote.
3. Positions within the alphabet are learned through practical usage. It is soon learned, for instance, that the letter *b* is near the beginning, *m* near the middle, *w* near the end. Repeated filing of words establishes such spatial relationships functionally.
4. When a word is filed, its first letter becomes significant. Not only does it represent a sound and serve pronunciation purposes but it also serves either a filing or a location purpose.
5. The subtlety of some sounds and letters is brought into sharp focus. To file (*k*) *car*, (*s*) *city*, (*ch*) *chief*, (*f*) *phone*, (*skw*) *squeeze*, (*sh*) *shake*, (*gh*) *ghost*, (*j*) *giant*, (*wh*) *who*, and (*th*) *then* makes consonant discrimination sharper. Also, filing words like (*a*) *apple, ate, are*; (*e*) *east, end, earn*, and so on requires special attention to vowels and the variability of vowel sounds.
6. All the attention directed to beginning letters, letter order, and the sounds that letters represent calls attention to the order of letters within words. Thus, sensitivity to spelling or the letter order within words is increased.

The day is almost at hand when the hideous-looking letters of alphabet charts no longer appear around the walls of the rooms of every first grade and other primary grades. Almost everyone who attended first grade before 1965 has seen a huge alphabet staring admonishingly across the room. The big capital letters followed by the sad and diminutive lowercase letters challenged each child. Not only were the letters large, much larger than anything ever produced by a child on paper, but also they were up so high and so far beyond eye level that they looked distorted.

At last, schools are providing each child with personal desk copies that are clear and readable and adjusted to their size. This alphabet helps in the early use of a file-box word bank, because letter location can be easily checked on it. From the desk alphabet and word-bank filing to the dictionary is an easy transition. Each child should have a copy of a desk dictionary, such as *Webster's Elementary Dictionary* (5). The children must have a real dictionary, not a "Pixie" dictionary.

Now some learning sport can be indulged in. The children can be asked to locate any letter and its first entry. Some are sure to have trouble with this, so teams may be formed. But their delight when they are successful is well worth the effort. If the alphabet has index tabs along the side, the dictionary is especially helpful. (Tabbed dictionaries cost a bit more, but the return far exceeds the cost.) All the children might locate the same word, one that all can read, of course. So the teacher might write *snow* on the board and have each child or each team locate it in the dictionary.

Once begun, interest in the dictionary persists. Some children locate each word in their word banks and enter the dictionary page number on the back of the word card. Some select one word under each letter entry in their word banks and locate that in the dictionary.

As time goes by and progress is made in the various phases of the approach, the likelihood of pupils turning to the dictionary increases. The building and use of the consonant key and, particularly, the vowel key results in more frequent reference. If the card vowel key is the same as the dictionary's, the children should be alerted that this is the card's source. This is a good time to show the bright ones how phonetic respellings make use of consonant substitution, the vowel key, and the diacritical marks. It is not at all uncommon for a number of bright first-graders to use a dictionary for pronunciation by the phonetic respellings. Some children begin to use the dictionary to edit their own creative writing. Caution must be exercised with this commendable practice; children should not get the impression that dictionary usage and perfect spelling is the object of creative writing. Such an attitude could have dire consequences. The purpose of creative writing is to express ideas in writing, not to teach spelling or dictionary usage or editing.

Introduction of dictionary usage is not delayed until third or fourth grade. As can be seen, elementary steps in dictionary usage can be introduced early in first grade and steadily augmented as circumstances and abilities warrant. Approaching the dictionary this way alerts children early in their school careers to one of the most functional tools in a scholar's life.

Not all the skills of dictionary usage are taught at this point, of course. An account of what can be done makes this quite clear. The refined skills of dictionary usage for learning etymologies, pronunciation, synonyms and antonyms, usage levels and dialect distribution, common English spellings and for consulting the many explanatory notes require special training and maturity. For some, this may be a lifetime process.

Roots in action

Printed language, like spoken language, is a form of symbolic condensation and is regulated by <u>interpersonal</u> <u>exchange</u> and <u>cooperation</u>. "Thanks to language," says Piaget, "the child has become capable of evoking absent

situations and of liberating himself from the frontiers of space and time
. . . also . . . objects and events . . . are experienced within a conceptual and rational framework which enriches the understanding of
them" (3, p. 89). From the time sounds are associated with specific actions
and the acquisition of language, children gradually enter an objective
universe. They do so by a series of adaptations of linguistic fitting and
alerting or internalizing and externalizing or assimilating and accommodat-
ing. In fact, it is to the degree that children are able to communicate with
language that they learn to cope with their social world and its unfolding
realities as well as with their inner lives.

Oral-language facility is acquired by children either spontaneously or
by elicitation in a world of increasing intercommunications with adults,
siblings, and peers. Facility with printed language should be acquired in a
similar way. Children can then adapt thought to others and to reality
more effectively. This is why the Language-Experience Approach to
learning to read provides a functional transition from oral language to
printed language for all children, almost regardless of their abilities and
backgrounds.

The communication of ideas, either spontaneous or elicited, provides the
teaching vehicle. Gradually, children discover the riches of the world of
realities through their own interpretation, that of their peers and teachers,
and, through books, that of authors. At first, their responses, oral and
written, are rudimentary and closely linked to actions, but, as they continue to use written language of their own creation and by others, they discover the need for certain rules. So they begin to make adjustments that
reflect certain common obligations.

Methods for decoding a printed word not recognized at sight are first
discovered and refined by decoding their own recorded language. Recall
and recognition are thus facilitated by authorship and semantics. Children
make ready and constant application when they read their own language
and then that of their peers and finally that found in books and other
printed sources. Thus, reading and word-attack application is closely
linked to interest and activity-related values.

Techniques for unlocking words are acquired functionally. When a
skill helps a reader along the printed pathway to comprehension, its
utility is recognized and its use becomes efficient. Word-attack skills are
acquired because they are functional and facilitate comprehension. Thanks
to printed language and the rich exchange among individuals that it
affords, the refinement of word-attack skills grows more functional. Rules

are not memorized or taught in isolation as a means of readying a child to deal with printed language. The lack of consistency within the majority of so-called phonic rules is recognized functionally. As a result, variability does not produce the anxiety of failure.

Apparently, then, phonics must be kept in perspective to recognize its contribution to reading and the learning-to-read process. The following generalizations about word-attack skills and phonics are timely and relevant.

1. Children should *always* read for meaning.

2. Words to be dealt with should *always* appear in meaningful context.

3. Context or meaning clues to word recognition should *always* be tried first when attacking a word not recognized at sight.

4. Phonic generalizations are useful while learning to read. This is true particularly if the printed words being dealt with are already a functional part of the subject's speaking-meaning or oral-language vocabulary.

5. Generalizations about structure are useful while learning to read. Knowledge of common inflectional changes and affixes helps the reader deal with words that are already part of his speaking-meaning vocabulary.

6. Ability to substitute consonant sounds, to recognize variations of vowel sounds as marked diacritically, and to blend sounds together are essential to dictionary usage.

7. A dictionary helps word recognition for both pronunciation and meaning. For pronunciation, a dictionary provides phonetic respellings of consonant substitution, diacritical vowel marking, syllabification, and accent. The dictionary also provides a diacritical key for convenience and accuracy. Meaning clues are provided through definitions, illustrative usages, word histories, and pictures.

8. Rules are so great in number and so complex in detail that only the most skilled phonetician is apt to know them all and use them correctly. All readers depend on a dictionary for help. Therefore, efficient use of the dictionary should be taught, starting with the first grade.

Conclusion

This chapter presents compactly the basic word-attack skill program of the learning reader. It explains and illustrates why acquisition of the fundamental skills is neither complex nor difficult. Each year some children starting to school for the first time have already learned to read and have developed, much on their own, functional word-attack skills.

As in all communication, word-attack learning should always give first attention to the use of context or meaning clues to recognition. This means that skills are first developed by using words selected from a language and a morpheme sound unit.

Word-attack skills serve a reader to help him reach into his speaking-meaning vocabulary and to use the dictionary. The first takes precedence in the early stages of reading instruction, because the children already possess large functional speaking-meaning vocabularies. As soon as the words met in print are not found in their speaking-meaning vocabularies, they must turn to a dictionary.

Sound pedagogical training is accomplished by using the children's speaking-meaning vocabularies and then gradually going on to the vocabularies of others as expressed in books, magazines, and newspapers. Sound psychological training comes by using practices of learning based on logical usage, meaningful repetition, meaningful transfer to new contexts, instant feedback, and frequent retention exercises.

The teaching of word recognition must have its roots in the pupils' actions. From the time children first associate sound—words—with specific actions and begin to acquire language, they gradually enter an increasingly more objective universe. Their knowledge must govern the purpose and action of functional word-attack-skill teaching. When it is, the utility of skills is recognized and their use becomes increasingly more efficient.

Bibliography

1. Cordts, Anna D. *The Word Method of Teaching Phonics*. Boston, Mass.: Ginn, 1929.
2. Jespersen, Otto. *Language: Its Nature, Development, and Origin*. New York: Macmillan, 1949.
3. Piaget, Jean. *Six Psychological Studies*. Edited by David Elkind. New York: Random House, 1967.
4. Thomas, Charles Kenneth. *An Introduction to the Phonetics of American English*. New York: Ronald Press, 1947.
5. *Webster's Elementary Dictionary*. Springfield, Mass.: G. and C. Merriam, 1966.

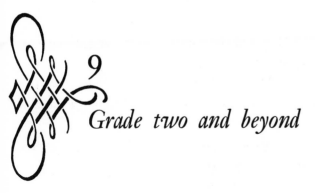

9
Grade two and beyond

The material presented thus far has dealt with the introduction and use of the Language-Experience Approach primarily in the first grade. This chapter tells in some detail how the procedure can be adapted and used in grades two, three, four, and on.

The chapter is in eleven major parts. The first part reviews the features of the program in the first year. The second part lists features that are characteristic of the second year. The third part describes the cycle of group and individualized Directed Reading-Thinking Activities. The fourth part tells about the dictating and recording suggested for second grade. The fifth part discusses creative writing and how it develops. The sixth part describes the developing use of word attack. The seventh part discusses the increasing importance of libraries as a source of reading material. The eighth part enlarges on the nature of sharing and how intra- and interschool sharing can be done. The ninth part presents a detailed account of how formal spelling is introduced and taught. The tenth part tells about third grade and beyond. The eleventh part explains how one of the principal assets of the approach is the progress in social behavior that develops in children.

The reader is asked to read the following objectives and make deductions about the answers. He must understand that his comprehension is determined largely by the degree to which he studies the objectives and makes them his. The intellectual commitment that results will help keep him on course and sharpen his comprehension.

1. Describe the first-year features of the Language-Experience Approach.
2. Tell about the signs of progress that are germane to this approach during the first year.

Upon reading the second part, the reader should be able to meet the following objectives:

1. Tell how the summer away from school between first and second grades can influence reading achievement.
2. Name the nine features of the second-year program.

Upon reading the third part, the reader should be able to meet the following objectives:

1. Explain how the individualized and group DRTA cycles cause children to examine their reading interests carefully.
2. How does a child get to know himself better?
3. Describe how the group DRTA's become more sophisticated and scholarly.

Upon reading the fourth part, the reader should be able to meet the following objectives:

1. Tell why dictating is continued in second grade and how it is different from dictation in first grade.
2. Explain how and why children can be recorders or secretaries.

Upon reading the fifth part, the reader should be able to meet the following objectives:

1. Describe what happens when creative writing is reintroduced and how changes occur.
2. Explain how editing attempts increase and why.

Upon reading the sixth part, the reader should be able to meet the following objectives:

1. Describe how the word-attack skill program is extended and refined.
2. Explain why dictionary usage increases.

Upon reading the seventh part, the reader should be able to answer the following objectives:

1. Tell why and how the Language-Experience Approach makes increasingly heavy demands on libraries.
2. Discuss the increasing importance of individual visits to the library.

Upon reading the eighth part, the reader should be able to meet the following objectives:

1. Explain how each planning session produces change.
2. Describe how the reading and collecting of ideas is influenced by sharing time.
3. Explain why it is important to have different ways of sharing.
4. Tell why it is timely to introduce a judging board.

Upon reading the ninth part, the reader should be able to meet the following objectives.

1. Describe in detail how spelling levels are determined.
2. Describe the test-study and self-correction methods.
3. Explain why it is essential that instruction in spelling be differentiated.

Upon reading the tenth part, the reader should be able to meet the following objectives:

1. Distinguish between features that develop in the third grade and beyond.
2. Describe how and why the three-draft idea becomes functional.
3. Discuss the use of a schedule chart.

Upon reading the eleventh part, the reader should be able to meet the following objectives:

1. Describe the differences apparent among children who are taught in an action-oriented school.
2. Explain why the socialization of behavior resulting from the Language-Experience Approach is so significant.

A comment heard repeatedly in one form or another was recorded in a statement of a second-grade teacher. She had taught in her community for many years and enjoyed an excellent reputation as a teacher. She had mastered the use of basic-reader materials and did as efficient a job as one can do with their limitations. At a staff gathering of all the second-grade teachers in her district late one September, she stood up and said, "I have never had so many children who knew so many words and know what to do when they get to a 'new' word." It was evident to all that she was enthusiastic about this and that she was giving it her tacit endorsement. Her first measure of achievement, though, was "words known," her second "attacking an unknown" word. This is typical of persons oriented to basic readers rather than reading measured by attitudes, comprehension, library usage, resourcefulness, cooperative communication, interests and tastes, and the like. Her appraisal of achievement is indicative of that of many teachers, both experienced and new.

Test results, as reported in the Appendixes, provide evidence of the possibility of objective appraisal of basic-reader and language-experience approaches. The achievement of children measured at the end of the first year, in the beginning of the second year, and on a carefully controlled replication study showed astounding performances in the language-experience programs. The tests used in these studies measured only certain limited aspects of reading achievement (1, 5). Not measured were the children's regard for reading, their resourcefulness as readers, their range of interests and tastes, their versatility with language, and their cooperative and cooperative sharing. Furthermore, the measure of achievement in creative writing was an adapted test and, while results showed excellent achievement, a test with more validity and reliability might have shown even greater progress.

End-of-the-year appraisal by first-grade teachers was enthusiastic but not wildly so; this always happens where the Cognitive Approach is newly adopted. The calm conviction registered by the teachers testifies convincingly to their success. It is true, of course, that the Hawthorne effect may operate but it is tempered by the self-regulated firmness of the teachers' convictions; by the fact that the teachers were not specially selected; by their subsequent teaching, which seldom, if ever, reverts to former practices; and, of course, by the knowledge that the effect can operate in all efforts. Closely related to the success of interest and activity is the self-evaluation that exerts its influence on teaching practices and beliefs; it may be said that success breeds success.

The first year

The principal features of cognitive-reading instruction are the degree to which teaching practices take advantage of the language wealth of children derived from their personal, social, and cultural experiences and interests and curiosities; talent for individual concentration and effective group collaboration; the feelings of mutual respect engendered; and intellectual capacity. The approach is centered in activity and respect for work that results from explicit or tacit accord. Skills are acquired functionally where understanding and communication are the aim. As a result, the skills are not just for verbal parroting and are truly respected in practice.

The principles of the approach are pragmatic and didactic communication. Dictation permits children to recount first-hand experiences arranged by the teacher, recount old experiences, and create stories. Accounts of fresh experiences elicited by the teacher can be less demanding than created stories in that the pupil has only to tell back. The ease with which accounts and new creations are made increases as children realize that their ideas and language are not only sought but accepted. Certainly the child respects the teacher, but there is also mutual respect between them.

The dictations provide a chronological record of performance. Each child can readily see his improvement from week to week and month to month. Any child can look back at any time and react, as one boy did, by saying "That's how I did when I was little." The evidence of progress is constantly available and reassuring: It shows changes in amount dictated; quality of dictation by sentences, vocabulary, and order of ideas; number of words underlined as known; and nature and quality of illustrations.

In addition, a child can reread his own dictations and those of his peers. He can compare his version of an experience with those of others.

The word bank provides a constant source of scholarly gratification and reassurance, too. The number of words known is a source of ego strength and fosters effort. The word bank is a treasure house—a word miser's cherished repository of wealth. Its alphabetic order is prestigious because it simulates understanding of the dictionary. The words can be used for auditory and auditory-visual discrimination training. The words provide the wherewithal of the creative assembling of ideas on a word-card holder. Questions can be addressed to the teacher and to classmates, and sentences and stories can be structured.

The classroom and school libraries provide many books, magazines, and newspapers in which words learned as early as the first day of school can be found or cut out. Before too long, entire books can be read. They can be read orally, to individual classmates, and to the entire class.

Auditory word attack, started on the first day of school, puts to work the phonological wealth the children have already acquired but now makes it more precise. Auditory-visual training links letters and the sounds they represent in the context of words. Consonant substitution rapidly enriches the word bank as different words become the base of large word families. Vowel variablility helps add words, helps in the pronouncing of words, and helps make spelling more accurate in creative writing. Dictionary usage is a marvelous ego-building source for budding scholars; new words as well as words from the word bank can be found there. The vowel key can be used in phonetic respellings.

Creative writing makes authors of the students. Now, whenever opportunity allows, a pupil can record his own ideas and no longer has to wait for a teacher to take his dictation. He can save his own writings and share them with his classmates and family. He can write messages of all kinds. He can use capital letters and periods and question marks; sometimes he can even use quotation marks and exclamation marks. His handwriting improves, as does his spelling. He approaches writing without anxiety of failure and yet is gradually led to evaluate his own writing.

The group Directed Reading-Thinking Activities give him an opportunity to show not only that he can say words but that he can think. He examines evidence and makes educated guesses. He knows how to prove he was right and how to change his mind if he is wrong. He does not fear being wrong because he is sharpening his thinking. He sees how his classmates evaluate circumstances, make predictions, prove points, and change their minds. He enjoys the intellectual challenge of give and take.

All in all, he has engaged in many activities that have challenged him, aroused his confidence, and showed him how to be resourceful and persistent. He has enjoyed reading about many things and sharing with others. He has felt that he was respected by his classmates as well as his teacher. From the start, his language and his ideas were accepted. Gradually, he changed some of his language as well as ideas, because he realized he could achieve things better that way. In brief, he has emerged as a young scholar intent on discovering and mastering man's accumulated knowledge in a steady, self-regulated, teacher-directed, affectively tempered way.

The second year

The principal features of the eclectic approach to reading instruction during the second year are similar to those of the first. Yet they are different because of increased maturity among the children and the reminiscent effect of the summer on the skills and abilities acquired.

THE SUMMER AWAY

School records show and teachers' opinions confirm that when children return to school in the fall to start their second year most of them have lost many of the skills acquired in first grade. This is especially true of reading skills. It is not at all uncommon in many school districts for all second-grade children to reread the last two levels of basic readers they had completed the previous year and reperform the skill activities. This review period usually continues for the first 6 to 8 weeks.

This practice reflects quite obviously on the nature and quality of learning and instruction in first grade. Not only have the memorized skills been forgotten in disuse but the attitudes toward reading so glibly voiced by children at the end of first grade have failed to prevail and now need to be shored up with coaxing.

Evidence in the Appendix corroborates the contrary fact that children nurtured on the eclectic approach not only maintained their skills and abilities but improved them. Their attitudes toward reading and creative writing were such that they practiced during the summer and consequently showed improvement. Of course, not all improved, but so many did to such a degree that overall they contributed to a resounding success story.

The opening of second grade in the fall did not expose the children to an extended period of review. The motivation was refreshingly stimulating. Some skills, such as how to deal with words not recognized at sight and word-attack skills, were reviewed. Also reviewed were skills of determining interests, selecting materials, and sharing. All this was done while reading, though, and not as isolated drills on warmed-over material.

THE FEATURES

At the beginning of the year, a new cycle of Directed Reading-Thinking Activities was activated and rotated monthly. The first month of school was devoted to an all-out language-arts effort that might also be referred to as individualized instruction founded on self-selection. October, the second month, introduced group Directed Reading-Thinking Activities and basic readers. On each succeeding month, emphasis and practices were alternated.

Dictation was initiated in September. For most of the students, dictation did not occur with the same frequency as it had in first grade.

Creative writing was reactivated and pursued in much the same manner as in first grade. Noticeable changes began to occur, however, and were increasingly more evident as the year proceeded.

Word-attack training was continued, extended, and refined as required by the growing vocabulary demands of the children and the materials they read. And, of course, this included dictionary usage.

Library usage, both in the classroom and in the school library, was reactivated.

The features of self-selection were refined and extended through structured planning, more selective choice of interests, and improved ways of sharing.

Formal spelling instruction on selected word lists differentiated according to ability was introduced in mid-October.

Among the seven- and eight-year-olds and children older, increased maturity and scholarly astuteness led to refined and creative reading and communication.

The progress and socialization of behavior resulted in increased mutual respect and a subordination of self to the laws of reciprocity.

Each of these features will be dealt with separately in the rest of the chapter; the activities will be enlarged on and conclusions will be drawn.

The new cycle

A distinguishing characteristic of cognitive reading is the manner in which it utilizes group and individualized instructional procedures. Both approaches have distinct advantages and entail practices that are excluded if just one or the other is used. In other words, any sound program of reading instruction must include both procedures.

It is imperative that the directing of reading activities start in the fall through activation of individualized self-selection practices. Many important opportunities for the teacher to learn about the pupils in her class are thus provided. The children also have a chance to examine themselves and their interests and abilities in the atmosphere of discovery.

A classroom library is available again and filled with books selected by the teacher and the librarian. The books vary in subject, covering a range of concepts in the sciences, social sciences, literature, and mathematics at different levels of readability.

The children reexamine their reading interests and abilities for a month, starting with the recounting of summertime activities, particularly reading activities, perhaps in the public libraries. School libraries are increasingly being kept open through the summer, too, and children may have availed themselves of such reading opportunities. Children who read will welcome talk about the reading they have done. Children who had limited or perhaps no opportunity to read will have had some experiences worth relating. Everyone's life has some episodes worth telling about.

This kind of warming up leads directly to an examination of the books in the classroom library, perhaps as a review led by the teacher. From this to a declaration of interests or preferences is an easy next step. Books are chosen from the classroom library by some; others may want to visit the school library. This visit is purposeful because each child has some idea about what he would like to find.

Word-attack skills learned in first grade are reviewed. Auditory-discrimination activities are used rather extensively. The word-family idea is reactivated with its use of consonant substitution and vowel variability. How to deal with a word not immediately recognized is also reviewed.

Sharing sessions are introduced, with short sessions held daily for a week or two. Then more structured sessions may be planned for the end of the month. This requires planning, preparation, and scheduling.

Depending on achievement levels, much use is made of dictated stories. Word banks are reopened or special word banks are begun for unusual words.

Sharing sessions about summer activities are held and creative writing about them is begun. Most of the children are eager to write. Some need reassurance. Again the children are urged to spell words the way they think they are spelled so that production is not stifled. Spelling this way shows quite clearly whether sounds have been associated effectively with letters. The spelling in the creative writing provides the best clues as to what phonic skills must be retaught.

Throughout September, the teacher is doubly alert. She notes levels of performance and inventories word-attack skill by noticing the nature of requests for help, responses to skill inquiries that she makes directly, and responsiveness to daily skill-training sessions. Specific needs of specific pupils are identified. She listens to sharing in front of the whole class and in small groups. But, particularly, she has especially helpful sharing sessions with each child. She notes the kinds of books they select for reading, the nature of each pupil's interests, and the efficiency of his book-card record-keeping. She asks each child to read aloud to her privately and to the class.

By the end of the month, both the teacher and the pupils will have discovered many things. Pupils will have started reading at a pace they can maintain, devoid of artificial pressures. It is almost like getting back into a swimming pool at the start of a new summer season by easing in gradually. Pupils find self-appraisal worth while and as a result of it approach reading and all language-arts activities cooperatively, confidently, and in a scholarly way. In addition, of course, the teacher learns a great deal about each child—his interests, initiative, word-attack skill, reading level, and resourcefulness. For both pupil and teacher, September is a marvelous way of getting acquainted at a pace that each can maintain.

In October, group Directed Reading-Thinking Activities are initiated. The children are grouped for levels each member can attain without frustration. Some can handle third-reader material with ease, some do best with second-reader books, and some may do best at the first-reader level. Three or four groups are organized: membership should not exceed ten in each.

The important goal of group instruction is to teach children to read in an intellectually critical way. They must learn to set purposes for reading, to examine material and select relevant facts, to weigh evidence so as to prove or disprove conjectures, to suspend final judgment until all available evidence has been examined. This is what group instruction is about. It poses a tremendously challenging opportunity. If inquiring, critical, and creative scholars are to be developed, this is when and how to begin.

Intragroup action provides the testing group, as all examine the same material. A pupil must take a position in the presence of the group and then prove or disprove the validity of his position by supplying evidence from the reading. The group and the teacher audit each performance and provide censorship. Each pupil is urged to establish and defend a position over and over again, so that he may achieve critical and creative reading performances.

It soon becomes apparent that what is done with the materials intellectually is more important in many ways than the material itself. A reading *process* is being taught. This is why basic readers can be used. Advantage lies with the use of well-structured material designed for purposeful scholarly reading, however.

It becomes apparent also that a group need not meet each day for directed reading-thinking sessions. Active participation in groups of eight or ten meeting only every other day is best. The anxieties that some teachers experience as they try to crowd three group sessions daily into time that barely allows for two are not worth while. Some teachers establish only two groups with as many as fifteen children in each, but this is self-defeating. If a group exceeds twelve, interaction is drastically limited. Circumstances do not allow it to be otherwise. Such grouping for DRTA reflects eventually on the quality of the teaching.

For the rest of the year, activities are alternated from month to month. One month, emphasis is on self-knowledge through individualized instruction and sharing sessions. Another month, emphasis is directed toward re-fined thinking habits acquired through group interaction. In all, there are five cycles in a 10-month term. More cycles can be planned if the change is made every three weeks. (Some schools prefer this because it coincides with a 6-week report-card schedule.)

Dictating and recording

Dictation is continued in the second year for two reasons. All the children benefit. Some of the slow children require the continued word learning that comes from dictation.

Children love creative writing. It is an excellent means of expressing ideas and it has lifetime social, pedagogical, and professional value. But it slows down the process and reduces the quantity of expression. Dictation, on the other hand, permits greater freedom of expression without impos-ing the demands of writing and spelling and the increased sensitivity to syntax and grammar that are demanded by creative writing. Dictation tends to become longer than creative writing, too. Length is not really the objective, but providing helpful detail for a reader or listener is, as is clarity of expression. Furthermore, oral expression develops communica-tion skills also of long-term value; more and more people are becoming active participants in civic affairs. Dictation to a "private secretary" has a steadying and inviting influence. A pause to think is accepted, a change of wording can be made, and effort can be concentrated on what is said more than on how it is said. All this helps the child learn to speak co-herently.

There are always some children, however, who need to continue dicta-tion, word learning, and word-bank approaches initiated in the first grade. *The eclectic approach to reading instruction does not and cannot elimi-nate individual differences.* It can and does permit individuals to achieve at rates in keeping with their potential. The fast learner moves at his own pace and shares with others and has time to help others not so fast. The slow learner engages in the same kinds of activities as the bright children and also shares and helps others. The slow learner delights in dictating, treasures the notebook in which he arranges his typed copies in chrono-logical order, covets his word bank, and engages successfully in many word-attack sessions.

Whereas the fast learner dictates only once a week or once every two weeks, the slow achiever dictates two and three times a week. It is not uncommon for a slow learner to dictate to a faster one. Such teaming up is priceless. The first has an opportunity to express himself, to collaborate with a peer who thus has a chance to combat achiever's arrogance, and to see that even the bright students are not perfect. The high achiever lends a hand and realizes the psychic return that he thus gains; he learns to listen attentively and to hold someone else's idea in mind while he writes, to keep the quality of his handwriting at a very high level, and to do his very best in spelling. Similarly, much can be said for bringing to the room capable fifth-graders and sixth-graders to perform the same activities as helpers. These students become excellent aides and are always impressed with the talents that even slow learners display.

Tape recorders may be used for dictation but are not always effective. For a while, the novelty of recording creates a considerable amount of interest, but the impersonality of tape recorders soon leads to ineffective returns. The problem of transcribing can prove to be too much of a challenge, too. Pupils are impatient to get back their dictation, and if its return is delayed for a few days, they become disinterested.

Creative writing

The second year, as in the first, pupils write, write, write. At first, when they start writing in September, one can look for a period of adjustment. Handwriting needs refining. Spelling is less accurate than in the previous spring. Ideas are not as orderly. Thus, the first year's skills must be reviewed. Some handwriting practice sessions are needed, but not in which all practice the same letters. Each pupil works on those he has had difficulty with. Some may practice *ou* or *or*, *y*, *m-n*, *J*, *p-q*, or *h-k*. The practice must be aimed at specific needs identified in each person's creative writing.

Using the consonant key for construction of word families and the vowel key for recognition of variability helps sharpen spelling skills. Some letter arrangements are phonologically more orderly than others, but evidence indicates that children taught as described here do as well with phonetically irregular words as with regular words (Cramer report, Appendix B). This is an interesting and gratifying scholarly return and high endorsement for the practices described. Accordingly, as the month goes by, word-attack training begins to yield success in spelling in creative writing.

The length of any one creative-writing attempt must not falsely be taken as the chief measure of writing eminence. Length varies from topic to topic, pupil to pupil, and purpose to purpose. Uniformity of length is no more to be looked for than uniformity in the expression of ideas.

Topics to write about are as abundant as they were in first grade. Current events, locally and nationally, afford much stimulation. School happenings, playground episodes, home activities, relatives, trips, visits, special-events days, all provide topics of interest. More and more, though, children begin to record ideas learned and experiments done in curriculum areas other than the language arts.

Even in first grade, some editing was done. Children noticed on rereading, for instance, that a word had been missed and they were shown how to insert it by using the caret ($\wedge$). Oral rereading sometimes alerts them to pauses and idea or sentence endings, and so periods are inserted. Occasionally, a spelling error is detected. This occurs frequently when another pupil reads an account and experiences recognition difficulty. Such changes are made with greater frequency in the second grade, as pupils show increasing interest in form as well as idea.

Creative-writing accounts are posted for others to read; places in the classroom are set aside for this. Similarly, papers are posted in school corridors or in the library or in exhibit cases. Posting creates interest and desire to write well. Some children ask to rework their writing before it is posted. Thus, by force of circumstance and function, the value of preparation of a second copy is introduced. *Formal editing should not be introduced,* however. This confuses some and stifles others. Let the growing demands of the sharing circumstance provide a natural communication impetus. Preparing a second copy serves a useful purpose, but it can readily defeat all purposes if it becomes a drudge.

Time must be allowed in the school week for sharing of writings. This can be done by the author's reading aloud or by exchange of papers. The latter must be done with caution, because children are not equally competent.

Word attack

As long as the speaking-meaning vocabularies exceed reading vocabularies, word-attack skills have great utility. Gradually, as the reading vocabulary exceeds the speaking vocabulary, and as precision of meaning takes on increasing importance, dictionary usage becomes essential. This does not occur for most children, though, until the spiraling curriculum demands of the fourth grade are faced.

In September, it is timely to review all the skill activities (as referred to in Chapter 8). One should always start with auditory discrimination of beginning sounds (single consonants, blends, digraphs, and vowels). Then proceed with ending sounds (inflectional and derivative changes), vowel sounds (particularly medial vowels, both single and double), and parts of words (syllables). As the year progresses, increased attention to word parts will prove useful when attacking unknown words and in creative writing.

Auditory-visual training is just as useful at this level as earlier. Sounds must be linked with the letters used to represent them. The word-family way of dealing with consonant substitution and vowel variability is every bit as practical at this level as earlier, too. Much effort can be devoted to this. Teams can be formed. Competitive group activities can be arranged. Word-family construction increases ability not only to substitute letters but also (perhaps more important) to blend sounds together into pronunciation units. The ability to blend sounds is required for effective use of phonetic respellings in the dictionary, and the training is started at this level.

Dictionary usage proceeds in much the same way as in first grade. The vowel key is used, phonetic respellings are used, word meanings are checked, and, occasionally, word spellings are obtained. Now and throughout the year, much intellectual pleasure can be derived from examining different meanings of words like *stand* (44 different meanings), *run* (103), *dress* (6), *truck* (11), *true* (19), *recórd* and *récord* (20), *draw* (39), and *doll* (3). The meanings that are within the children's grasp will invite and obtain much interest.

By this time the efficiency of guide words can be introduced. Pupils begin to realize how helpful guide words can be, if they have learned to turn to the dictionary for help.

Just as in the first grade, word-attack training must occur daily, in contexts either phonetic or semantic, and in new situations so that transfer skill can be acquired immediately.

Library usage

Weekly library visits are not made as perfunctory trips. They are anticipated and planned. "What do you want in the library and why are you going?" must be kept in mind for each pupil. In turn, the librarian is more than a book custodian, she helps the children decide and locate what they want.

The complaint about the cognitive approach to reading is that the children always exhaust the school's library resources. A ratio of five books per child soon becomes inadequate and ten or fifteen books per child are needed. It is soon discovered, too, that the readability range of books for second graders must be extended beyond what is usually allowed for. Above all, it is discovered that the interests of the children range more widely than was thought and goes beyond fiction to nonfiction.

The librarian takes advantage of class visits to the library to tell children about new books, tell stories, show pictures and exhibits, and so on. The different ways of sharing the knowledge that can be acquired in a library must all be viewed.

Individual visits to the library are permitted to some. Pupils who come on their own must know something about book location, the card index, checking-out procedures, and behavior that shows regard for others using the library. Individual visits are a privilege and are to be treated that way.

The demands on the school library are so great in schools where reading is taught this way that it would seem advisable to have two libraries in an elementary school. One library could service the first two grades, the other, grades three through six. This goal may be achieved someday.

Special features

Once the cycle of instruction has been initiated—to individualized in September, group Directed Reading-Thinking Activities in October—the changes from month to month are made with ease. As the children grow in reading ability, classroom poise, and independence as young scholars, changes occur within each of the subsequent four cycles. The individualized phases are marked by changes in planning, preparing, and sharing. The group phases are marked by changes in the nature and quality of the purposes for reading and their subsequent attainment.

PLANNING

By the time the second period of individualized instruction is initiated in November, the children have learned a great deal about themselves and school. As a result, plans for the month (or 3 weeks) and each succeeding period are structured more precisely. The greatest influences on the plans are interests, increasing abilities, and the use of different ways of sharing.

Each subsequent planning session is marked by more thoughtful expression of interests on the part of the pupils. Use of the library and the selection of books does not stop during October. Children continue to read but mostly on their own, without formal planning or sharing. So the idea "to just read" in November takes on different meanings. As a consequence, each planning session results in a more careful self-examination of likes and dislikes and ambitions as well as closer attentiveness to what classmates prefer and why. It becomes apparent to the children that one does not just read but that one reads about something. This realization focuses attention on what to read, on interests, and on major concepts. The read-about-something realization gradually effects a move from fiction to nonfiction and reflects the influence of the other areas of the curriculum—arithmetic, science, health, music, art, history, geography.

In November, a 2- or 3-day planning session begins the new cycle. Pupils declare and explain their interests. A list of interests is posted. Such planning sessions promote not only self-examination but also teaming up. Children influence each other, so if two or three indicate that they want to

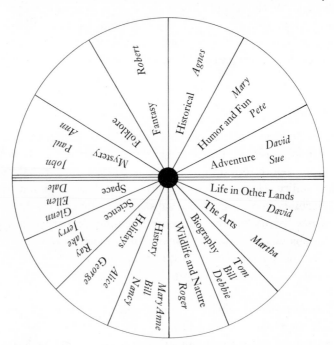

Planning Wheel

read about pilgrims, for instance, they may get together on the selection of materials and the plans for sharing. Interestingly enough, when they are permitted to express their preferences, children seldom select only one or two areas. Usually eight or more are voiced. Each child's name is added to the list of interests. This list stays posted for the month and is retained for reference at future planning sessions.

Each planning session produces changes. They become more serious in that pupils give more thought to what they want to do and why. One effective planning variation is the planning wheel. The upper half of the wheel lists fiction interests, the lower half nonfiction. Pupils' names are recorded in each spoke, according to interest.

PREPARATION

Visits to the classroom, school, and community libraries are accomplished more purposefully each month. Children know what they want and are more discriminating about their choices.

Reading and collecting ideas occurs with an eye to sharing time. No longer are they reading just for themselves. This reading-to-share objective promotes more selective reading and appraisal, even among the least able. They, too, give thought to what they might share with the class.

If two or three pupils are pursuing the same reading interest, they read and meet and read again and participate in small seminar sessions. This kind of planning and sharing promotes rereading and reflection and other visits to the library. It helps children to get their facts straight.

How to share becomes crucial and requires careful planning. It is indeed gratifying to see how thoughtful even seven-year-olds can be about what will interest the class and how they should make their presentations. This often leads, in turn, to changes in sharing.

SHARING

By midwinter and spring, sharing time consumes 3 or 4 days. It is the culmination of the month's reading, studying, and preparation. How to catch and hold the class's attention becomes as important as the reading and searching. Children become producers and directors.

Ways of sharing are numerous. One of the finest lists available was published by Amy E. Yensen (7); Jeannette Veatch's is useful, too (6).

A good procedure is to select eight or ten ways of sharing and examine them. Then from that list, a child or team can select what they think is appropriate for their purposes and abilities. Of course, caution must be exercised so that not all will choose the same means of sharing. The decisions are made on a class basis and seldom need arbitration. Among the most popular at the second-grade level are puppet shows, TV skits, panoramas, plays, demonstrations, and radio shows. Puppet shows are a marvelous means of getting timid souls to participate. The security of the curtain can raise a voice and vary its intonations. In another month, ten additional ways of sharing can be examined and used. If this kind of regulation is not made, popular ways are overused.

Once a way of sharing has been selected, preparation for it must be made. The cooperation of children is always astounding. In order to share with the class something that will be reasonably new, some degree of secrecy must be exercised; children display unusual integrity in this regard. Each knows that the other is preparing, yet each is so busy that he is preoccupied with his own preparation. Preparation time becomes rehearsal time and is like the rehearsal for a play production. Children coordinate their efforts and have dry runs. Even the solo performers need and use preparation time.

Equipment needed must be provided. Some require a table; others need a chalkboard support for a mural, an easel for exhibiting, a lectern for reading, a tape recorder or overhead transparencies for demonstrating.

Time must be checked. Most productions are short but even so it is wise to alert children to the fact that all need an opportunity to share and no one should monopolize the time.

By the end of the year, schedules can be made. Children can list the nature and approximately the time of their presentations. This promotes careful thinking about sharing.

By spring, a fascinating thing that can be done is to visit other classrooms and present sharing performances. Interroom sharing arouses a great deal of interest. One sharing day a week can be set aside for it. Not all presentations can be shared, of course, so thoughtful decisions must be made. How to select the presentations to be shared raises questions of evaluation. Criteria for selection must be declared that go beyond a subjective "I liked it." Thus, in a very functional and purposeful way, value judgments are required. Not only must choices be made but the number of choices must fit the time available, so length of presentation takes on new meaning. In addition, everyone must be considered, because interroom sharing must not be monopolized by a few clever ones. In short, much sound thinking is required. Conditions for judging are: it was interesting, no time was wasted, everyone could see and hear, and so on. Once such conditions have been declared, they naturally influence future presentations, for which preparation is made with these criteria in mind.

GROUP DIRECTED READING-TRAINING ACTIVITY

By the time the second group DRTA occurs in December, performance becomes increasingly more sharp and effective. Divergent-thinking opportunities evoke more predictions that are plausible and more responses. Children begin to see how, even with limited information, many courses of action are possible. Responses become more varied but more likely.

As the amount of evidence increases, the children become more selective and objective in their use of story facts. Their predictions, fewer in number, display a more astute use of ideas and reflect the influence of plot convergence.

Predictions are seldom made without basis. When a conjecture is stated, it is usually backed up with a reason. In other words, a child might say, "I think the girl will win the race, because she is big for her age, she likes the outdoors, and it says she has been practicing secretly." Predictions of this kind provide selected evidence to support conclusions. If a child agrees with someone else's predictions, he does not say only "I agree with Jim"; he also adds why he agrees. Or, if he disagrees, as someone did about the previous prediction that the girl would win, the challenge is made politely and respectfully. The challenging prediction is also supported by evidence: "I think Mark will win because he won before, and this is the first time a girl has been in such a race."

Direction of predictions from the teacher should influence thinking toward objective appraisals. She asks why a prediction was made if it has not been supported. She constantly varies the amount of information supplied to the reader for prediction purposes. If children have been asked to read all of a story except the last page or the climax page, the predictions about plot outcome should reflect the amount of information available.

While predictions become more qualitative, allowance must be made for subjective responses. Some child may feel that a certain outcome will occur, even though he cannot say why he feels as he does. Intuitive responses are acceptable as long as they are recognized as such.

Spelling

To spell a word is to produce its established letter order correctly. The spelling of a newly created word is not determined by some master plan designed by a board of linguistic and phonetic authorities. It usually reflects an attempt at coding sounds by using letters to represent the sounds. Regardless of the source, once a spelling has been declared, it becomes a fixed and permanent letter order to be used correctly on all occasions. Correct spelling distinguishes one word from another and facilitates ready and efficient communication.

First in the language-experience program, the children are exposed to words to be read. They also enjoy the unique experience of seeing their talk written down. Each word that the teacher writes down from their dictated stories is printed letter by letter. Thus, they can see that each word has a fixed letter order. When a word is repeated, as *Snow White* was, for instance, it is always formed in the same way. Thus the children are exposed to more than words; they are exposed to spelling and letter order. It is fortunate, of course, that this should happen from the beginning of their reading-instruction program. Every time, thereafter, when they dictated they saw words being formed by placing letters in certain fixed orders. If, as happened on occasion, a teacher made an error, it was immediately corrected, so they could conclude that correct spelling is important.

Reading words requires reaction to word configurations. The shape of words is determined by their letters. Some words are long, have many letters; some are as short as one or two letters; some have capital letters while others do not. One boy said he remembered that *Snow White* had big letters at the beginning of both of its words. He saw that his name did, too. Some words have endings that look alike, some look different. The boy who saw *snow* in the word *snowy* reacted to the word's ending. Some words look somewhat alike: *in* and *on, fort* and *feet,* and so on. Word form provides visual stimulation and requires <u>visual</u> <u>perception</u>. The more accurate that perception becomes, the more selective children are about words and the better the words are remembered.

Likenesses and differences in letters and the sounds they represent are taught from the very beginning of school. Auditory and auditory-visual discrimination helps focus on the distinctions. Word-family activities help make distinctions clearer.

When creative writing is introduced, letter order within words takes on new significance; the knowledge that sounds are represented by letters can now be used. Words are spelled by children largely as they sound, and often they are right or almost right. Many words are spelled correctly because the children have seen them so often. They notice, too, that some of their sound-letter spellings need only a bit of changing to be right. As the year progresses, their word-attack skills improve, their sound-letter sensitivity becomes more acute, so their spelling improves. Test results, referred to earlier and reported in Appendix B, show that, at the end of the first year, the spelling ability of all the children is astoundingly good. The pragmatic approach yields the returns predicted, without the stifling of creative writing by spelling demands.

In mid-October of the second year, "formal" spelling can be introduced. All the previous functional spelling, reading experience, and word-recognition training provide sufficient readiness. It must be kept in mind that formal spelling has to be introduced in such a way that it will not stifle creative writing. Instruction has to be differentiated. To impose the same word list on all children would be disastrous, if not utterly ruinous. Accordingly, each pupil's instructional level has to be found. This is easy to do and is interesting for the children.

First, a spelling list—such as ones published in most language arts series or spelling series for use in elementary grades—should be obtained. In the first and second grades, a sample of twenty words is proper. At each level beyond that, samples of twenty-five words should be used.

A sample should be fair and unbiased. If, at the first-grade level, the total number of words in the list is two hundred and the size of the sample wanted is twenty, divide two hundred by twenty. This means that, if one selects every tenth word in the list, an adequate and unbiased sample of twenty words will have been compiled. Follow a similar procedure at each grade level until the list is complete. (See Appendix C for an example of a complete list.)

In testing the class to determine ability levels, each child should have a sheet of paper on which he can put twenty words in a column. The following instructions should be well understood: "I will pronounce or say a word and will speak it only once. As soon as you have heard the word, spell it by writing it on your paper. If you are not sure of the spelling of a word, try it anyway. You may be right. If you don't know the word at all, just draw a line." These instructions may be repeated and illustrated on the chalkboard until all understand, but the testing situation should not be made to seem a penalty or create anxiety. All that is wanted is that the children are urged to do the best they can. It should be stressed that each word will be spoken only once. Allowance must be made for instances in which a child really does not hear a word, and then it is repeated, but these are definitely exceptions. Because this is functional spelling and patterns must be set correctly from the start, the words are *not* put into sentences and no effort is made to distinguish homonyms.

Children who spell 70 percent or more of the words correctly will then take the second-grade level list. On the first day of testing, taking two lists will most likely be enough of a challenge. Testing then continues the next day and until all in the room spell correctly less than 70 percent of a list. The following distribution is likely to occur in a class of thirty children:

Number of Children	Instructional Level
5	1
12	2
8	3
5	4

This means that in this room there are four spelling groups each at a different level. Each child is assigned to a level according to his skill.

Spelling instruction can now be initiated with each child at his instructional level. Now the test-study and the self-correction methods are introduced. The test-study method proceeds as follows. On a Monday, each group is administered a list of twenty words taken from the master spelling list. The teacher has four lists and proceeds one at a time from list to list. The children in the first group spell the first word pronounced; the children in the second group spell the second word spoken; the third group the third word, the fourth group the fourth word.

Each word is spoken only once. Now the children are instructed that, if a word like *one* or *won* is spoken, they must ask which one is meant. This gives the teacher an opportunity to reply with "How many do you know?" If the child knows both, you can then indicate which word is meant. This may all sound a bit complex, but the children catch on to it quickly. Whenever they are writing functionally, they must know whether to use *one* or *won*, also. No one will stand by and tell them. Therefore, for spelling instruction they must learn from the beginning how to be self-reliant and resourceful.

The teacher must pace the pronunciation of the words at an even tempo and allow enough time for each child to write. Classes and teachers tend to establish their own tempos. No child must be frustrated by the pacing, though.

Why is a word spoken only once? Spelling is largely a rote conditioned-response reaction. One does not pause while writing and repeat a word once or twice; one just writes. When a word to be spelled is spoken, the pupil must be free and ready to spell it at once. Chances are good that he will be much more successful this way.

While administering the list, the teacher should not walk around in the room. A fixed position should be established for all spelling occasions. The teacher should always stand there and speak the word clearly and without distortion.

As she proceeds through the word lists, she may orient the group occasionally by saying, for instance, "This is word number five" or "ten" and so on. This helps all pupils stay together.

When the four lists have been dictated, the <u>self-correction</u> phase is introduced. Each child is now given a typed copy of the words he was just asked to spell. This means, of course, that the first group must have five lists, and so on. Each child then checks his spellings against the list. This way he discovers his own successes and his own errors. He learns to recognize and deal with his own needs. Because each child is at his own instructional level, he is apt not to miss more than three or four words; that is, he spells sixteen or more words out of twenty correctly without first attempting to memorize the list. He achieved this well because of his reading, phonic letter-sound, and creative-writing abilities.

If a word is misspelled, a check mark ($\checkmark$) is placed next to it. The number of misspelled words is then placed at the top of the page; if none were misspelled, this is indicated with a o. In the beginning, a quick check by the teacher is needed to see how they have done, but, once the technique is learned, an occasional spot check will do. Childern are basically honest and have a tremendous amount of integrity. A bit of policing not so much to uncover dishonesty as to discover honest oversight is sufficient. If the teacher finds a word misspelled that has not been marked, she points this out but does not tell the child which word it is. All she does is change the number at the top of the paper. Then the child must check his words again to find the misspelled word.

Each misspelled word is studied immediately. This study procedure follows the usual method that has been used for many years. First, the pupil studies the correct letter order, repeating it over and over. Then he closes his eyes and visualizes the word while he repeats the spelling. He restudies the word while looking at it. Then he *covers both* the misspelled word and the correct word and writes the word again, next to the misspelling. Then he checks to see if he is right and repeats the act, as follows:

thes $\checkmark$ this   this

In the beginning, all this takes a bit of time, but it is worth every second of it. In a month or so, the children will have caught on so well to the idea that everything will proceed easily and efficiently.

That is all for Monday. On Wednesday, the same procedure is followed. Everybody spells the same words again, even if they had a perfect paper on Monday. If a child spells all words correctly on both Monday and Wednesday, he is through for the week. If he does not, he is tested again on Friday. If a child misses the same word on Wednesday that he missed on Monday, he studies it more intently on Thursday. The period of delayed recall from Monday to Wednesday showed that the word had not been established well enough for retention and needed more reinforcement.

Thus, the week's activity permits a number of psychological learning actions to occur. First, the test-study method takes advantage of each pupil's reading ability, visual-perceptual word-recognition ability, sound-letter word-attack training, creative-writing experience, and rote establishment of word letter order as evidenced by conditioned-response reproduction. Second, the self-correction method takes advantage of the individual discovery of success and failure, focusing on specific personal errors. The self-correction employs first-hand oral and visual clues, oral and visual imagery, repetition, and double checking. Further, because each child performs at his instructional level, the number of errors made is not so large as to be frustrating, usually no more than three. The second check on Wednesday provides a delayed-recall retention check to see how effective the previous learning has been. In addition, each of his skills is reactivated. Pupils who show twice that they do know the spellings are excused and so rewarded for their knowledge. The third check on Friday again yields evidence of retention and accuracy of recall.

Additional delayed-recall checks should be made biweekly or monthly. On these occasions, the words missed in the previous 2 or 3 weeks are used again in the test-study procedure.

When spelling is taught this way, it becomes a pedagogical pleasure and a learner's challenge rather than a drudge and a frustration. Rate of progress varies according to each child's level of achievement. Bright children may be spelling a fifth-grade list by the end of the year. The opportunity to proceed at a pace in keeping with their ability spurs all, but especially the bright students, and the achievement gap between them and the slow learners becomes increasingly larger.

Instruction can be varied by giving the bright children twenty-five or even thirty words to spell each week. Or, if they continuously achieve perfect scores on Mondays and Wednesdays, they can be given a new list on Fridays. On the other hand, it has been found quite helpful to reduce the number of words per week for the slow ones. Administering only ten or fifteen words helps them along. It is better to attain a perfect score on ten words with regularity than to be overwhelmed by twenty words.

Differences in the size of the lists does not complicate instruction. When the ten words have been presented to the slow learners, one among them quietly distributes the check lists and they start checking their productions. By the time the bright ones are finished with their dictation, the teacher is free to move among the slow ones and check their achievement while the bright ones correct their performance. The adjustments facilitate administration, correction, study, and double checking as well as the teacher's directing time.

At the third- and fourth-grade levels and beyond, the spelling gap between the top performers and the others widens even more. Good teaching increases individual differences. It is not uncommon for fourth-grade classes to have some children being instructed at the ninth- and tenth-grade levels. In a fourth-grade class in Seaford, Delaware, for instance, all the children were spelling words above the fourth-grade level, with three of them spelling ninth-grade words.

If tape recorders are available, a teacher can tape Monday's words prior to the spelling lesson. When spelling time occurs, all she need do is turn on the tape recorder. This frees her to watch how the children perform. In the second grade, and to some degree in the third grade, it seems better to have the teacher dictate the list. She can adjust the pace of her dictation and repeat a word if necessary; this kind of adjustment avoids frustration and keeps everyone going at a steady pace.

Third year and beyond

Once the cycle of instruction has been introduced as described for the second-grade level, it serves as the pattern throughout the middle grades. Each school year should start with individualized instruction—examination of interests, self-selection of materials, study and research, preparation for sharing, and sharing—that continues for at least 3 weeks. Then group instruction—all reading the same material; setting purposes; reading, proving, and disproving conjectures—also takes place for about 3 weeks. This then is the alternating plan for the year.

Dictation continues in the third grade once a week and gradually shifts to once every 2 weeks, especially for the average and above average pupils. The others continue with dictation once a week. Creative writing continues in the third grade with two marked changes beginning to show: First, the writing attempts are more and more recording and reporting in which the pupils write about some experiment in science, health, or biology or write about some current social or political event. In other words, their writing, like their reading, shows a marked movement toward nonfiction and objective content. After all, *this is to be expected, since reading is a process and not a subject.* Second, they show increasing delight in composing plots and contriving stories reflecting human relationships but also reflecting some animism. This seems like a new way of expressing egocentric talk and dreams. These changes become more apparent in the fourth grade. Nine-year-olds can be astonishingly detailed and accurate in their recording of events and experiments and clever and original in their plot contrivances.

Some editing occurs in first-grade creative writing and continues in the second and third grades, but, by the fourth grade, specific attempts at editing are defined and enacted. Draft copies take on increasing merit, from necessity. As the amount of writing increases and the nature of the writing changes, pupils become more preoccupied with the content of what they say. As a result, handwriting suffers, as do spelling and grammar. Their urgency is to get their ideas recorded. Once recorded, rereading shows the need for mechanical adjustments. So, a second copy is made in which adjustments are made in spelling, punctuation, capitalization. This is followed by a desire to clarify expression and to make semantic changes. Pupils begin to realize that what they write can be said in different ways by adjusting a sentence or two or even a paragraph. This brings on the third copy.

Posters can be made to show what one does and how one does it. A Three-Draft Poster might show:

Draft One: Write
Put down ideas

Draft Two: Correct
Adjust ideas
Express thoughts more clearly
Correct punctuation

Draft Three: Polish
> Adjust punctuation
> Adjust capitals
> Improve handwriting
> Correct spelling
> Improve expression

All this must be done without stifling the recording of ideas, of course. To write is still the major objective. Gradually, to write correctly takes on importance. Editorial suggestions from the teacher are made individually and respectfully. If the need for a correction in spelling, punctuation, or capitalization is detected, a mark is placed in the margin at the beginning of a line. The pupil then finds his own needs and corrects them. This kind of spotting by the teacher is usually sufficient. It must be kept in mind that the range of performance among fourth-graders or nine-year-olds shows a great deal of variance—frequently about six levels. Not all perform or respond in the same way, and the teacher's understanding of this variance in editing is reflected in her suggestions to individual pupils.

Sharing sessions show marked improvement. They are better organized and rehearsed and show increasing sensitivity to the audience. Props are more carefully planned and prepared. Scheduling is more sophisticated. Schedules, such as the following, of a rather formal nature are posted.

Pupils	Interest	Props	Time
John and Bill	pulleys and ropes	table pulleys ropes	20 min.
Walter	glass	table chart glass	10 min.
Sarah, Helen, and Mary	dances	chart game dance floor	15 min.

Children begin to team up more frequently and offer more intricately planned and rehearsed presentations. Their timing is accurate. Their use of props is studied and shows increasing sensitivity to clarity and interest.

In the fourth grade, critics can be appointed at each sharing time to keep an eye on things. The critics—usually three pupils—report on each presentation by noting two reactions: the things they liked best and the changes that might be made for another time. Both responses keep attention focused on the positive and deemphasize the negative: Comments must be constructive.

Time to share takes on new significance. Four days are now allowed and all the reading and language-arts time is used for sharing. Even spelling may be suspended for the week. By November, sharing sessions may be organized as follows:

> Tuesday: intraclass
>
> Wednesday: intraclass
>
> Thursday: interroom
>
> Friday: all fourth grades

On Tuesday and Wednesday, pupils share with each other in a room. On Thursday, certain performances chosen in each room are presented in a neighboring classroom. On Friday, each room selects one presentation to be performed in the auditorium. It is truly inspiring to sit in an auditorium with 120 fourth-grade children and see how attentive they are to presentations and to hear how they applaud in appreciation. It is thrilling to be backstage and see how the polished performers stage a production in front of their peers.

By the fourth grade, even the group DRTA's are different. Less time is allowed for them; only 2 weeks may be allowed at a time, with 4 or 5 weeks allotted to individualized reading. More and more, group DRTA's occur with material other than basic readers. Science and social studies lend themselves particularly well to directed reading-thinking processes. In addition, by this time the children have become so schooled in the procedure that they can serve periodically as teacher-director. They do a superb job as teachers and know how to make their peers predict wisely, read carefully, and offer sound proof. The teacher is free to observe how each group is doing and to see how well she is being imitated.

Of course, attention must be given to refining word-attack skills and developing concept recognition. Word-attack skills will have to be applied with increasing frequency on words that either are not in the children's speaking-meaning vocabularies or are in the speaking vocabularies but only vaguely in the meaning vocabularies. Attacks now focus on pronunciation accuracy and identifying the meaning that fits context. Skill in the use of prefixes, suffixes, and root words augments the word-attack repertoire. But reference to dictionaries must be taught, for identification of pronunciation and meaning. Dictionary usage is continually stressed as an important tool in a reader's armory.

Versatility in reading to improve efficiency must be taught as a discipline essential to all scholarly reading. Children must learn to establish purposes for reading and how to adapt their rate of reading to the nature and difficulty of the material. Therefore, they must be taught how to survey, skim, scan, and study. For a detailed account concerning the teaching of versatility see (4, ch. 10).

The progress and socialization of behavior

Piaget begins a section in his book *Six Psychological Studies* with the title "The Progress and Socialization of Behavior" and the statement: "In an activity-oriented school, where the children are at liberty to work either in groups or alone and to talk while working, one is struck by the difference between these children and classes of younger children" (2, p. 39). If the last phrase were changed to "and classes that are not activity-oriented," then the statement would serve this book: The best way to describe this difference between classes is to refer to the reactions of visitors. Visitors are nearly always astounded by the individual concentration children exhibit when they work by themselves and the effective collaboration they show when they work in a group.

As Piaget says, "True discussions are now possible in that the children show comprehension with respect to the other's point of view and a search for justification or proof with respect to their own statements" (2, p. 39). "True discussions" occur with amazing frequency in the cognitive approach to reading instruction. The children substitute reflection and deliberation for impulsive behavior, which is of utmost importance in the development of intelligence and emotion. A system of values, closely related to realities and results, one that is based on mutual respect and reciprocity, gradually emerges for each pupil. The children attribute equivalent personal values to each other, and this kind of respect produces honesty and tolerance between peers and friends. It shows regard for rules and regulations essential to study and intercommunication for efficient functioning in a classroom, a library, a school, or even a community. It leads to forms of conduct and moral feelings that emanate from within, are less subject to external dictation. Individuals see the why and how of subordinating themselves to the laws of reciprocity.

Of all the benefits that derive from the use of the Language-Experience Approach and the broader cognitive approach, the progress and socialization of behavior is by far the most significant. Children will perform as described if they are given the proper opportunity, encouragement, and pedagogical direction.

Conclusion

This chapter tells in some detail how the Language-Experience Approach, the eclectic approach, or the cognitive approach is employed in grades two and beyond. The more skillful and sophisticated the children become, the more the purpose and opportunity to integrate the language-arts increases. The results are constantly more fruitful and functional.

The review of the features of the first-year program should be examined carefully and contrasted with the features for the second year. Competence in communication creates changes in the quantity and quality of pupils' work.

The dictation of accounts and stories never really ends. The demands of dictation are so different from creative writing that developing the skill must continue. Similarly, creative writing shows marked changes in writing style, language, and topic. The influence of the total curriculum is increasingly felt.

As curriculum and reading demands continue to present concepts beyond the immediate experience of the children, dictionary usage takes on mounting importance. Pronunciation demands increase as does precision in meaning.

The more refined that reading interests and tastes become, the greater are the demands on libraries. Inquiry reading for research takes children into many books and sources.

When at last formal spelling is introduced, the most practical procedures available are used: test-study and self-correction. Instruction must be carefully differentiated, so that pupils may progress according to the abilities of each. The spelling program might truly be titled "functional spelling."

In the final analysis, it is the poise, confidence, and scholarly modesty of the children that is most striking in a Language-Experience Approach. The children develop a system of values based on mutual respect and reciprocity.

Bibliography

1. Bond, Guy, L., and Robert Dykstra. "The Role of the Coordinating Center in the Cooperative Research Program," *The Reading Teacher,* vol. 19, no. 8 (May, 1966), pp. 565–568.
2. Piaget, Jean. *Six Psychological Studies.* Edited by David Elkind. New York: Random House, 1967.
3. Stauffer, Russell G. *Directing Reading Maturity as a Cognitive Process.* New York: Harper & Row, 1969.
4. Stauffer, Russell G. *Teaching Reading as a Thinking Process.* New York: Harper & Row, 1969.
5. Stauffer, Russell G. "The Verdict: Speculative Controversy," *The Reading Teacher,* vol. 19, no. 8 (May, 1966), pp. 563–564.
6. Veatch, Jeannette. *Reading in the Elementary School.* New York: Ronald Press, 1966.
7. Yensen, Amy E. "Attracting Children to Books," *Elementary English,* vol. 33, no. 6 (October, 1956), pp. 332–339.

IO

Special uses of the language-experience approach

Five special uses of the Language-Experience Approach, or eclectic approach, will be dealt with in this chapter. Each use is as productive, in its way, as the developmental approach described in the previous chapters. Each is concerned with a different population, yet each group possesses cognitive wealth that makes the use of this approach practical and successful. The five groups are: preschoolers, immature six-year-olds, special-education children, clinical cases, and adult illiterates or semi-illiterates.

Once more the reader is asked to read the following objectives and conjecture about answers. By now, the reader must know that he increases his comprehension of a chapter to the degree that he makes these objectives his objectives. He realizes that by doing so, personal and social commitments result that regulate his reading and keep him on course.

1. Explain how preschoolers are being educated even though they may not be receiving formal schooling.
2. Tell how curriculum for preschoolers is structured.
3. Describe how the use of language helps free preschoolers from domination by their perceptual world.
4. Explain how experience charts can be used and how their use at this level differs from what is done later.

Upon reading the part concerned with immature six-year-olds, the reader should be able to meet the following objectives:

1. Explain how immature six-year-olds may be identified.
2. Describe how they may progress when their potential is utilized.
3. Tell about the nature and complexity of their dictated accounts and compare them with structured materials.

Upon reading the part concerned with special-education children, the reader should be able to meet the following objectives:

1. Describe special-education children and how they are identified.
2. Explain how the Language-Experience Approach honors them.
3. Tell about the nature and complexity of their dictated accounts and compare them with structured materials.

Upon reading the part concerned with clinical cases, the reader should be able to meet the following objectives:

1. Explain how the use of the Language-Experience Approach differs from the use of the Fernald Tracing Approach.
2. Explain how the therapeutic possibilities inherent in the Language-Experience Approach serve the instruction program.

Upon reading the part concerned with adult illiterates and semi-illiterates, the reader should be able to answer the following objectives:

1. Tell how on-the-job training can be especially helpful in promoting learning-to-read instruction.
2. Describe how adults of different age levels and with different jobs provide a good instructional nucleus.
3. Tell about the nature and complexity of their dictated accounts and compare them with structured materials.

Preschoolers

In the circumstances in which individual differences are dealt with in practice as well as in preachings, the word *preschooler* takes on a narrower meaning. It then refers only to children who are not old enough to meet the age required to attend school. It does not mean that preschoolers are all alike or that all are unresponsive to teaching. Piaget's descriptions of the preoperational child and his egocentric ways of discovering his concrete world and his gradual movement intellectually from percepts to concepts is probably the most detailed and carefully examined description available (see Chapter 1). His stages of intellectual development are sufficiently open ended to allow for the fact that children of the same chronological age show different levels of ability, knowledge, and skills as a function of the rate and quality of the learning experiences they have encountered.

Education, in its broadest sense, is going on constantly between infancy and school age. Children are educated by the people they know, parents, peers, other adults; by the environment in which they live, home, neighborhood, countryside; by the games they play and the performances of others; and by the ideals and ideologies of the culture in which they live. Their education is characterized by constant interaction between people and environment. In this time, they learn a great deal, in keeping with their potential.

Educational efforts now being planned recognize this education and how it influences different individuals, and educators are setting out to make it more formal. As a result, kindergartens are a required part of many educational systems. In addition, social and economic impetus is affecting the establishment and development of nursery schools. Thus, at ages three and four, children are being taken away from the privacy and natural selections of home and neighborhood to the public and less personal surroundings of the school. Children are introduced to an objective world and brought together with a teacher and her methods in order to pursue common tasks.

The curriculum for these young folks, particularly those children of kindergarten age, is structured to give each a chance to grow individually and socially and to learn in a systematic way by competing and sharing with each other. It is developed to recognize that percepts and concepts can be designed and presented to have relevant educational content. More and more the curriculum is providing the child with experiences and stimuli that will help him realize his mental capacities at his own time and pace and that will give him an opportunity to practice and perfect his emerging mental abilities through action.

"With the appearance of language," says Piaget, "behavior is profoundly modified both affectively and intellectually" (8, p. 17). With the aid of language, a child can reconstruct his past actions and anticipate his future actions. This has three consequences, Piaget goes on to say. It heralds the onset of socialization of action, the internalization of words, and the internalization of actions.

Even though much of the language usage among young children is rudimentary and linked to acts and deeds, they are able to communicate with others. They do so in most instances without really learning to take the point of view of others. So they talk not only to others but to themselves.

The activities planned for a preschooler can capitalize on his language development by providing many opportunities in which children can participate actively by doing things with others and talking about what they are seeing and doing. They can engage in and go beyond imaginative and imitative play. They can ask questions and need many opportunities to do so. In short, they can be led to engage in many activities as individuals, or as an individual in a group, and to talk about them.

By the time many children are four or five years old, their talk about things they have done and have seen or imagined can be recorded in dictated stories. Many children are quite responsive to requests to dictate or react to experiences, much as six-year-olds are. Their ideas can be recorded and read back immediately to them. Illustrations can be made by the children to accompany their dictation or pictures prepared by adults can be used. The illustrations that accompany dictation help children recognize interests when they want to reexamine a dictated account at a later date. They can locate their own story about pets, for example, because they recognize the picture. The picture symbol system reinforces and helps recognition of the printed-word symbol system. All this is done without formal attempts at word-recognition training and retention. The children refer to their dictation and see it over and over again. Such repetitive contact has a tremendous value, because intellectual curiosities and abilities are exercised spontaneously through actions that encourage unfolding intelligence.

Stories are recognized. Ideas are recalled. Soon, words are recognized and remembered and the recognition of printed words will have started. Bright four- and five-year-olds begin to recognize words and read them just as they recognize "ice cream," "Bonanza," and the like from seeing and hearing them repeatedly on television.

A kindergarten teacher can accumulate many group and individually dictated stories and read and reread them with the children. First-hand experience stimulation for the stories and the vividness of the experience, because they were unique or emotionally charged (Halloween, Thanksgiving, Christmas, for example) foster interest and facilitate recognition. Given such opportunities, many children begin to recognize words and to read.

It is important when planning activities for preschoolers that they participate in some kind of action and then use language to describe the action. Feeding animals, caring for plants, assembling puzzles or toys, seeing puppet shows, making paper hats, painting, playground activities, singing, visiting, all can promote cognitive activity. Dictation about what they experienced can then be made after the action and participation has occurred. Telling about an experience after the event and in the absence of the original stimulus facilitates expression and avoids simple "I see" or "I do" expressions. Thus, language usage is subject to the primacy of perception and action.

An excellent program for preschoolers resulting from stimulation provided by such things as Head Start and Title I funds was organized in Cambridge, Maryland,[1] involving four- and five-year-olds learning together in circumstances integrated through both pupils and teachers. The one word that best describes their program is "action." Children, interacting with each other by thought, word, and deed in a structured-unstructured pedagogical program, act and react to innumerable experiences that encourage and permit a multisensory approach. All movement, thought, and emotion is in response to circumstances that have been promulgated by the teachers and teacher aides. The pupil-teacher (teacher aide) ratio is such that much pupil-adult contact can occur throughout the day.

The children, constantly encouraged to use language to name things, ask questions, issue commands, and assert beliefs, increase their language use while seeing, hearing, smelling, tasting, feeling, and are thus freed from domination by percepts; they anchor percepts symbolically, manipulate them reflectively, and carry out deeds in thought. Thus, they become more reflective and less impulsive. In the words of Piaget, language helps them interiorize an action, object, or place.

Everyday oral reading to the children occurs; the teacher and her aides take turns reading aloud. Nursery rhymes and the like are frequently used and the children chant them together whenever the rhymes are suitable. Listening centers are also available for voice records and music tapes.

The teaching rooms of the children in this program, as miniature action centers, replicate the multiaid idea of a modern library. Books and magazines are available. Easels and drawing boards are available for creative expression through brush, crayon, and pencil. Private places are available for the child who wants to be alone for a time. Games and toys with movable parts are about. Each room has a wash bowl in a corner for experiments as well as cleanliness. Seeds are watered, animals are fed, and nature is observed.

[1] Mrs. Dorothy Nave, Mrs. Judith VanCrobber, and Mr. Thomas Flowers organized and directed the program under Superintendent James G. Busick.

Experience stories, largely recounts, are recorded, posted, and read. Some children show facility at creating stories and this, too, is encouraged, but by and large the children tell about something they have experienced and acted upon.

The total environment provides sources for motivation, physically and geographically as well as socially, culturally, and historically. Located on the eastern shore of Maryland off Chesapeake Bay, it has a wealth uniquely its own and the children are learning to act and talk about their own acres of diamonds.

The immature six-year-olds

No one questions the value of two premises basic to teaching: teaching at the level of the learner and early diagnosis and prevention of learning disability. In reading instruction, these two principles have been stated and restated innumerable times. One of the staunchest advocates of them is Emmett Betts (1). Others are Donald Durrell (4), Arthur Gates (6), Guy and Eva Bond and Miles Tinker (2, 3). In fact, there is hardly an authority in the field who does not advocate these principles.

In almost every unselected population of children required to attend school at age six, a certain portion of that population does not possess the maturity of physiological, intellectual, or emotional development, to be responsive to the kind of formal teaching-learning that is started in most first grades. Test results on six-year-olds obtained before they entered first grade have shown a disparity of readiness of as much as 5 years. These findings are not astounding; neither need they be disconcerting. Where individual differences are recognized and the instructional program is paced accordingly, many problems are resolved.

The range of potential among six-year-olds shows that a certain number are well advanced beyond the statistical and somewhat mythical average of a whole population and that, similarly, some are less ready. Both need to be taken into account if sound pedagogical practices are to be used. The previous nine chapters refer again and again to how the superior child is given numerous opportunities to produce at his expectancy level. This seems to be a major advantage of the Language-Experience Approach —each child's cognitive potential can be used to the fullest. Instruction does not require all children to move as one; instruction is not adapted to the average and below-average populations in a vain attempt to keep a convoy of scholars together. This book has also indicated over and again how slow developers can use to the fullest their cognitive wealth by engaging in the same kinds of learning activities as the average and superior children are doing but at their own rate of assimilation and accommodation.

Early identification of maturity for beginning-reading instruction can be considerably accurate. But constructive use of information about individual differences among six-year-olds and preschoolers seems lacking in too many instances.

A particularly successful plan has been used in the Seaford, Delaware, schools. The account that follows is based on real situations; the same practices and procedures have been used in many schools and with similar success.

Seaford is a town of about 8,000 people in southern Delaware. It is the home of DuPont Nylon. The total integrated school population is approximately 3,200. There are three elementary schools, a junior high school, and a high school.

All pupils starting school at West Seaford Elementary School were assigned indiscriminately to four different first-grade classrooms and tested and studied by their respective teachers. At the end of the first 3 weeks of school, the first-grade teachers met with the reading consultant for the district to compare notes. Then, out of the total population of beginners, twenty-three were identified who seemed by all evidence (teacher's judgment, informal tests, standardized tests) the least mature. The twenty-three were assigned to an experienced and able teacher and they stayed together as a group for the rest of the school year.

Intelligence quotients for the twenty-three, as determined by SRA Tests of General Ability[2] resulted in a range of scores of from 111 to 78 (two pupils were untested). Scores obtained by the school psychologist with the Wechsler Intelligence Scale for Children (WISC)[3] on thirteen in the group ranged from 88 to 51. Lee-Clark Reading-Readiness Test[4] scores ranged from mental age 3–1 to 5–1, with an average score of about 4–4. In chronological age, the pupils ranged from six years, two months, to seven years, six months. One physically handicapped boy was nine years, two months old.

Patricia Derrickson, their teacher, worked with the children on a

[2] Published by Science Research Associates, Chicago.
[3] Published by The Psychological Corporation, New York.
[4] Published by California Test Bureau, Los Angeles.

readiness program much like that described for preschoolers. She soon noted that pupils could talk more and dictate better if they were telling about something they had done or something they had experienced. As the teacher put it, "The more exciting and vivid the experience and the more a child participates in an event, the better the recall for the telling of a story."

A list of the experiences she and the pupils engaged in throughout the year that tended to be more or less exciting were:

1. walks to
   collect leaves
   mail a letter
   buy a gift for a new baby sister
   buy a Christmas gift
   buy food for a party
2. visits to see
   a live turkey
   the same turkey in the school cafeteria broiler
   and take a ferry ride
   and take a fire-engine ride
   Douglas's pony
3. parties for
   Halloween
   Valentines Day
   birthdays
   Christmas
   celebration of fruits (an all-apple party, an orange party, a pineapple party, a watermelon party)
4. pets brought to school by parents, for example, a
   rabbit
   duck
   puppy
   parakeet
5. attendance at and participation in a toy show
6. watching a kite being put up and flown
7. reenacting and retelling stories and nursery rhymes
8. watching a touring group of University of Delaware dramatic-arts majors presenting "Alice in Wonderland" and "Gingerbread Boy" to all the Seaford school children

Mrs. Derrickson soon discovered that even in this group there existed marked differences. In a short time, she noticed that five achieved far better than the others. Their stories were longer; their sentences were better; their ideas were more related. Most significant was their rate of word learning compared with that of the rest of the class. By Thanksgiving, these five knew the following number of words: 45, 41, 38, 34, 33. These words had all been learned through dictated stories. Most of the techniques described in this book were used. The children kept their own story notebooks, had their own word banks, wrote stories, performed word-recognition skill-training activities, and so on.

These five children along with the rest of the class were tested individually on the Monday and Tuesday before Thanksgiving. The teacher had each child, one at a time, bring to her his word bank and pronounce each banked word. On the Tuesday following Thanksgiving, these children were retested by a visitor. Post-Thanksgiving testing, in spite of the 120 hours of forgetting time, yielded almost the same scores as obtained on the pre-Thanksgiving test.

At the post-Thanksgiving session, one of the girls performed in an interesting and gratifying way. One of the words in her word bank puzzled her, and she could not recall it. Before the examiner could even consider stopping her, the girl was up off her chair and on her way to the front of the room. On the right side of the room, the teacher had filed by interest area the stories that had been dictated by individuals and groups. The girl took down a set of stories, flipped through them rapidly, found her story, and located the word. She quickly replaced the stories and came running back to the visitor, actually sliding the last 3 feet, and shouted the word. All this added up to an astonishing show of resourcefulness and eagerness.

First, the girl knew she did not know. Second, she was undaunted by this failure to recognize the word in isolation. Third, she remembered when she had learned the word and the context in which she had learned it. Fourth, she selected the right set of stories, located her story, and located the unknown word. She did this so fast that she could not have read each word in the story. Apparently she was doing some form of skimming to locate the word. Fifth, she had the presence of mind to replace the stories. Sixth, she remembered the word and told it to the examiner.

In reading and reflecting on the report of this girl, the reader should be sure to keep in mind that this class represented a specially selected group of children who seemed the least mature of 120 pupils at the beginning of the year. These are the children who, under traditional approaches, would invariably have needed special remedial help.

In this group of twenty-three, the largest number of words known by any one pupil by Thanksgiving was 45, the least was 2. The average for the class was twenty-three. Only three pupils in the class knew fewer than 16 words, the number usually introduced in a first preprimer. Notice, too, that the five top pupils possessed a recognition vocabulary that was about equal to the vocabulary total of a second preprimer, 36 words.

The accompanying table shows the word-learning progress of the twenty-three pupils at different times (the end of November and January, the middle of March, the end of April, and the first week in June). Word knowledge was tested by presenting words in isolation. Testing recognition this way is more demanding on recall than testing them in context, so, in a sense, the test is a better measure of known words than are most standardized primary reading tests.

	NUMBER OF WORDS KNOWN				
Pupil	*November*	*January*	*March*	*April*	*June*
1	33	89	129	167	257
2	45	74	101	145	202
3	41	90	130	181	246
4	38	83	126	177	233
5	34	74	120	141	187
6	24	57	108	126	166
7	23	53	75	94	129
8	22	49	85	123	171
9	17	40	62	103	133
10	21	53	76	114	149
11	30	51	70	126	157
12	23	45	71	102	138
13	22	45	72	94	123
14	18	43	60	84	110
15	21	45	90	108	138
16	26	59	—	113	136
17	23	51	73	85	118
18	12	38	62	82	105
19	20	35	62	72	75
20	7	16	28	43	62
21	9	20	23	30	36
22	2	4	13	20	25
23	25	41	65	67	97

The steady progress throughout the year, along with the end of the year totals, represents astounding figures for a specially identified population of this kind: the range of words known, 25 to 257; the average score, 139 words. If the five bottom scores are deducted, the average shoots up to 170 words. This represents the progress made not by a typical low group but by a low-low group.

In addition, the top six people were started in the third preprimer of a basic-reading series on February 3. An adapted group DRTA procedure was used. By the end of the school year, these six had completed the second primer unit. The pupils read the first two preprimers independently.

The next five pupils were introduced to a third preprimer on April 1. The next six pupils were introduced to a second preprimer on the same date. With these pupils, an adapted group DRTA was also used. In both instances, the adaptation was occasioned largely by the need for the teacher to ask more leading questions. Gradually, the pupils began to catch on and do their own examining of clues and making of conjectures. By the time the top six had reached the primer level, they were performing in a reading-thinking way that was quite satisfactory.

The following are stories dictated by a member of the top group:

Cafeteria

I saw some butter
Some chicken. A great
big stove. Some potatoes
and gravy.

Jack-O-Lantern

We made a
Jack-O-Lantern. We put eyes
in it, and nose, a mouth.
We made him a hat.

Turkeys

We saw turkeys. We
went to see Mrs.
Colbourn. All of us
saw horses and a bull.
We saw a little horse.

To the Fire House

I went to the
fire house. I looked
around. I got a hat.
And I got a balloon.

Mother

She cooks potatoes.
She washes clothes. She
sets food on the table.
She reads books to me.

Shopping Center

Jerry has a girl
baby. We saw some ice.
We bought Jerry a baby
pin. We bought Nancy a
telephone. I saw Thelma,
Jean, and Barry. We
looked at the birds.

Christmas Story

When I woke up my mommom was there. I got a corner store for Christmas. And some houses to go on my train. George and Sandy gave me a school and stuff for the train, and some pajamas from Santa Claus.

Monkey

We got him last night from Edith and Bruce. He stayed with us last night. He turned over Mommy's paint. We leave him out in the wash room. Daddy tied him.

Birthday

Mommy is going to give me a projector, and Daddy. JoAnn is going to give me the slides. I am going to show it to Peter and Judy. Light the candles by myself.

Cat

My cat lays down on my leg while I am watching TV. When he sees Rip he runs up the tree. He watches the Flintstones with me. Every time he sees the Flintstones move, he scratches the TV. Every time my cat gets some meat from Mommy, Chipper get it.

The preceding stories may be contrasted with the following, dictated by a pupil in the bottom group:

Cafeteria

We see fried chicken.
We see butter.
Biscuits.

Cafeteria

He put the tables down.
He put the other tables down.

School

We went walking around school. Seen the library. Seen the kids.

Trick or Treat

We eat popcorn. We eat marshmallows. We drink tea.

Mother

My mother cooks. She cooks on the stove. We wash our hands before we get up to the table.

Christmas

I got something for Christmas. I got a doll baby. And shirts and pants. Number blocks. Toys and candy in stockings.

Hearts

We hanged them <u>up</u>. <u>We</u> put them on <u>a</u> <u>string</u>. <u>We</u> put them on <u>a</u> big <u>heart</u>. <u>We</u> put <u>the</u> <u>hearts</u> on <u>a</u> <u>string</u>.

Father

His name is <u>Earl</u>. <u>He</u> <u>goes</u> <u>to</u> work. <u>He</u> stays home some time. Sometimes <u>he</u> <u>goes</u> <u>to</u> work. Sometimes <u>he</u> <u>goes</u> <u>to</u> store for <u>Mommy</u>.

Picnic

<u>We</u> <u>are</u> <u>going</u> <u>on</u> <u>a</u> picnic. <u>We</u> <u>are</u> <u>going</u> <u>to</u> <u>eat</u> <u>on</u> <u>Mrs.</u> <u>Derrickson's</u> porch. <u>We</u> <u>are</u> <u>going</u> <u>to</u> eat our lunch <u>and</u> throw <u>the</u> bags away.

The words underlined are the words recognized by the pupil. In this room, pupils always marked only words known. It was thought wisest to have them constantly underscore their successes.

These stories were all kept in individual notebooks. At the end of the year, each pupil had a dated chronological account of some of his reading efforts for the year. Also, he could go back and reread any story any time during the school year. Reading books could be exchanged in class, and they were.

These pupils did creative writing just as prescribed for other more successful pupils. They enjoyed it equally well. As a matter of fact, when they got the feeling of writing, they went on a "writing bender" for a while, just writing and writing.

The following year, the same teacher, Mrs. Derrickson, stayed with the group. She knew the pupils so well that she could pick up where they left off. One change occurred, though: the top six were placed in other second grades and absorbed into new classes and new groups. Interestingly enough, a visitor to the school could not identify the six pupils in the other rooms. This is evidence of how well they fitted into the new arrangement. All teachers, of course, were well posted concerning what was happening but a little skeptical about how the pupils would fit in. By the end of September, however, they, too, were convinced of the progress of the six and how well they had matured.

At the end of the second year with the same teacher, the remaining seventeen pupils were assimilated into other grades. All but four went on to third-grade classes; the four remained in second-grade classrooms. The pupils were assigned in such a way that only two or three of the group were in the same room. Progress was still reported as being most favorable.

Of course, the teaching time during both years was divided according to a planned curriculum. Art and music, physical education, arithmetic, and science were also taught. So all pupils were busy with a number of things.

The attention spans of the group, particularly the first year, were short. Needed more than tolerant patience was an adjustment of expectancies. Once the teacher's experience had led her to expect according to the "spans" of pupils like this, rather than like those of the rest of the population, she was calmer and more even-patterned in her acceptance of the children. Most first-grade teachers are thought of as mother-surrogates, as indeed they often are, and in this instance the label was most appropriate. The teacher became their "mother in school," firm and determined, attentive and devoted, affectionate and warm.

The classroom in which these children met was a typical room. It was in the wing with other first- and second-grade sections. The children mixed freely with each other, shared the playground, went to the cafeteria together, and had the same principal.

The parents and guardians of the children needed some special attention, too. At the very beginning of the program, when the pupils had been identified, each parent was seen privately and told about the plans. Parents were asked to agree but were not coerced. In a number of instances, there were requests to "think it over." In each instance, this involved a return visit and an unhurried interview. All the parents eventually agreed to the plan.

During the school year, all reports were made in interviews with the parents present. They were told about the word-learning process, the experience stories, the library hour, the visits, and so on. An interview guide form was drafted to help keep the records straight about progress and about what was said when. End-of-the-year changes and adjustments were similarly explained.

Administrative understanding and approval were required, of course. The superintendent was luckily an interested participant. On a number of occasions, he sat in with the teachers and he provided help as needed in community contacts.

The school principal was intimately involved. She lent a hand in screening and selecting the pupils, arranging transportation, and contacting parents. Trips were planned with her approval and her assistance.

The district's reading consultant was closely involved in every phase of the program. Her constancy and knowledge were a steady source of guidance and help. She frequently stood by when small group visits were made. All in all, this was an all-school enterprise.

In brief, then, it is apparent that in many ways what was done here was similar to the program of an ungraded primary school. Instruction was geared to the level of each pupil in as many ways as possible. Some pupils spent 4 years in the primary grades rather than 3. Teachers planned and worked together and literally teamed-up on these pupils.

Special-education children

Some children are classified as in need of special education because their genes set limits on their potential for intellectual development. Many states provide special instruction for such children by using teachers with special training and by placing the children in separate rooms of the school attended by more typically developing children. It is of special significance that the attitudes and efforts of the teachers who work with these children favor enriched environments and varied programs that maximize the potential of these individuals.

J. McV. Hunt's book *Intelligence and Experience* (7), particularly Chapter 8, shows why it is advisable to realize that children change and the process of change itself is open ended as well. Teaching according to this understanding can offset unwarranted generalizations about fixed intelligence and response. Hunt points out how parental behavior, for instance, is probably a much more important influence than such traditional indexes as parental education, social-economic level, and number of books in the house. Similarly, it may be pointed out that very probably teachers' behavior is a much more important determinant of rates and amount of development than are traditional indexes.

Enthusiasm about results of using the cognitive wealth and potential of children advantageously, as they are in this approach, has been expressed many times here. Enthusiasm was no less great from the use of the Language-Experience Approach with special-education children. In two schools in Cecil County, Maryland,[5] two classes of special-education children have been studied for 3 years with results gratifying beyond all expectation.

In each instance, the teachers were previously unacquainted with the techniques of the Language-Experience Approach and were educated in it while in service. In one school, the same teacher has taught the class for 3 years. In the other, a new teacher was introduced each year. Yet, in both circumstances, results have been exceptional. In the second school, much

[5] Holly Hall Elementary School, Elizabeth Maloney, Principal. Rising Sun Elementary School, Naomi England, Principal.

of the transition to new teachers was effected with the help of the school principal.

Most significant of all the changes that occurred in these schools was the attitude of the children and, in turn, the atmosphere in the classrooms. Children who had been withdrawn, belligerent, or extremely reticent began to share and team up, to be more thoughtful and tolerant of each other, and to talk and participate in discussions. On many occasions, Ralph Wachter, the County Coordinator of Special Education Classes, and I visited these rooms and were astounded and unbelieving of what we saw. In February of the first year, on the occasion of one of our visits, the teacher suggested to us quietly that we single out a particular boy and ask him to read his latest dictated experience recording. I did so and was pleased with his oral reading, the ease and enthusiasm with which he read. Then I suggested he go to the back of the room and read to the supervisor, and, without a moment's hesitation, he did so. This was a lad who had for 2 years been known throughout this school as the most close-mouthed child ever to attend. This is cited as illustrative of the changes that occurred in both rooms in both schools.

What did the teachers do to effect these changes? No more than has already been described, except to adapt the technique to the children. More action experiences were engaged in that permitted seeing, feeling, and hearing over a longer period of time. For example, rather than bring in a turtle for a day or two, a turtle was kept for weeks as a pet. Of course, he was attended to. Leaves were collected and examined and mounted; this was done almost daily for a while. Each experience evoked oral language.

When the children sat down to talk with the teacher to tell about an experience, they did so privately. These children can talk, they have reactions to experiences, and they have ideas. In the privacy of a face-to-face confab, they talk. The delight they exhibit when they see "their talk" being typed and when they can hold their own materials is indeed gratifying. Pride of authorship, of doing, of constructing verbally evokes deep-seated affective responses.

These children showed special delight when they found a word in a magazine or book that they learned to recognize through a dictated and recorded account. The "look Mom, I can read" radiance is energizing as well as illuminating.

All the activities of the approach are engaged in by these children but at a slower pace and with much more repetition than with more typically developing children. Auditory and auditory-visual training occurs. Word banks are built. Word-card holders are used. Listening posts are used to listen to music as well as to oral reading. It was not at all unusual to see one of the children go to a listening post and listen over and over again to a favorite selection. The freedom to do so, to put on the record, and to listen had a decidedly calming effect.

Construction activities also proved fruitful. From assembling a jig-saw puzzle, a block puzzle, a Halloween mask, Christmas tree decorations, a pen for a pet, a phonic booth, and a map to dictation and to creative writing was an easy and desired step.

Much oral reading to the class was done by the teacher, by the principal, and by other visitors. Tape recordings were sometimes made of such readings and then the children could listen again at their convenience.

While the most significant change was in attitude and atmosphere, almost equally significant was the nature and quality of the ideas dictated and recorded. The samples that follow are indicative.

R. C., a nine-year-old boy in 1969, was placed in a special-education class in September, 1967. Stanford Binet test results showed he had an I.Q. of 75 in 1965. WISC test results in November, 1968, yielded an I.Q. of 80. When he was admitted to the special education class in 1967, he could not read a word. The following is some of R. C.'s work:

The Dog

If I saw it out there in the yard, I would
throw a rock at it. It was on the table trying
to get at the bottle. It had its feet on the
table. Then it was trying to get at the pan.
You could see the shadow on the ground under
the table. And it looked funny. If it was
getting in the pan I would scare it. I would
sneak under the table and scare it.   (Dictated September 12, 1967)

The Planetarium

We visited the Planetarium last Friday. The
guy showed us the stars and the moon and the
planets. We had to sit back in the seats and
look up in the air.

The guy got shocked on the machine. It has
holes in the top. The top looks around. The
guy can make it turn around backwards and
frontwards. The guy can make it face up in
the air.

The Planetarium is round and big. The

top is a hole. It looks funny when you look
up.

    We saw the moon and the stars. There were
words up in the hole; the sun turned down to
the ground. We saw the man and the dog. We
saw the bull and the little puppy. He was
standing in one place. The guy said, "Venus
is the closest one to the moon."   (Dictated February 18, 1969)

> Robert Nov, 20 1968
>
> The Thanksgeving Turkey
> I am a Turkey. I am a pretty
> Turkey. I ham after a Boy and
> a girl.

> Bambi
> Bambi like to Be a fawn
> Bambi saw a man in The bushs
> Bambi was scared to death.
> He was to starte to run. The man
> shiot Bambi in the log.
>
> March 13, 1969
> Bobby

    The teacher describes R. C. as a very clean boy and well cared for. His special interest is fire engines. He dictates, writes creatively, and draws pictures of his experiences frequently. Much of the time he seems to be off in a world of make-believe. He is currently reading at a second-reader level.

J. T. is a ten-year-old with a Stanford Binet I.Q. of 56. He, too, was admitted to the special-education class in September, 1967, as a nonreader. He is a friendly, easy-going fellow who gets along well with everyone. He is in a foster home. Some of his stories follow:

I Hearded Something

I make noise and I saw the star. And
you tore it apart. And we do the watch the
flowers in it. And we watch, we sit down.
And we go outside. We send dollar. We
have horse.   (Dictated September 27, 1967)

Sad

Somebody make me mad. Mrs. Williamson
write on the board. We copy it down. Mom
makes me sad. She spanks me.   (Dictated January 11, 1968)

The Inauguration

We saw Nixon and the White House. We
saw the parade. And we saw marching. We
saw the daughter and his wife.   (Dictated January 23, 1969)

Snow

I like snow. We make a snowman. Robin
kicked our snowman down. We wear boots
outside. Joe Towers and Bill Billings and
Harry Towers and Bill Carter and Betty Lou
Mullins and William Carter, we played in the
snow. It was cold out there.
    I jumped in the snow. I fell down. Lots
of snow was on the ground. And Mommy likes
snow. Janie likes snow and Bud Barrett likes
snow. Bud's birthday is tomorrow.
    Everybody likes snow in my room. Mrs.
May likes snow. We sat down and watched TV
and I go by the window watching it snow outside.
The snow melted.   (Dictated February 10, 1969)

J. T. has done very little writing, but he has made attempts at it. He does "I like" stories because these are two words he can write and spell.

R. M. is an eleven-year-old girl with a WISC I.Q. of 56. She is reading comfortably now at a second-reader level. Here is a sample of her creative writing from November 20, 1968:

> Rosemary
> *rosemary*
>
> the thanksgiving turkey
> I ran a way no boby
> rit me,
> People will get you,
> People will shoot turkey,
> Pillogrim love turkey
> they seve: turkey
>
> Nov. 20. 1968

Another R. M. is an eleven-year-old girl with a WISC I.Q. of 62. She, too, is reading comfortably at the second-reader level. The following is a story she wrote on March 14, 1969, and read to me on my visit to their room:

> The car rake
> We saw a car rake The boy
> was hart he was Bleding
> very very bad he had cuts
> in back of his head
> he was in paeen he was
> harting to
>
> RoseMarie
> March 14 1969

F. J. is a twelve-year-old boy with a WISC I.Q. of 73. He was known for years by his terrible temper, but in the past 2 years, this has changed to spells of stubbornness along with a marked effort at trying to learn. He is now reading comfortably at a third-reader level. The following is some of his work:

The Puppy
Mrs. Ryan brought a little puppy to school
today. And it was a German Shepherd. And it
was brown and black. And I like him very
much. And after recess we got to see him.
And Mrs. Tippett got him out of the box and
untied him. Robert asked the teacher could
he pull him.
　　And we all petted it and I held it. And
Rose Marie took it from me and dropped him
down on the ground.
　　And Mrs. Tippett wanted to see him one
more time. And then Mrs. Tippett took the
little puppy back to his house and tied
him up again.　　(Dictated September 7, 1967)

The Planetarium
We went to the planetarium yesterday. We
saw nine planets. And there was a little
arrow that went around and pointed to the
planets. It went around the sun, too. And
he said, "If you lived on Jupiter you would
only have a birthday every 12 years."
You cannot throw a ball as far on Jupiter
as you can on Earth. It is about 30,000
miles long and 7,000 miles wide. And
everything looks like real.　　(Dictated February 2, 1968)

Examination of the items reproduced here shows how productive such children can be. The quality of their language and the nature and range of the experiences dealt with provide impressive evidence. These children can talk and act and think effectively. One of the astonishing outcomes is the self-regulation they display. Their rooms buzz with activity and with interpupil cooperation. They seem particularly sensitive to the rights and feelings of others and display a strong *esprit de corps* for their classmates.

Clinical cases

I first began to appreciate the efficacy of the Language-Experience Approach in 1950, when I started using it clinically as a process that was in a sense an intermediate step between the Fernald technique (5) for tracing each word and the basic-reader approach of most developmental classrooms. The incidence of nonreading that may cautiously be characterized as caused by visual aphasia or dyslexia is very small, but it is with the people who are so affected that the V-A-K-T Fernald approach seems most effective. Some means other than tracing is needed for the larger number of children who are not dyslexias but who, for other causes, are almost nonreaders. These are the children who, because of strained circumstances at home, emotional conditions, educational practices, physiology, or slow development, failed to learn to read. They need the equivalent to good first teaching and therapy to offset the attitudes acquired by failure.

The Reading Study Center at the University of Delaware used the Language-Experience Approach with such pupils almost exclusively by modifying the Fernald technique. This permitted a more advantageous use of Montessori methods, with their interest in the welfare of the child. The constructive effort to liberate the seriously handicapped readers from the Fernald Tracing pedagogy, on the one hand, and the boring repetition of basic-reader practices, on the other, has been effective. For these children, both were as detrimental to their growth in their ability to learn to read as a poor diet would have been to their physical growth. The Language-Experience Approach, with its emphasis on the cognitive wealth of these readers, most of whom were bright or superior intellectually, proved functional.

Nine-year-olds, with histories of 4 years of school failure and the resultant trauma in the home and at school, see by this approach that they can acquire learning techniques by using their abilities more effectively. These children invariably have excellent verbal facility, can think and reason, and are indeed creative. Failure in reading has so suppressed these capabilities, however, that other means of expression are usually acquired. Many of them become aggressive and literally strike out against a society that frustrates them and does not show them how to use their abilities to advantage. Some withdraw and harbor deeply seated grudges. All are anxious and highly suspicious. When they experience clinical success over and over again, their attitudes change, their personalities change, and their achievement changes, sometimes by leaps and bounds. The biggest obstacle is usually their early failures and their poor self-image.

The Language-Experience Approach takes advantage of their interests and tastes, their language facility, their insightfulness and intelligence, and, in general, their ability to do. The materials they dictate are *theirs*. The vocabulary is not a substandard variety foisted on them but reflects *their* fluency and accuracy of usage. The words they recognize and remember are identified by them. The words they wish to learn in a deliberate attempt to add to their vocabulary are of *their* choosing. The word-attack skills they learn are applied to their vocabulary. Everything that is done features their abilities and their choices.

All this in an atmosphere of mutual respect. The children are not patronized or treated solicitously but are treated as human beings for whom regard is shown when and as it is merited. In many ways during the early months of any child's program, the therapeutic aspects of the approach contribute more to success than the pedagogic aspects. As ego strength is acquired and confidence is restored, achievement is accelerated and is reflected in school performance. Heads go up, shoulders go back, and smiles are direct and self-assured. Tasks are engaged in more diligently and for increasing lengths of time.

Printed material is introduced early but largely through the medium of "status type" materials such as newspapers, magazines, and the like. They are used, just as in first grade, to identify words learned. Gradually, too, without undue pressure, books are introduced. Because these children are not isolated from a regular school program, they continue to have contact with books. When they start bringing their school textbooks to the clinic to seek help with them, then a big forward step has been made.

Clinic instruction is carefully coordinated with the school program. Schools are cooperative. Because the clinic teaching program operates only 4 days a week and only from 8 to 11 A.M., most children do not miss much of their ordinary school program. Classes are adjusted so that, if they miss any school teaching time, it will be that in reading, spelling, and English rather than in arithmetic, science, or history.

As the teaching program shifts from an exclusive use of dictated materials and some use of creative writing to books, the skills of reading-thinking are taught. If children in the clinic can be grouped—occasionally one or two can—then they are enlisted in group DRTA training.

Research and discovery reading is also used. These clinically trained children become quite receptive to visiting the library, both the materials center in the clinic and the university library. Once the pupils have progressed this far in confidence and ability, the end of the clinic training is in sight. Many can return to their classrooms for full-time participation with only an occasional visit to the clinic for reappraisal.

Adult illiterates and semi-illiterates

The Language-Experience Approach lends itself particularly well in teaching adult illiterate and semi-illiterates to read and communicate more effectively orally as well as in writing. This is because the method takes advantage of the language facility that eighteen-year-olds and people older possess and because it uses to good advantage their experiences, interests, attitudes, and motivation.

Children in the primary grades who fail in reading become painfully aware of their failure and develop various defenses and anxieties. Adults, faced with the need to provide for themselves in a society that places increasingly high premiums on literacy, become keenly aware of their differences and disabilities. On the one hand, they seek help urgently, almost desperately, and yet, on the other, they are highly suspicious and wary. For most of them, attempts have been made to teach them to read but without success, and, as a result, their response to "one more try" is guarded.

Conventional reading materials are not appropriate in most instances. Booklets and pamphlets with simple syntax, grammar, and semantics are readily recognized as simple. Adults resent a "Look, John Doe, look. See the gun. The gun is loaded" approach. They are quick to see the mask and its falsity.

When the disadvantaged person is given an opportunity to be a producer, however, to use his own interests, to choose his own vocabulary, to articulate his own experiences, he is quick to notice the degree to which his wealth has been recognized and honored. By tapping his experience-language wealth, his thinking is fostered and this, in turn, becomes stimulating to him.

If on-the-job training is given to him in addition to his recording, typing, and using his ideas to develop recognition and comprehension, then dramatic progress is shown in both of his educational efforts. The on-the-job training takes on additional significance and vitalizes his interest, because he is asked to talk about what he is doing and, in turn, to internalize his knowledge and experience. The ideas that he voices and the nomenclature that he uses become comprehensible in print and excite further attempts at use (9).

The words he learns can be located in print in various places, much as at the first-grade level. Words like *cocoanut, banana roll, seasoned, teaspoon, safety, railroad shop, National Bank, maternity, diploma, bureau, elastic, spark plug* can be found in brochures about different jobs, publicity materials, sales material, booklets, and books. Transfer from a typed account of dictation to other material can be immediate and effective. Word banks can be initiated, scaled, of course, to the level of the learners. Adults are just as responsive to activities that foster vocabulary growth as are children.

Newspapers and magazines can be used almost from the beginning. Known words can be located and underlined. A prize comment from one twenty-two-year-old, after 2 months of training, was obtained one day when he said he had done something at breakfast he had never done before. He had bought a newspaper and read.

If adults of different age levels and different job skills are taught together, interest in what different members of the group are doing, saying, and reading can run high. A nurses' aide can read back her account of her experiences for the day and a gas-station attendant can read about happenings on his job. As skill is acquired, typed accounts can be exchanged and read silently. Such actions and interactions stimulate interest and motivation and also develop reading skill and facility in different areas.

Mrs. Ruth Goodman, a graduate student of the University of Delaware, serving as coordinator of Adult Basic Education for the Wilmington Public Schools, collected innumerable samples of adult dictation and much evidence of adult progress. Interestingly enough, much of the dictation served also as a healthy catharsis for the individuals involved. The approach provides an opportunity for them to air their thinking about various topics. They are quite responsive to the fact that they have the sole attention of the instructor while dictating. Here are some of the accounts dictated by adults:

Progress in Adult Education
My progress in Adult Education has been wonderful.
The opportunity for another chance to finish my education. I want to finish my schooling so I'll be able
to get a better job, help my children with their school

work. Of course we know times have changed. In this
generation the children learn different from what we
did. If we don't have the education, how are we going to help them? I've asked a lot of my friends to
come, but they just laugh and say I've been once or
I don't need any more schooling. Some people just
don't understand the advantage we have to help our
children. It's no shame trying to better our education. Many times I wished I had stayed in school.
Now that I can continue, someday I hope to get a
good job. I would like to work with an IBM machine.
I have to know more than I know now, so while I have
the opportunity I am going to take advantage of getting my education that I missed in order to get the
job. Do not let anyone stop you from coming to school;
even if you are late, come anyway. It's better to get
a little in a short time than to lose a lot in a day.

I wish we had more days to go in the week because
this program is the best that ever happen for our
community. I do hope more people will take advantage
we have taken.

B. W.

I am coming to night school to get a better education which I wasn't able to get when I was younger.
Well, I was able, but as a teenager you don't think
too much about education; seemed to me there were
better things in life than finishing school, but now
I know that I was wrong. Now I am going to school
and taking up typing, etc., and I think I can make a
better future for me and my two kids.

G. C.

The Engine
Today our teacher showed us how to take the
engine apart. We are learning the names of some
of the parts of the engine. Someday I'll know
the engine and how to fix it. I'm going to get
a better job and be a mechanic. We saw how the
gas line connects with the engine, the carburetor,
and the manifold. I am learning things to look
for when the engine breaks down. We saw a film
and some pictures of parts of engines.

M. S.

Employers Should Consider the Handicapped
It is very hard for a man to obtain a good job
in any factory if he has any limb missing. For
instance, there is a man I know who had an accident
where he was working. He lost a thumb and some use
of his right arm. He lost his job and now has had
trouble finding a new one. Employers turned him
down because of his accident.

I feel that employers should give men like him a
chance to prove themselves. They are not exactly
handicapped. They can do just about anything a
normal man can do, but what some employers don't
realize is that it hurts a man's pride and lowers
his morale and makes him feel less like a man.

J. McC.

Conclusion

It should be apparent that whenever the wealth of an individual is used as
a base for intellectual growth through skill development, sound progress
is made. Principal to the use of the language-experience-cognitive-emotive
wealth of an individual is the attention it gives to starting at the level of
the learner. Thereby, it utilizes the entire process by which an individual
organizes his thoughts, interests, and ambitions. In a broad sense, the
approach is like the Socratic method, with its painstaking and systematic
development of thought through inquiry from earliest beginnings to
points of highest development. The mind and interest of the individual is
engaged and this is what is vital to the process.

Preschoolers can take a long stride forward in their acquisition of concepts and language usage as they free themselves from domination by their
perceptual world. While they act and interact, see, feel, hear, smell, and
taste, watch and listen to others, respond to adult guidance, and express
themselves creatively, they acquire a storehouse of experiences and language that serve communication at different levels.

The immature can grow at a pace in keeping with their potential. Without being pressured, their wealth is used and converted to serve more
functionally. Instead of being shunted aside, they are helped along by
steps that they can take successfully. On many occasions, paced learning

based on known wealth results in unexpectedly rapid growth. But above all, it allows for steady growth rather than stagnation.

Clinical cases, filled with the anxieties of failure and frustration, are encouraged to be producers and see more clearly that they possess many strengths. For them, the recognition that they have language and experience that are useful is considerable stimulus for further effort. One more big try seems worthwhile as heads go up, shoulders go back, and new vigor is evident in every stride. Recognizing words in print is done through their own semantic trail. Word-attack skills are based on their phonological wealth, syntactic power, and ability to transfer knowledge. By means of Directed Reading-Thinking Activities, a high level of motivation and interest is generated, because their thinking strategies and skills have been focused on.

Adult illiterates and semi-illiterates are not stupid but only unlettered. The Language-Experience Approach capitalizes superbly on the fact that these people do not lack the power to absorb ideas and impressions. To the contrary, it builds upon their ideas and impressions and the oral language facility they have acquired. As a result, a sufficient motivation to learn to read is generated and the successes that result become effective reinforcers. Their response is very much controlled by the consequences of their reading success. By utilizing job-oriented activities, their reading successes are immediately related to behavior needed for success in real-life situations.

Bibliography

1. Betts, Emmett A. *Foundations of Reading Instruction.* New York: American Book Co., 1946.
2. Bond, Guy L., and Eva Bond. *Teaching the Children To Read.* New York: Macmillan, 1945.
3. Bond, Guy L., and Miles A. Tinker. *Reading Difficulties, Their Diagnosis and Correction.* New York: Appleton-Century-Crofts, 1957.
4. Durrell, Donald D. *Improving Reading Instruction.* New York: Harcourt, Brace & World, 1956.
5. Fernald, Grace M. *Remedial Techniques in Basic School Subjects.* New York: McGraw-Hill, 1943.
6. Gates, Arthur I. *The Improvement of Reading.* 3rd ed. New York: Macmillan, 1947.

7. Hunt, J. McV. *Intelligence and Experience*. New York: Ronald Press, 1961.
8. Piaget, Jean. *Six Psychological Studies*. Edited by David Elkind. New York: Random House, 1967.
9. Stauffer, Russell G., and Ronald Cramer. "Reading Specialists in an Occupational Training Program," *The Reading Teacher*, vol. 20, no. 6 (March, 1967), pp. 525–531.

APPENDIXES

A

Science activities to motivate individual language experiences

MEASURING WEIGHT

Equipment: Small jar lid, simple wooden frame, spring, string or wire, several pennies, nickels, buttons, pieces of apple or other fruit or vegetable.

Directions: Compare the weight of small objects to the weight of one, two, three, or four pennies or other coins.

MEASURING TEMPERATURE

Equipment: Thermometers, pan of water.

Directions: Put the thermometers in the pan of water. (Do they measure the same degree of temperature?) Put the thermometers in different parts of the room. (Do they measure the same degree of temperature?)

MEASURING TIME

Equipment: Stop watch, simple pendulum, small objects of different weight.

Directions: Count how many times the pendulum swings in one minute. Lengthen and shorten the string to see how length affects the movement. Put different weights on the pendulum. See if this makes a difference in the movement.

BOTTLE OF FLIES

Equipment: Two mayonnaise jars with a large hole in each lid and the lids locked back to back, flies.

Directions: Put flies in one jar. Make one jar dark, make one jar cold, think of other ways to make the jars different and see what will make the flies go from one jar to another.

SEEDS

Equipment: Moistened sponge in covered dish, variety of seeds.

Directions: Put rows of seeds on the moistened sponge. Notice the different things that happen to them from day to day.

WHAT HAPPENS?

1. *Equipment:* Small jars, cups, or glasses; stirrers; water; variety of substances such as sugar, salt, baking soda, olive oil, vinegar, rubbing alcohol, scouring powder, carpet tack.

   Directions: Put a substance in water. Stir. Observe what happens. After testing each substance by itself, try mixing two or more. (Does anything different happen?)

2. *Equipment:* Cold water, hot water, cups, teaspoon, stirrer, salt, sugar.

   Directions: Add sugar to a cup of cold water, a teaspoon at a time. Stir after each spoonful until the sugar ceases to dissolve and some stays in the bottom of the cup. (How many spoonfuls were you able to dissolve?) Now do the same with a cup of hot water. (Did anything different happen?) Now do the same with salt, first in cold water and then in hot water. (Did anything different happen?)

3. *Equipment:* Lemon juice or vinegar, baking soda, spoon, two jars of water.

   Directions: Put the soda in the water. Add vinegar. (What happens?) Now put the vinegar in water first. Add soda. (What happens?)

DID THEY MIX?

Equipment: Half a glass of water, olive oil, teaspoon, detergent, stirrer.

Directions: Add a teaspoon of oil to half a glass of water. Stir. (Did they mix?) Now add a teaspoonful of detergent. Stir slowly. (What happens?)

WHY DID THEY GET CLEAN?

Equipment: Oil, cold water, soap.

Directions: Rub oil on your hands. Rinse your hands with cold water. (What happens?) Wash your hands with soap and cold water. (What happens?)

WHAT HAPPENED LATER?

Equipment: Glass of hot water, sugar, pencil, string.

Directions: Dissolve all the sugar you can in a glass of hot water. Tie a string to a pencil and lay the pencil over the glass so that the string hangs in the sugar water. Set the experiment aside for a few days. (What happened?)

TESTING

Equipment: Red and blue litmus paper; jars of lemon juice, vinegar, sour milk, ammonia water.

Directions: Dip a piece of red litmus paper into each jar. (What happened?) Dip a piece of blue litmus paper into each jar. (What happened?)

WHAT MAKES ICE MELT FASTEST?

Equipment: Crushed ice cubes, four jars or cups, thermometers, salt, sugar, vinegar, alcohol, teaspoon.

Directions: Put a thermometer in each cup. Put one crushed ice cube in a cup. Add one teaspoon of salt. Now do the same in another cup with the sugar, then each of the other ingredients in turn. Watch the thermometers.

CHEMICAL DETECTIVE

Equipment: Sand, chalk, crushed chalk, iron filings, salt, baking powder, baking soda, sugar, flour, magnet, water in a cup, litmus paper, two small pieces of glass.

Directions: Put each of substance through many tests. Touch them, rub them between fingers, touch them with the magnet. (How are they alike? How are they different? Would you like to make a chart?)

RING AROUND THE BATHTUB

Equipment: Two jars with lids, eye dropper, distilled water, tap water, liquid soap.

Directions: Add a drop of liquid soap to a jar of distilled water. Close the lid and shake the jar. Do the same with a jar of tap water. Keep adding a drop of soap at a time until you have suds in both jars. (Which needed more soap?)

FUN WITH MAGNETS

Equipment: Pendulum made of a magnet tied to string; other magnets of different sizes; several small objects such as coins, buttons, nails, hair pins, stones, paper clips.

Directions: Use the different magnets to see in how many ways and directions the pendulum will move. Then see which of the small objects can be attracted to the magnet on the pendulum.

ROLLER

Equipment: Two round cans or boxes, drinking straws.

Directions: Lay some straws all the same direction out on the table. Place the cans or boxes on the straws so that their length is perpendicular to the straws and so that they do not touch. Blow between the containers. (What happens?)

CAN YOU MAKE A WHISTLE?

Equipment: Drinking straws, scissors.

Directions: Flatten one end of a straw. Cut off the flattened corners. (Now how can you make it whistle?)

A NEW WAY TO GROW A PLANT

Equipment: Plant leaf, pin.

Directions: Pin the leaf to a corkboard, wall, or desk, wherever it will get plenty of light. Watch what happens over a period of time.

Some sources of simple science experiences

1. *The A.A.A.S. Science Book List for Children.* Washington, D.C.: American Association for the Advancement of Science, 1963.
2. Cornell Science Leaflets. (Published four times a year.) Ithaca: N.Y.: New York State College of Agriculture, Cornell University. Titles include: *Amphibians, Ancient Sea Life, Birds, Chemicals in Action, Electricity and Magnetism, Food Chains, Keeping Animals in the Classroom, Let's Measure, Light, Little Climates, Making Black and White Photographs, Plants Without Flowers, Reptiles, Science Experiments in the Classroom, Seeds, Simple Machines, Sounds, Weather.*
3. Milgron, Harry. *Explorations in Science.* (A book of basic experiments.) New York: Dutton, 1961.

4. Hone, Elizabeth B., *et al. Teaching Elementary Science: A Source Book for Elementary Science.* New York: Harcourt, Brace & World, 1962.

5. Neal, Charles D. *Exploring Light and Color.* Chicago, Ill.: Children's Press, 1964.

6. Parker, Bertha M. *Science Experiences.* Evanston, Ill.: Row, Peterson, 1961.

7. Podendorf, Illa. *101 Science Experiments.* Chicago, Ill.: Children's Press, 1963.

8. *Science and Children.* Journal of the National Science Teachers Association.

9. *Science for the Eight to Twelves.* Washington, D.C.: The Association for Childhood Education International, 1958.

10. *700 Science Experiments for Everyone.* UNESCO publication. New York: Doubleday, 1958.

B

Effectiveness of Language-Arts and Basic-Reader Approaches to First-Grade Reading Instruction

ABSTRACT

The purpose of this study (U.S.O.E. Project 2769) was to compare a language-arts approach to beginning reading instruction with a basic-reader approach. English teachers, semanticists, psycholinguists, and librarians as well as reading teachers have for many years talked about the need to consider reading, writing, listening, and speaking skills in all sound teaching practices. This study was undertaken to determine whether this approach to language and communication would be effective from the beginning of reading instruction.

OBJECTIVES

The general objective was to determine the effects of the two methods of beginning reading instruction on first-grade children. The following specific questions were posed. It was asked first of all whether there would be a significant difference in:

1. the performance of two treatment groups as measured by the Stanford Achievement Test
2. the performance of boys and girls as measured by the Stanford Achievement Test
3. attitudes toward reading of the two control groups
4. the oral-reading performances of a random sample of the two groups
5. word-recognition ability of a random sample of the two groups

6. writing mechanics, spelling, and total number of running words between random samples of the two groups on a measure of written language
7. the number of words spelled correctly, the number of different words used, and originality, interest, and story consistency between random samples of the two groups on a written language measure
8. reading achievement between the two groups when readiness-test results and intelligence-test results are held constant

In addition, these questions were posed:

1. Will any pretest measures be good predictors of achievement?
2. Will the presence or lack of kindergarten experience be associated with a significant difference in reading achievement between the two groups?
3. Will there be a significant difference in achievement between the two treatment groups when pupils are regrouped according to the Terman classification of intelligence?
4. Will there be a significant difference in achievement between the two groups when the segregated black children are removed from the experimental population?
5. Will there be a significant difference in achievement as measured by the Stanford Achievement Test when both treatment groups are compared with a national sample?
6. Will there be a significant difference in achievement as measured by the Stanford Achievement Test when the segregated black population has been removed from the experimental population and this group, along with the control population, is compared with a national sample?

PROCEDURE

In this study, the language-arts approach applied to the first treatment group was designed to utilize to the fullest the children's facility to communicate through: oral language (speaking and listening); written language, or dictation, and creative writing; artistic ability in drawing and painting; dramatic ability such as in creative dramatics, puppetry, and so on. Intensive word-attack training was initiated at the beginning, using words derived from the children's spoken and written vocabularies. Group reading instruction, to develop the thinking-reading skills required for reading for information, was introduced by means of basic readers as soon as a group of children could read at a first-reader level. When this stage of reading ability was attained, then reading instruction time was divided equally between group instruction using basic readers and individualized instruction using self-selection from a library and creative writing.

The teachers in the second treatment group, the basic-reader population, were asked to continue to use the basic reader series they had used in previous years. They were asked to make a special effort to follow the instructions outlined by the basic-reader teacher's manual.

There were 528 subjects in this study. All children were at least five years and eight months of age on September 1, 1964. Because of absences and population mobility, only 433 pupils received full pretest and post-test analysis. In the experimental, language-arts population, there were 232 subjects, 119 boys and 113 girls. The total included a segregated black population of 27 boys and 44 girls. In the control, basic-reader population, there were 201 subjects, 117 boys and 84 girls.

Twenty first-grade classrooms in three towns in southern Delaware were involved. The location of the experimental population was Seaford, in which all the first-grade classes participated, ten in number. This meant, of course, that all ten first-grade teachers were involved, and it helped neutralize the Hawthorne effect to a degree, since not all ten were equally enthusiastic about the language-arts approach.

The control population was divided equally between Georgetown and Harrington, about 20 miles from each other. There were five classrooms in each town. The Ginn basic-reader series was used in Georgetown, American Book Company's Betts basic readers in Harrington.

Central library facilities were available in each school. In Seaford, there were two part-time library aides. A.L.A. minimum standards for books available to children were met in all instances.

The following pretests were administered: Murphy-Durrell Diagnostic Reading-Readiness Test, Research Edition, 1964; Metropolitan Readiness Test, Form A, 1965; Thurstone Pattern-Copying Test, Experimental Edition; Thurstone and Jeffrey Identical Forms Test, Experimental Edition; Detroit Word-Recognition Test, Form B, 1953. The Pintner-Cunningham Test of Mental Ability, Form A, 1964 Revision, was also administered, using the publisher's revised norms of May, 1965.

The following post-tests of achievement were administered, in the order named, late in April and early in May, 1965, during the week the 140th teaching day occurred: San Diego Reading-Attitude Inventory; Stanford Achievement, Primary I, Form X, 1964; Gilmore Oral-Reading Test, 1951; Fry Test of Phonetically Regular Words Oral-Reading Test, 1964; Gates Word-Pronunciation Test, 1942; Karlsen Phonemic Word Test,

1964. In addition, a creative-writing sample was obtained from each child.

The Attitude Inventory and the Stanford Achievement Test were administered to each child in the study. The others were administered only to randomly selected populations.

Means, standard deviations, and analyses of variance and covariance were computed as required. Computations were made by a Schie Scientific Data Systems (SDS 9300) Computer located in the computer center at the University of Delaware.

RESULTS AND CONCLUSIONS

The Stanford Achievement Test was the principal test of achievement used in all the studies, and only the table reporting its results is presented here.

Means and test of significance of stanford achievement test, primary i, Form X, for boys, girls, and total populations of experimental and control groups

	EXPERIMENTAL		CONTROL		*Mean*			*Level of*
	N	*M*	*N*	*M*	*Difference*	*df*	*t*	*Significance*
WORD READING								
boys	119	18.07	117	15.20	2.87	222	2.81	.01
girls	113	20.12	84	16.89	3.23	117	2.64	.01
total	232	19.07	201	15.90	3.17	398	3.95	.001
PARAGRAPH MEANING								
boys	119	17.53	117	15.02	2.51	207	2.01	.05
girls	113	20.90	84	16.96	3.94	186	3.18	.01
total	232	19.17	201	15.83	3.34	397	3.74	.001
VOCABULARY								
boys	119	19.46	117	17.96	1.50	234	1.50	none
girls	113	19.51	84	19.32	0.19	197	.21	none
total	232	19.49	201	18.53	0.96	428	1.43	none
SPELLING								
boys	119	9.60	117	7.98	1.62	234	1.87	none
girls	113	12.19	84	10.16	2.03	197	2.43	.02
total	232	10.86	201	8.89	1.97	431	3.19	.01
WORD-STUDY SKILLS								
boys	119	33.96	117	31.99	1.97	234	1.26	none
girls	113	36.56	84	36.18	0.38	197	.23	none
total	232	35.22	201	33.74	1.48	431	1.31	none
ARITHMETIC								
boys	119	29.67	117	34.91	−5.25	234	−2.23	.05
girls	113	32.55	84	38.92	−6.37	197	−2.86	.01
total	232	31.07	201	36.58	−5.51	432	−3.33	.001

Pretest results showed that the total control population was significantly older than the experimental population, the boys making the difference. There was no significant difference in mental age between the total experimental and the total control populations. On the readiness tests, the Murphy-Durrell test of phonemes and the Metropolitan alphabet test, the total experimental population scored significantly higher than the total control population. The control population scored significantly higher on the Thurstone and Jeffrey Identical Forms Test. There were no significant differences in performance on the Murphy-Durrell tests of letter names and learning rate, the Metropolitan subtests of word meaning, listening, matching, numbers, copying, and the Thurstone Pattern-Copying Test. On the Detroit Word-Recognition Test, the experimental population made an average score of 16.8 words, with a range of from 3 to 38 words. The control population made an average score of 5 words, with a range of from 1 to 32 words.

Post-test results and the resulting analysis of findings are presented as answers to the fourteen questions asked as Objectives, in sequential order.

1. The experimental population earned significantly higher scores (at the .01 level of confidence) than did the control population on the tests of word reading, paragraph meaning, and spelling. The populations were equal on the tests of word-study skills and vocabulary. The control population scored significantly better on the arithmetic test. It can be tentatively concluded from this that the language-arts approach to reading instruction is likely to result in better achievement in reading and spelling but not in vocabulary and arithmetic.

2. The boys in the experimental population scored significantly higher than the boys in the control population on the tests of Word Reading and Paragraph Meaning. There were no differences on the tests of Word-Study Skills, Spelling, and Vocabulary. Again the control group was significantly better in Arithmetic. The girls in the experimental population scored significantly higher than the girls in the control population on Word Reading, Paragraph Meaning, and Spelling. The groups were about equal on the tests of Word-Study Skills and Vocabulary. Again the control group scored significantly better on the Arithmetic test. It might be concluded that girls may fare better with the language-arts approach and that boys will show up particularly well in reading.

3. There was no difference in attitude toward reading as expressed by the two populations, either as a total population or on a boy or girl basis. It can be concluded, tentatively, that both approaches produce about the same attitude toward reading.

4. On an individually administered test of oral reading, the experimental population scored significantly higher than the control population on accuracy but not on rate of reading. It may be concluded that the language-arts approach will produce good oral reading.

5. On each of the three measures of word-recognition ability, the experimental population random sample scored significantly better than the control population sample. To the degree that these measures represent a good appraisal of skill, it might be concluded that pupils taught by the language-arts approach are apt to fare better at attacking new words in isolation than are children taught by a basic-reader approach.

6. The results of the random sample experimental population on a measure of written language were significantly better in writing mechanics, spelling, and total number of running words than those of the control pupils. It may be concluded that giving extensive opportunity to dictate, write creatively, and read the writings of classmates was a more effective way of teaching certain writing skills than using a basic-reader approach.

7. Results showed that in each of the areas tested the experimental children scored significantly higher than did the control children. It can be concluded that the language-arts approach will produce better results in the number of different words used and spelled correctly and in originality, interest, and story consistency than will the basic-reader approach.

8. When readiness and intelligence were held constant, the experimental population scored significantly better on all measures except Word-Study Skills of the Stanford Achievement Test and on rate of oral reading. When the black children were excluded, the experimental population again scored significantly better on all tests except Word-Study Skills. It may be concluded, therefore, that the language-arts approach yields high returns almost regardless of readiness or capacity.

9. Results showed that, of the pretest measures reported, the test of intelligence provided the best prediction evidence for success in reading, spelling, vocabulary, and arithmetic. The two readiness tests provided significant predictive evidence for the experimental population and in good part for the boys of the control population. It may be concluded tentatively that achievement can be predicted.

10. In both populations, the children with 100 or more days of kindergarten experience performed significantly better than children with no such experience. In addition, the children of the experimental population with kindergarten experience performed significantly better than the similar group in the control population. It may be concluded, then, that

kindergarten experience does make a difference in the achievement of children faced with the demands of beginning reading instruction and especially so if they are taught by the language-arts approach.

11. It can be concluded that children in the average and above-average groups taught by a language-arts approach will make better progress than those taught by the basic-reader approach. Only in Arithmetic did the children in the basic-reader program perform better. In the low-average group and the group of below 70 I.Q., the children made about equal scores.

12. The unsegregated experimental population performed significantly better on all tests than did the control population. It can be concluded that the performance of the segregated black children was not influenced sufficiently by the language-arts approach to avoid having their scores materially lower than the mean achievement scores of the total experimental population.

13. Both approaches to reading instruction produced achievement records comparable with the average group of the Stanford Achievement standardization population. It can be concluded that both methods of reading instruction are effective ways of teaching beginning reading.

14. It can be concluded that the language-arts approach did not sufficiently influence achievement of the segregated black population to avoid having their performance materially influence the mean achievement scores of the total experimental population. The unsegregated group in the experimental population showed marked superiority over the control population in the comparisons with the national sample. It can be concluded that the language-arts approach is a most effective way of teaching reading.

In general, it may be concluded that the language-arts approach to beginning reading instruction is effective. It produced excellent results in reading performance, word-attack skills, spelling, vocabulary development, written communication as promoted by creative writing, and handwriting. Furthermore, the technique can be used effectively with all children.

The fact that all the first-grade teachers in the Seaford School District participated in this study provides much support for the idea that all teachers can learn to use the language-arts approach effectively. In the beginning, not all the teachers were equally enthusiastic about the approach or participation in the study. At the end of the year, all the teachers were highly enthusiastic about the language-arts approach and almost evangelistic about their conclusions.

Tests are needed that will show more adequately the language skills acquired by means of the language-arts approach. The principal test used in this study did not have either the breadth or depth to give a true measure of language achievement. Sound tests of reading attitudes, creative writing, writing mechanics, word-attack skills on words in context, critical reading, and reading tastes are still needed.

Effectiveness of Language-Arts and Basic-Reader Approaches to First-Grade Reading Instruction—Extended into Second Grade

ABSTRACT

The purpose of this study (U.S.O.E. Project 3276), with W. Dorsey Hammond, was to test the hypothesis that there is no significant difference between the effects of language-arts and basic-reader methods of primary reading instruction when extended and applied at the second-grade level. The language-arts approach was designed to utilize children's oral-language facility and experience and their creative-writing facility to develop a reading vocabulary, word-attack skills, and written-communication skills. The second treatment group, the basic-reader population, used basic readers, study books, and teacher's manuals designed to develop and maintain a reading vocabulary, word-attack skills, and comprehension at the second-grade level.

OBJECTIVES

The general objective of this (longitudinal) study on the same population was to determine the effects of the two methods of reading instruction on second-grade children. The following specific questions were posed. It was asked whether there would be a significant difference in:

1. intelligence as measured by the Kuhlmann-Anderson Intelligence Test in September of the experimental year

2. performance of the two treatment groups as measured by the Gates Primary Reading Tests in September of the experimental year

3. performance of the boys and girls of the two treatment groups as well as within the treatment groups as measured by the Gates Primary Reading Tests

4. writing mechanics, spelling, number of running words, and number of different words used between a random sample of the two treatment groups on a measure of written language in September of the second-grade year

5. originally, interest, and story consistency in the creative-writing sample between a random sample of the two treatment groups in September of the experimental year

6. attitude toward reading as measured by a Reading Attitude Inventory in May of the experimental year

7. performance of the two treatment groups as measured by the Stanford Achievement Test, Primary II, in May of the experimental year

8. performance of the boys and girls of the two treatment groups as measured by the Stanford Achievement Test, Primary II

9. eagerness to read and maturity of reading between the two treatment groups as measured by an eagerness-to-read scale and a maturity-of-choice scale

10. the number of books read between the two treatment groups in February of the experimental year

11. oral-reading performance of a random sample from the two treatment groups in May of the experimental year

12. word-recognition ability of a random sample from the two treatment groups in May of the experimental year

13. writing mechanics, spelling, number of running words, and number of different words used between a random sample of the two treatment groups on a measure of written language in May of the experimental year

14. handwriting skill of the two treatment groups in May of the experimental year

15. originality, interest, and story consistency in the creative-writing sample of a random sample population of the two treatment groups in May of the experimental year

16. reading achievement between the two treatment groups in May of the experimental year when the scores on the Gates Primary Reading Tests administered in September of the experimental year are held constant

17. reading and spelling achievement between the two treatment groups in May of the experimental year when scores on the Stanford Achievement subtests administered the previous May in first grade are held constant

PROCEDURES

In second grade, the technique known as Directed Reading-Thinking Activity was used with groups primarily to teach critical thinking and comprehension skills. Individualized Directed Reading-Thinking Activity was used primarily to teach the important skills of selecting, reading, and sharing. Creative writing was an important part of the instructional program. In addition, word-recognition training was emphasized to provide the reader with the tools to recognize new words in both the group and individualized reading sessions. The second-grade teachers alternated group instruction, using basal readers and self-selection from the library on a monthly basis. Children were grouped for spelling instruction; the approach was a test-retest self-correction method.

The basic-reader series used in the control classrooms had been in use in the control schools in previous years.

There were 389 subjects in this study. Only children who received full pretest and post-test analyses in both first and second grades were included. In the experimental population, there were 206 subjects, 104 boys and 102 girls. In the control population, there were 183 subjects, 100 boys and 83 girls.

Twenty classrooms in three towns in southern Delaware were involved in the study. Eleven classrooms used the language-arts approach and nine classrooms used the basic-reader approach. In Seaford, the location of the experimental population, all the second-grade classes participated. The control population was divided between Georgetown and Harrington, about 20 miles apart. The Georgetown School District involved its total second-grade population of four classes, and the Harrington School District involved its total second-grade population of five classes. The three communities are similar in social-economic make-up. In Georgetown, the Ginn basic-reader series was used, in Harrington American Book Company's Betts basic readers.

A central library was available in each school. A.L.A. minimum standards for books available to children were met in all instances.

The following pretests were administered in September of the experimental year: Kuhlmann-Anderson Test of Intelligence, Form B, 1963; Gates Primary Reading Test, Form I, 1958, Word Recognition, Sentence Reading, and Paragraph Meaning; a creative writing sample.

The following tests were administered in May of the experimental year: San Diego Reading-Attitude Inventory; Reading-Interest Scale; Stanford Achievement Test, Primary II, 1964; Gilmore Oral-Reading Test, 1951; Fry Test of Phonetically Regular Words Oral-Reading Test, 1964; Gates Word-Pronunciation Test, 1942. In addition, a creative-writing sample was obtained from each child.

The Attitude Inventory, the Reading Interest Scale, and the Stanford

Achievement tests were administered to each child in the study. The other post-tests were administered to a random sample drawn from each treatment group.

RESULTS AND CONCLUSIONS

Analysis showed that there was no significant difference in chronological age between the experimental and control populations.

The pretest results and the post-test results and the analysis of findings will be presented as answers to the seventeen questions asked as objectives.

1. The total language-arts experimental population had a significantly higher raw score on the intelligence test than the basic-reader control population (.05 level of significance or below). The boys in the experimental population had a significantly higher score than the control boys, and the girls in the experimental population had a significantly higher raw score than the control girls.

2. The total experimental population earned significantly higher scores on the Gates Primary Tests of Word Recognition, Sentence Reading, and Paragraph Meaning. These findings support the finding of the first-grade study, which demonstrated a significantly better performance by the language-arts treatment group than by the basic-reader treatment group on most measures of reading achievement.

3. On the Gates Word-Recognition Test, the experimental boys earned significantly higher scores than the control boys, the experimental girls significantly higher scores than the control girls. On the Sentence-Reading Test, the experimental girls received significantly higher scores than the control girls. There was no significant difference between the boys of the two treatment groups. On Paragraph Meaning, there was no significant difference between the boys of the two treatment groups or the girls of the two treatment groups. When divided by sex, three of the six interactions were significantly in favor of the experimental groups. The three interactions that were not statistically significant approached significance in favor of the experimental population. The results suggest that the significant difference in favor of the language-arts approach found at the end of first grade tended to hold up during the summer months. In both the experimental and control groups, the girls received significantly higher scores than the boys.

4. An analysis of the creative-writing performance of a random sample group from each treatment indicated that the language-arts group wrote significantly longer stories, used a significantly more varied vocabulary,

spelled significantly more words correctly, and exhibited a significantly better performance in writing mechanics than did the basic-reader group. These results strongly suggest that the language-arts approach develops a greater facility in written communication than does the basic-reader approach.

5. The creative-writing samples of the experimental population were significantly more original in content and consistent in story sequence than the samples of the control population, according to an independent rating. There was no significant difference in the interest level between treatment groups.

6. There was no significant difference in attitude toward reading between the two treatment groups.

7. The experimental population received scores significantly higher than those of the control population on the subtests of Word Meaning, Science and Social Studies Concepts, Spelling, Word-Study Skills, and Language. The control population achieved a significantly higher score on the subtest of Arithmetic Computation. There were no significant differences on the subtests of Paragraph Meaning and Arithmetic Concepts. An examination of the performance of the total populations of the two treatment groups indicates that the language-arts pupils were reading better at the end of second grade than were the basic-reader pupils, as measured by the Stanford Achievement Test.

8. The boys of the experimental group received significantly higher scores on the subtests of Science and Social Studies Concepts, Word-Study Skills, and Language. The control boys had significantly higher scores on Arithmetic Computation. There were no significant differences for the subtests of Word Meaning, Paragraph Meaning, Spelling, and Arithmetic Concepts. The experimental girls earned significantly higher scores than did the control girls on subtests of Word Meaning, Science and Social Studies Concepts, Spelling, Word-Study Skills, and Language. There were no significant differences for Paragraph Meaning and the Arithmetic subtests for the girls. The results suggest a rather strong trend in favor of the experimental group, particularly for the girls.

9. The results indicate that the experimental girls and the total experimental population exhibited a greater eagerness to read than did the control girls and the total control population. There was no significant difference between the boys of the two treatment groups. On the measure of maturity of reading choice, the experimental boys were rated significantly higher than the control boys; there was no significant dif-

ference between the girls or the total populations of the two treatment groups. Of the six interactions on eagerness to read and maturity of choice, the three significant findings were in favor of the experimental treatment group. These findings suggest that the language-arts approach fosters a greater interest in reading and, with the boys, a greater degree of maturity in selecting reading material than does the basic-reader approach.

10. The experimental boys read significantly more than the control boys, and the experimental girls read significantly more than the control girls. The total language-arts treatment group read significantly more than the total basic-reader treatment group.

11. On an individually administered test of oral-reading accuracy and oral-reading rate, a random sample from the experimental population scored significantly better than a random sample drawn from the control population. It may be concluded that the language-arts approach produces more accurate oral readers and faster readers than the basic-reader approach at the second-grade level.

12. On two individually administered tests of word recognition in isolation, the random sample experimental group received significantly higher scores than the random sample control group. It may be concluded that the language-arts approach fosters greater facility in word recognition than does the basic-reader approach.

13. An analysis of the creative writing in May of the experimental year indicated that the experimental population used a significantly more varied vocabulary in both the number of different words used and the number of polysyllabic words used. The difference in spelling performance between the two treatment groups closely approached significance. There was no significant difference in writing mechanics or in length of stories. The latter finding was a curious one, because classroom observation had suggested that the language-arts children wrote more often and wrote consistently longer stories. Part of the answer may lie in the fact that the children in both treatment groups had a story read to them and were asked to write only an ending. The mere writing of an ending might have acted as a restriction by not allowing children to develop their own plots and story characters.

14. There was no significant difference in quality of handwriting between the two treatment groups.

15. On independent ratings of originality, interest, and story consistency in the creative writing sample, the random sample experimental

group rated significantly higher on each measure than the random sample control group. It may be concluded that the language-arts approach, which puts special emphasis on written-communication skills, yields more interesting creative-writing performances.

16. When the Gates Primary Reading Test administered in September was used as a covariate, the Word-Meaning subtest of the Stanford Achievement Test administered in May remained significant in favor of the experimental population, and the Paragraph-Meaning subtest became significant in favor of the experimental population. The Word-Study Skills subtest did not reach significance when the Gates scores were held constant.

17. An additional approach to covariate analysis in this study was to hold constant comparable subtests administered in May of the first-grade year with the Stanford Achievement subtests in May of the second-grade year. The following interactions summarize these findings. When the Word-Reading subtest administered in May of first grade was co-varied, there was a significant difference in favor of the experimental population on the Word-Meaning subtest. When the Paragraph-Meaning subtest administered in May of first grade was held constant, there was a significant difference in favor of the experimental population on Para-graph-Meaning in May of the experimental year. When the Spelling sub-test scores and the Word-Study Skills subtest scores obtained the previous year were held constant, there was a significant difference in favor of the experimental population. It may be concluded that the adjustment of pretest differences tend to support previous findings favoring the experi-mental population in May of the experimental year.

In general, it may be concluded that both the language-arts approach and the basic-reader approach are effective means of instruction in second grade. Even though both are effective as measured by the tests used in this study, an examination of the data suggests quite clearly that the lan-guage-arts approach is the more effective of the two. There were many statistically significant differences in performance between treatments, and all favored the language arts-approach with the exception of Arith-metic subtests for boys on the Stanford Achievement Test. The standard-ized-test results yielded evidence of the superiority of the language-arts approach when extended into second grade. Some of the nonstandardized test results, such as the analysis of written-communication skills and read-ing tastes, also favored the language-arts approach.

Certain Differences in the Syntactic Structure of Creative Writing at Four Elementary Grade Levels

ABSTRACT

This study, a 1968, unpublished doctoral dissertation of W. Dorsey Hammond at the University of Delaware, investigated certain aspects of syntactic structure in the creative-writing performance of chlidren in second, third, fourth, and sixth grade.

The sample consisted of 120 children enrolled at the Seaford Special School District in southern Delaware. Fifteen boys and 15 girls were randomly selected from each of the four grades. The enrollment at each grade level was approximately 350 students. The children randomly selected from the second, third, and fourth grades had followed a Language-Experience Approach to reading instruction with an emphasis on written-communication skills. The sixth grade sample had had a limited exposure to a language-experience curriculum.

Beginning with the last week in October, the writing produced during daily creative writing sessions by all the children enrolled in grades two, three, four, and six of the Seaford Special School District was placed in individual file folders. Each teacher of these grades was given a set of instructions in regard to obtaining the creative-writing samples. No specific writing topics were given. Each story was dated and signed by the writer. At the end of November, the file folders containing the stories written by all the children were collected by the investigator. Approximately 500 words written by each member of the random sample were used in the analysis.

Analysis of the data yielded the following findings:

1. There was a statistically significant effect for grade in the mean length of single-clause T-units. The mean length of single T-units increases as a function of older grade levels.

2. There was a statistically significant effect for grade in the mean length of multiclause T-units. The mean length of multi T-units increases as a function of older grade levels.

3. There was a statistically significant effect for grade in the ratio of multi T-units to single T-units. The ratio increase as a function of older grade levels.

4. There was statistically significant effect for grade in the combined total of adjective, noun, and adverb clauses. The use of three types of subordinate clause increased as a function of older grade levels.

5. There was a statistically significant effect for grade and a statistically significant interaction of sex and grade for adjective clauses. There was a significant effect for grade in the use of both noun and adverb clauses. The use of noun and adverb clauses increased as a function of older grade levels.

6. There was a statistically significant effect for grade in the number of different types of verbs used. There was an increase in the number of types of verbs used as a function of older grade levels.

7. There was a statistically significant effect for grade in the use of unmodified nouns and pronouns. The use of unmodified nouns and pronouns decreased as a function of older grade levels.

8. There was no significant effect for grade, sex, or interaction in the use of adverbials.

9. There was no significant effect for grade, sex, or interaction in the use of prepositional phrases.

10. Mean T-unit length was a better syntactic predictor of the grade level of children's writing than mean sentence length, mean clause length, or subordination ratio.

The following conclusions were reached:

1. Children in older elementary grade levels used different types of verbs more frequently and fewer unmodified nouns and pronouns than early-grade children.

2. Early-grade children used adverbials as well as prepositional phrases with about the same frequency as older-grade children.

3. Older-grade children tended to write longer single T-units and longer multi T-units.

4. As children progressed through the elementary grades, the ratio of multi T-units to single T-units increased, the total number of subordinate clauses used in writing increased, as did the use of adjective, noun, and adverb clauses. Use of adjective clauses, however, varied inconsistently with sex at different grade levels.

An Investigation of the Spelling Achievement of Two Groups of First-Grade Classes on Phonologically Regular and Irregular Words and in Written Composition

ABSTRACT

This study, a 1968, unpublished doctoral dissertation of Ronald L. Cramer at the University of Delaware, investigated the spelling ability of two groups of first-grade classes in terms of achievement on phonologically regular and irregular words and spelling achievement in written composition. Although neither group of classes received formal spelling instruction, each received reading instruction according to a different method. The two reading-instruction methods were the language-arts approach and the basic-reader approach.

Twelve specific hypotheses were tested. The first four predicted that spelling performance on phonologically regular words would be superior to spelling performance on phonologically irregular words for both groups in February and May, irrespective of the reading-instruction method employed. The next four hypotheses predicted that the classes taught reading according to the language-arts approach would achieve significantly higher spelling scores than the classes taught reading according to the basic-reader approach; these hypotheses applied to regular and irregular words in February and May. The last four hypotheses predicted that the language-arts classes would achieve significantly higher spelling scores in written composition than the basic-reader classes; these hypotheses applied to two types of word category in February and May.

The sample consisted of 21 first-grade classes located in three school districts in southern Delaware. Ten of the classes received language-arts reading instruction; eleven received basic-reader reading instruction. The class was the unit of sample.

Two spelling lists were constructed. One consisted of forty regular words, the other consisted of forty irregular words. The spelling lists were administered to the classes in February and May, 1966. Written-composition samples were also obtained in February and May. Ten written-composition samples were randomly drawn from each class and analyzed for spelling accuracy. All data were analyzed using T tests of differences between means.

Analysis of the data yielded the following.

1. The language-arts classes did not spell regular words significantly better than irregular words in either February or May of the first-grade year.

2. The basic-reader classes spelled regular words significantly better than irregular words in May of the first-grade year. The difference between means was significant at .05 in May. They did not, however, spell regular words significantly better than irregular words in February of the first-grade year, although differences approached significance .10.

3. The language-arts classes spelled regular words significantly better than the basic-reader classes in both February and May of the first-grade year. The differences were significant at .01.

4. The language-arts classes spelled irregular words significantly better than the basic-reader classes in February and May of the first-grade year. The differences were significant beyond .05 in February and at .01 in May.

5. The language-arts classes achieved significantly higher spelling scores in written composition than the basic-reader classes. The differences were significant at .01 or beyond in both February and May of the first-grade year. Significance was confirmed on both running and different word categories and held whether proportion or raw scores were analyzed.

The findings of this study support the conclusion that the language-arts classes spelled regular and irregular words with nearly equally proficiency whereas the basic-reader classes spelled regular words with somewhat greater facility than they spelled irregular words. Furthermore, the language-arts classes spelled both regular and irregular words significantly better than the basic-reader classes when performance on the phonological spelling lists was directly compared. Finally, the language-arts classes spelled words in written composition with significantly greater accuracy than the basic-reader classes when performance was directly compared.

C*

	I		*II*		*III*		*IV*
1.	come	1.	table	1.	news	1.	choose
2.	to	2.	you	2.	things	2.	witch
3.	he	3.	bed	3.	six	3.	fit
4.	mother	4.	must	4.	teach	4.	burned
5.	and	5.	had	5.	roof	5.	forest
6.	was	6.	water	6.	farmer	6.	raise
7.	in	7.	many	7.	walked	7.	learn
8.	do	8.	five	8.	ready	8.	given
9.	it	9.	other	9.	part	9.	everyone
10.	can	10.	much	10.	carry	10.	turkey
11.	with	11.	house	11.	place	11.	cost
12.	on	12.	pull	12.	laughing	12.	below
13.	like	13.	saw	13.	wall	13.	marks
14.	see	14.	cry	14.	year	14.	belong
15.	I	15.	man	15.	holding	15.	sometime
16.	have	16.	hope	16.	watched	16.	raised
17.	we	17.	her	17.	Mrs.	17.	eight
18.	here	18.	eye	18.	early	18.	blame
19.	of	19.	where	19.	out	19.	bathing
20.	at	20.	more	20.	sitting	20.	field
				21.	clean	21.	leaders
				22.	gray	22.	silk
				23.	stores	23.	bake
				24.	cream	24.	rose
				25.	light	25.	neck

* This informal spelling inventory is based on the American English Language Arts Series published by Holt, Rinehart and Winston, New York, 1960.

V	VI	VII	VIII
1. delay	1. central	1. practically	1. considerably
2. owner	2. prevent	2. astonish	2. appearing
3. laid	3. profit	3. colonies	3. regardless
4. seventeen	4. serving	4. affect	4. development
5. parties	5. directly	5. instance	5. existence
6. study	6. material	6. lowest	6. adopt
7. airplane	7. wherever	7. propose	7. domestic
8. having	8. adventure	8. arriving	8. financial
9. strike	9. canvas	9. employ	9. pursue
10. bucket	10. pleased	10. puzzle	10. disappointed
11. pride	11. we're	11. using	11. application
12. level	12. burden	12. disagree	12. subscription
13. candle	13. bushel	13. collected	13. cooperation
14. claim	14. shipment	14. bandage	14. located
15. feather	15. purchase	15. legal	15. kindergarten
16. island	16. active	16. chop	16. missionary
17. waste	17. manager	17. trout	17. forwarded
18. neighbor	18. precious	18. remained	18. introduced
19. pleasure	19. jewel	19. behavior	19. grieve
20. taste	20. illness	20. personally	20. evidence
21. American	21. million	21. madam	21. percentage
22. preach	22. peach	22. lecture	22. supreme
23. moment	23. risk	23. straighten	23. duly
24. gay	24. solo	24. bond	24. institute
25. steady	25. dearest	25. energy	25. moderate

D

Book-list sources

Adventuring with Books. Champaign, Ill.: National Council of Teachers of English, 1960, and supplement, 1963.

A Teacher's Guide to Children's Books, by Nancy Larrick. Columbus, Ohio: Charles E. Merrill, 1960.

Basic Book Collection for Elementary Grades, 7th ed., by Miriam S. Mathes, *et al.* Chicago, Ill.: American Library Association, 1960.

Best Books for Children, compiled by Mary Turner. (Revised annually.) New York: Bowker.

Bibliography of Books for Children, edited by Sylvia Sunderlin. Washington, D.C.: Association for Childhood Education International, 1968.

Books for Beginning Readers. Champaign, Ill.: National Council of Teachers of English, 1962.

Books for Brotherhood. (Issued annually.) New York: National Conference of Christians and Jews.

Books for Children: 1960–1965. Chicago: American Library Association, 1966.

Catalog of the Best Books for Children. Wellesley Hills, Mass.: Junior Reviewers, 1956.

Children and Books, by May Hill Arbuthnot. Chicago: Scott, Foresman, 1957.

Children's Books for $1.50 or Less. Washington, D.C.: Association for Childhood Education International, 1967.

Children's Books Too Good to Miss, by May Hill Arbuthnot, *et al.* Cleveland, Ohio: Western Reserve University Press, 1953.

Children's Catalog, 11th ed., edited by Dorothy H. West and Rachel S. Wilson. Bronx, N.Y.: H. W. Wilson, 1967.

Children's Literature: A Guide to Reference Sources. Washington, D.C.: Library of Congress, 1966.

Fifty Years of Children's Books, by Dora V. Smith. Champaign, Ill.: National Council of Teachers of English, 1963.

Gateways to Readable Books, by Ruth Strang, Ethlyne Phelps, and Dorothy Withrow. Bronx, N.Y.: H. W. Wilson, 1966.

Good Books for Children, 3rd ed., by Mary K. Eakin. Chicago, Ill.: University of Chicago Press, 1966.

Growing Up with Books. (Revised annually.) New York: Bowker.

Growing Up with Science Books. (Revised annually.) New York: Bowker.

"One Hundred and One More Books for Beginning Readers," by Elizabeth Guilfoile. *Elementary English* (November, 1964), pp. 370–372.

Proof of the Pudding: What Children Read, by Phyllis Fenner. New York: John Day Co., 1957.

Reading Ladders for Human Relations, by Muriel Crosby. Washington, D.C.: American Council on Education, 1966.

Subject Index to Books for Primary Grades, by Mary K. Eakin. Chicago, Ill.: American Library Association, 1967.

Trade Books for Beginning Readers, by Martha O. Condit. Bronx, N.Y.: H. W. Wilson, 1960.

Poetry sources

Index to Children's Poetry, by E. J. Brewton and Sarah Brewton. New York: Bowker, 1942.

Subject Index to Poetry for Children and Young People, by Violet Sell. Chicago, Ill.: American Library Association, 1957.

Periodical and newspaper sources

The Booklist. Monthly. American Library Association, 50 E. Huron St., Chicago, Ill.

The Calendar. Quarterly. Children's Book Council, 175 Fifth Ave., New York.

Elementary English. Monthly, October–May. National Council of Teachers of English, 704 S. Sixth St., Champaign, Ill.

The Horn Book Magazine. Bimonthly. Horn Book, 585 Boylston St., Boston, Mass.

New York Times Book Review. Weekly. Semiannual issues (November and April or May). New York Times, New York.

Paperbound Books in Print. 4 issues a year. Bowker, 62 W. 45th St., New York.

School Library Journal. Monthly (except July and August). Bowker, 62 W. 45th St., New York.

Magazines and weekly newspapers for elementary grades

Guide to Children's Magazines, Newspapers, Reference Books. Rev. ed. 1968. Association for Childhood Education International, 3615 Wisconsin Ave., N.W., Washington, D.C. 20016.

American Childhood, 74 Park Street, Springfield, Mass. 01105.

The American Girl, Girl Scouts of the U.S.A., 830 Third Avenue, New York, N.Y. 10017.

Animal Kingdom, New York Zoological Society, 30 East 40th St., New York, N.Y. 10017.

Arts and Activities, 8150 North Central Park Ave., Skokie, Ill. 60076.

Audubon, National Audubon Society, 1130 Fifth Ave., New York, N.Y. 10028.

Boy's Life, Boy Scouts of America, New Brunswick, N.J. 08903.

Child Life, Review Publishing Co., 1100 Waterway Blvd., Indianapolis, Ind. 46202.

Children's Digest, Parents Institute of Parents Magazine, 52 Vanderbilt Ave., New York, N.Y. 10017.

Children's Playmate, Children's Playmate Magazine, Inc. Cleveland, Ohio. 44114.

Highlights for Children, 37 East Long Street, Columbus, Ohio. 43215.

Humpty Dumpty's Magazine, Parents Institute of Parents Magazine, 52 Vanderbilt Ave., New York, N.Y. 10017.

Jack and Jill, Curtis Publishing Co., Independence Square, Philadelphia, Penna. 19108.

My Weekly Reader, edition for each grade. American Education Publications, 1250 Fairwood Ave., Columbus, Ohio. 43206.

National Geographic, National Geographic Society, 1146 16th St., N.W., Washington, D.C. 20036.

National Geographic Society School Bulletins, National Geographic Society, 1146 16th St., N.W., Washington, D.C. 20036.

Nature and Science, American Museum of Natural History, Central Park West at 79th St., New York, N.Y. 10024.

Nature Magazine, 1216 16th St., N.W., Washington, D.C. 20036.

Pack-O-Fun, 14 Main Street, Park Ridge, Ill. 60068.

Plays, The Drama Magazine for Young People, Plays, Inc. 8 Arlington Street, Boston, Mass. 02116.

Popular Mechanics, 250 West 55th St., New York, N.Y. 10019.

Ranger Rick's Nature Magazine, National Wildlife Federation, 1412 16th St., N.W., Washington, D.C. 20036.

Scholastic Magazines (edition for grades one through five), 33 West 42nd St., New York, N.Y. 10036.

Wee Wisdom, Unity School of Christianity, Lee's Summit, Mo. 64063.

Index

Abercrombie, M. L. Johnson, 143
Achievement, 12, 107, 140–141, 204
  pacing of, 165, 237, 246
  research on, using the Language-Experience Approach, 268–281
Action, 2, 12, 13, 14, 16
  based on group discussion, 174
  defined, 13
  developing word recognition and, 200
  kindergarten program and, 235–236
  Piaget's views on, 13, 14, 234
  role of in learning process, 12, 13, 14, 64, 73, 108, 109, 197–198, 229, 234
  special education and, 247
  value of pupil, 13, 108
Adams, Hazel, 116
Adapting to children's needs, 21, 29–36, 42, 79, 237–238, 246, 253–254; see also Individual differences, teaching for
Adult illiterates, reading program for, 255–258, 259
  attitudes of, 255
  dictated stories of, 257–258
Affective characteristics, 35–36, 85
Alliteration, see Auditory discrimination; Beginning sounds
Allport, Gordon W., 35, 36
Almy, Millie, 12, 13, 14
Alphabet, learning of, 66, 80, 196
  dictionary training and, 196
Alphabet charts, 196
Alphabetizing in word banks, 65–66, 75, 80, 195–196
American Association of School Librarians, 114, 115, 123, 125, 126–127
Analysis, of adjustment, 39
  of phonic development, 81, 94–95, 209

of progress, 96, 140–141, 203–204
of readiness, 25
  See also Creative writing; Evaluation; Readiness
Anatomy of Judgment, The (Abercrombie), 143
Anticipative mediators, 10
  See also Purpose
Assimilation, 13
"Attainment of Concepts, The," (Sigel), 7, 8, 12
Attitudes, of children, 28, 39, 78, 134, 247
  development of, 36–37, 51, 58, 64, 79, 119, 143, 149, 204
  intellectual, 7
  toward reading, 207
    failure and, 253–254
    research on, 268–281
Attributes, 11
Audio-visual aids, 116, 119, 212, 225
Auditory discrimination, 72, 75, 80, 181, 182–183, 186, 205, 209
  beginning sounds and, 185, 188–191
  defined, 182
  developing, 182–183, 185, 188, 214, 220
  ending sounds and, 184, 189
  rhyming words and, 183, 184–185, 187–188
  syllables and, 195
  vowels and, 192–193
Auditory-visual discrimination, 181, 184, 205, 220
  training for, 27, 72–75, 80, 183–188, 214
    beginning sounds and, 185–187, 188–191
    ending sounds and, 184–185, 189
    rhyming words and, 184–185
    vowel sounds and, 192–193
Austin, Mary C., 5, 11

293